Not j Alcoholic

Steven Midgley
and Clare Midgley

chipmunkapublishing
the mental health publisher

Steven Midgley and Clare Midgley

Published by
Chipmunkapublishing
United Kingdom

http://www.chipmunkapublishing.com

Copyright © Clare Midgley 2018

ISBN   978-1-78382-424-3

For Steven

Author's Note

I promised Steven his story would be told and this is it. A true story, much of it was difficult and painful to write but I felt compelled to do so.

Thank you, Steven for being the voice behind my right shoulder that gave me the courage to continue.

Acknowledgements

I wish to recognise the contribution that friends and family have made to this work. Without the patience of my husband Ian, I could not have continued, and I am grateful.

The encouragement and interest from Professor C sparked this story into life; thank you. Sincere thanks also to Jane and Andy for their support. As a family we also received sensitive support from our GPs and their staff, and in the last months from a caring CPN, thank you. Last but not least, I could not have completed this task without the support of a very skilled lady, Ann. Thank you all.

Clare Midgley March 2018

Steven Midgley and Clare Midgley

Part 1 An insane journey through life and lies

Written by Steven Midgley with commentary from his mother Clare Midgley

Steven's Facebook profile

Forward by Steven date unknown

CHAPTER 1: STRANGE CHILD

CHAPTER 2: THE NATURE OF THE BEAST

CHAPTER 3: THE STORM BREAKS

CHAPTER 4: IT'S GONNA GET YOU

CHAPTER 5: IT'S GOT YOU

CHAPTER 6: OUR MAN ON THE INSIDE (AGAIN)

CHAPTER 7: INTO THE GREAT WIDE OPEN

CHAPTER 8: FREE FALLIN'

CHAPTER 9: ANOTHER KIND OF WORLD

CHAPTER 10: THIS IS THE END...?

Part 2   The aftermath

Written by Clare Midgley

September 2011

In Mourning

November and December 2011

January 2012

February 2012

March 2012

April 2012

May 2012

June 2012

July and August 2012

September and October 2012

November and December 2012

Give a dog a bad name

Flaws in the system?

In conclusion

Glossary and resources

Steven's Facebook profile

The urban dream is no more than a lie, the people that matter are waiting to die. I will believe advertising the day my IQ has been permanently damaged by drink to equal that of a pan of tomato soup.

I'm a musician, a producer, a writer, a poet, a nutter, a drinker, an experimenter, an animal lover and I usually wake up a different person every day.

Two marriages down the bog but who cries over spilt milk? I'm harmless and enjoy a laugh as much as Spike Milligan did. The expert!

Religion: Pagan / Wiccan

Politics: Bollocks! And sod the so-called coalition.

'Don't let the bastards grind you down'.
Aaron J. Tandy is alive and well and living in Los Angeles.[1]

---

[1] Reference to Steven's chosen alter ego

Steven Midgley and Clare Midgley

Forward by Steven date unknown

When it's daft o'clock in the morning and you can't sleep, writing endlessly in notebooks and seeing the first rays of daylight before you feel remotely tired, you're probably manic. When you don't respond to tranquillisers and a large amount of strong liquor as a means to rectifying the lack of sleep, you're probably manic. When you can't put down the headphones and you've listened to half of your vast collection of albums whilst doing the strong liquor and tranquillisers, you're probably manic. When you simply can't get enough sex, and you don't even like or fancy the person, you're also probably manic, or maybe just a lucky drunken party animal.

If you can't face getting out of bed and languish there until gone tea time, you're probably depressed. If you're too paranoid to go out of your front door, you're probably depressed or have some other psychiatric disorder. If you've gone completely off sex and food, you're probably depressed. If you can't see any meaning to your existence, you are either depressed or a realist.

But there has to be something wrong when your mind won't stop racing and you're agitated. There's a pool of your own blood on the floor, because you've just cut your arms to pieces with a big knife. Then you really know there must be something wrong. Either depression, mania or the dreaded mixed phase of the illness. I hope to enlighten you about manic-depressive illness; the highs, the lows, the mixed episodes, the psychoses. And maybe I can give you some ideas about what you can do to help yourself, although I was never very successful. The illness isn't necessarily obvious to your immediate family, but there are often signs if they care to look. Signs you may not even see in yourself when ill, and others may need to fill in the blanks. I don't remember every manic episode I have had.

An example would be the time I was desperately picking up knife after knife and testing them for sharpness and cutting ability. My mother, who I wasn't even aware was there, was calmly taking them off me one at a time. In my confused manic state, I would just pick up another one. When I ran out of knives, rambling away to myself about suicide, I started on the medicines and pills. I rejected those inefficient enough not to be fatal by tossing them over my shoulder. My mother took these away and went to call for medical help. Unfortunately, the doctor decided I was too risky to visit, so wouldn't come out to our home. Mother was advised to give me Diazepam until I calmed down. Somehow, she managed this, without me being aware of it. I have no memory of this, and only since starting this book was it mentioned by my mother.

It is nine o'clock in the evening and Steven is agitated and unresponsive to questions or conversation. He is dressed just in his boxer shorts and is searching the kitchen cupboards and drawers. He empties the cutlery drawer onto the floor and is examining the knives. As he searches he is muttering to himself. He rejects knife after knife because even in his confused state he knows that it is difficult to do yourself in with a blunt butter knife. Giving up on the contents of the drawer he starts on the refrigerator. For some reason we have Paracetamol in the side shelf, he latches onto this and examines it carefully. His agitation increases as he realises what it is. He tosses it over his shoulder. Yet another ineffective way of alleviating his distress.

My sister is staying with us and she is resting on a bed settee in the dining room. I ask her if she is frightened. "No, it's only Steven. He wouldn't hurt anybody."

I phone NHS Direct and ask for help and a visit from a doctor. All I get is a doctor who phones back and asks about the situation. After he listens to me explaining Steven's history, he asks "What is he doing now?" "Well he's wandering around searching for something to kill himself with and seems very upset. He has just pushed a coffee table over because it hasn't anything on it that he is interested in." "I'm not coming out. He is a risk to me. Have you got any Diazepam?" Why the hell would a doctor assume that we have Diazepam in the house? Well that did it, no help for this family tonight.

My sister overhears the conversation as she keeps an eye on Steven's movements. "I've got some in my bag for my back-pain spasms. There will surely be enough for Steven as well." A genuine coincidence for which I'm thankful.

I am advised to give Steven Diazepam until he calms down, but no dose is quoted. I am too shocked and upset to argue the toss with the doctor. Steven needs help now. Nothing else is offered at all. And of course, you can't get access to the Mental Health Crisis Team unless a doctor calls them. The doctor again states that he would not feel safe coming out to us and I slam the phone down. My sister looks through her bag for medication and we find some 2 mg tablets. I look up the safe dosage on the internet and note that it is 2 to 10 mg, two to four times a day. My sister and I are following Steven around and popping tablets into his mouth at each opportunity. He is compliant and swallows obediently, his focus totally somewhere else that we cannot comprehend. He is still desperately searching for 'something'. After about 30 minutes we have got seven tablets into him and I begin to worry, as 14 mg is more than one recommended dose and Steven is not slowing down. I follow him into the bathroom, aware that we have scissors and nail files accessible to him. As he scatters toiletries from the shelves, his knees buckle, and he goes down like a felled beast. I cannot catch him or break his fall. He lands awkwardly, his lower spine connecting with the edge of the bidet and he slides to the floor. Ian has arrived home just in time to heave him up and lay him in the recovery position on his bed. We watch him carefully for the next two hours and he appears to be sleeping peacefully with normal breathing. It is a relief to give in and go to bed ourselves.

I have no idea why I didn't complain about the lack of support at this time or the doctor's attitude. I know that we didn't want to call an ambulance because we knew from bitter experience that Accident and Emergency was no place for a distressed and possibly manic Steven. It has always involved long waits in unfamiliar surroundings where we have never yet had access to a psychiatrist or a psychiatric nurse. So as usual we cope on our own.

Amazingly Steven wakes quite early the next morning without even a headache. He is bright and cheerful with no memory of his distress the evening before. He does however have a bruised back!

I can't think of what else I might have done that I've forgotten. On the other hand, you will always remember the black depressions, where every painful second lasts a hundred years or more. This illness wears many gowns as you will see.

I am strongly compelled to shed some light on this illness, which is much misunderstood by many people. It is not a simple thing to explain. Most people would put it down to basic madness, but there is a lot more to it than that. It is both exhilarating and crushing at times. It can be treated, but it can also kill you, and potentially you could kill others. You're born with the predisposition to this mental illness. However, the social stigma of what is now called bipolar disorder is needless and I hope this story may help others understand.

I know that some level of autobiographical information is necessary to determine the comings and goings of my moods, manias, depressions etc. but I will try and keep this to a minimum. Of course, it's going to be fairly heavily autobiographical, that can't be helped.

This is really the story of my life so far as I can recall it, so I'm going to have to bore you with some of that in order to paint a reasonably accurate picture. Many other books are in existence that will give you a medical picture of a sterile nature. Some are peoples' personal experiences, some well written, some poor. This book is meant to be a mixture of science and experience. This is a true and honest account of my tumultuous life as I recall it.

The reader must allow for the vagaries of memory when one is ill, drunk, medicated or just plain terrified. Now that I am again stable in mind, I feel that this is the right time to speak out. I do so with thanks to my parents and friends without whom I'd be long dead.

CHAPTER 1: STRANGE CHILD

I was about a year to 18 months old when I first recall feeling 'strange'. Lying in my cot, convinced that the 'monsters' that all children believe in were there waiting to attack and when the light went out would do so. Except I was wide awake and I saw them. They spoke to me and terrified me and prevented me from ever getting any sleep until daylight. Yet this was definitely no dream, nor an over-active imagination. It was the early onset of madness. My mother told me that one night I woke up screaming and she came to comfort me. I was convinced that it wasn't her, that she was a shape-shifting demon or a body-snatcher and screamed for her to get out. I do have a vague memory of this distressing incident.

My earliest memory was when I was younger than a year and I was being pushed in an old-fashioned pram past the old Woolworth's shop in town. My mother tells me she got rid of said pram for a pushchair before I was 10 months old and it surprised me that I could remember so far back. Apart from when seriously ill or plain intoxicated, as I sometimes would be as an adult, my memory of events, experiences, times and dates is near impeccable.

My parents were level headed. Apart from a serious spell of post-natal depression[2] and a confusion caused by side effects from painkillers for her back pain, my mother was warm and loving. So was my father, a very logical and dependable man.

As a toddler, people remember me as bubbly and highly inquisitive, restless, but never difficult. I wanted to know the ins and outs of everything, and when I got

---

[2] My post-natal depression was never officially diagnosed, and I survived so maybe it wasn't serious.

interested in something there was no stopping or distracting me. Even the local bin men knocked on the door to give me a present before my 2nd birthday. I was so fascinated with their wagon that I had spent all year waving at them on collection day. Then came the fascination with music, of which, more later. At age 3 I'd make my dad play the same LPs and tapes repeatedly. I don't know how that Genesis LP survived! I'd grab the tiny microphone and record myself singing my take on the hits of the time. The radio was always on in our house.

I was usually awake before the crack of dawn and didn't sleep much before it. I didn't think anything of it. I was a child and this was my life.

My mother and my father both read to me and taught me to read very early on, before any official schooling. This gave me the literature bug at an early age.

By the time I was ready for nursery, I would engage with what other kids were doing up to a point. I started getting distracted easily and thinking very deeply about random things. I would slip into my own world that no one else was permitted to enter. It was easier for me to engage when I found that they had a piano at the nursery, out of bounds to most. For some reason the pianist put me on her lap and let me play, tolerant of my attempts at music.

I never really saw much point in nursery, or indeed any other academy, but I learned a lot from my parents. One nursery teacher called me an idiot and a liar when I told her I'd grown an orange plant from a pip. "It's too cold in this country, don't be stupid!" But bless my mother, she brought said plant into class next day and extracted an apology from a very embarrassed young teacher.

I progressed to infants' school which was no more enjoyable than the nursery. I played with the other kids in my class for a while, but then I started to feel like I was on the wrong planet. A bit like the series 'Life on Mars' or 'Ashes to Ashes' which I would enjoy when they were broadcast over 20 years in the future.

It was about this time my grandfather bought me my first keyboard - a little wind organ that I took to like a duck to water. I'd be playing it all hours of the day or night, and I can't imagine how many batteries I must have killed in the process.

Steven has forgotten that this little keyboard was bought when he was just 3. He taught himself to play and this was the beginning of his passion for keyboards and music.

It was about this time I started to be haunted by dark thoughts not becoming of a 5 year old. My own mind had conspired to torture me to madness. I believed that I was evil. I thought about harming people. I didn't want to, and never did, but these thoughts tortured me to the limit of my endurance. Luckily for me they burned out as quickly as they came… for the time being.

Steven doesn't mention the death of his nanna Yvonne here which happened in November 1985 just before his 6th birthday. It affected him profoundly and I do now wonder if it contributed to his mental instability and possibly a personality disorder in later life. She had been poorly with breast cancer for about five years and we had been hopeful that she would reach a good stage of remission. During this time, she looked after Steven whilst I worked part time in a local bank. She chose to spend time with Steven, knowing that it might be all she had and some days it was a struggle for her. They had a close and loving relationship.

Not just an Alcoholic

On the day she died we were on our way to visit her. Ian pulled the car into the street and we saw the ambulance parked up, doors open but with no sense of hurry or urgency. Leaving Steven and I in the car, Ian went to assess the situation. He came back with the shocking news that nanna Yvonne had just died and the paramedics had given up trying to resuscitate her. Steven is anxious and wants to know why we are still sitting in the car. I quietly explain that nanna, who he knows has been very poorly, has just died. He struggles to absorb the news and insists we are wrong and wants to see his nanna. He is fighting me to get out of the car. Ian and I exchange looks and I help Steven out. Leading him by the hand I explain that nanna will not look the same as he remembers and that she is not really here anymore.

Yvonne is spread-eagled on the bed and everything is in disarray. We let him take in the scene and then lead him away. I explain that things are a mess because the paramedics have been trying to help nanna but now she is dead. She has gone to a place where she is not poorly any more. The distress of his grandfather upsets him further.

Many people may say that it is inappropriate to show a child of 5 a dead body, but I would not change the way we dealt with that part of the situation. Steven had a vivid imagination and dealt with the truth much better that pretence. He accompanied us to the church service and then to the cremation, but we left him sitting in a limousine with my father. We decided that the sight of a coffin on its way to the furnace might overwhelm him. This was a mistake. He bore a grudge for many years, talking about being excluded from the service and the opportunity to say goodbye to his nanna.

We seemed to jog along okay. I gave him many opportunities to talk about his Nanna and we did not avoid the subject. About three weeks after the funeral his grief finally showed itself. At evening bath time, I was chatting to him about nanna, and he turned on me with fists and feet, sending soapy water everywhere, screaming "She's my nanna, not yours!" I hurriedly wrapped him in a big towel, hugging him to me. We lay on his bed as he sobbed and fought me. Eventually he calmed, and we lay together in silence, except for his sobs and snuffles. It broke my heart to find my child so sad and distressed, but death is a fact of life and should never be hidden.

We moved home the following March, having been in the process of buying a house with a third bedroom where nanna could come to stay. Too late now to be of any help to her.

By the time I turned 6, mania hit again, not that I knew what it was. I became fanatical about horology. For a year I managed to pester family, their friends, my friends' parents and even the local watch repairers to help with what became a collection of over 86 clocks and watches. I would stay awake in my room all night maintaining my 'clock shop'. People would joke that walking past my bedroom sounded like there was a ticking time bomb nearby. How right they were. Apart from this obsession with timepieces, everything felt normal at this point. I eventually lost patience with the idea of becoming a top clockmaker and resumed normal life, as happy as anyone else, but not over happy. I developed a fear of what it would be like to be an adult, that the world would be a dangerous place by then and I probably wouldn't like it. Interesting…

Steven's obsession with clocks started much sooner than he remembers, about age 2 and lasted for over 10 years. He also had persistent night terrors about lights on his bedroom ceiling. He called them 'gliniks and gambis' and described them as walking scissors.

I was always a very nervous, neurotic child, but I had a perfect upbringing, so it must all be nature rather than nurture. But then that's manic-depressive illness for you, its biochemical, and although stress can trigger a mood shift it's already in there and doesn't wait for an invitation.

As I moved up through school, I had maybe two years of stable moods. My fascination with clocks was eventually replaced by the desire to collect every piece of vintage electrical fitting. This included old Bakelite two pin plugs, old three pin plugs, round pins, old valve radios and the like. I'm lucky not to have electrocuted myself. That danger would be faced when I was much older.

At this time, aged about 7 I had a severe personality clash with my teacher. In my head I'd already grown up enough to have sensible conversations with adults, and didn't appreciate this person talking down to me as if I were sub-human and unintelligent. I was always polite, but it seemed this person had it in for me. It wasn't just me being paranoid. On parents evening the offending teacher slated me to my folks and quite rightly, they defended me and backed it up with what I'd told them. After that, I never got a single bit of persecution. Well, not for a while.

Unfortunately, this is true. The teacher concerned was fresh from college, inexperienced and unable to form a useful relationship with Steven.

All through junior school I became more and more distracted. I had bags of energy but ditched playing with the other kids apart from the odd 'hello' and suchlike. I was happier in my own little world. In my mind I was on a plane flying somewhere, or I was a lord of the manor during mediaeval times, my imagination was my companion. I seemed to have boundless energy which had nowhere to go. School work was boring; I just wanted to do my own thing. By the end of my first year of junior school I was severely fed up.

At around age 8, I was still living in a dream world but was gathering friends, one of which became very close for a while. My spirits were heading upwards again and over the space of a few months I'd enthusiastically collected a myriad of car parts and badges from local scrap yards. I had carburettors and alternators, spark plugs and distributors all over my writing desk. I drew endless pictures of cars and designed a few as best as a child of that age could. I even submitted one to Ford who humoured me. What the hell was I thinking? I was a bit less neurotic during this period, and with hindsight I realise that I was enjoying a mild high. It was about this point that I became completely fascinated by street lamps. As a toddler the tall ones had seemed like evil giants to me. Now I wanted to be a lighting engineer. But then the darkness started creeping in and I was feeling strange again.

Steven is aged about 8 when he is featured with a photo in the local paper. He has written to the town council to ask if he can 'adopt' a local lamp post that sits isolated on waste ground near to our home. It has been there since 1954 and is showing signs of neglect. Steven is keen to smarten it up a bit.

My next teacher, when I was 9, was a very mercurial, sometimes temperamental Scotsman. He had an excellent sense of humour and an equally quick, if fleeting temper. He encouraged me a lot and let me get away with things that the others couldn't. He wasn't soft by any stretch, but this was a man who didn't mind having kids talk to him in an intelligent and adult manner. On the flip side he didn't mind playing the fool to get a few laughs and keep the interest of the whole class. I was put in charge of all the class electronics projects. Some kids at 9 didn't even know how to wire a bell up to a battery, but he asked me if I could make a 'test your luck' type machine for the school fête, so I did.

This teacher also turned out to be a music fan and a drummer. Encouraged by him, I brought my newest (and now much more professional) keyboard into class and gave a quick rendition of numerous requests. I don't read music when I play; I play by ear and vamp it if I get stuck. I asked him if he thought I'd played alright, had I hit any wrong notes? "Great – and there's no such thing as a wrong note. People who say that are referring to a right note in the wrong place."

Aged 10, everything seemed normal. But the summer of 1990 brought on a brief mania that made me obsessive about killing myself even though I wasn't depressed. I just couldn't stop thinking about it. These thoughts passed as the summer wore on only to be replaced by a deathly fear of the supernatural, which came and went. Unsurprisingly, as the summer turned to autumn, so did my mood.

1990 Its early autumn and suddenly I just lost interest in everything. I wasn't a person, more a human 'just being'. I was totally flat. Everyone was busy around me at school like whirlwinds and I felt like I was frozen in time, watching. Nothing was exciting, everything was a chore. I would spend school break times alone in the quietest corner of the playground, away from all the noise of those having fun, and gaze at the dying autumn leaves.

Academically I was still doing okay I was on the 'brainy' table and with 4 or 5 other kids running ahead of the class. I was approaching my last term in junior school before going into secondary school. We few 'brainy' kids were being given work intended for year 8 secondary students instead of the stuff the rest of the class were working on. This was fun at first but quickly became boring and pointless to me. I felt I'd been segregated from the class, even if the other 'brains' on my table didn't. My teacher for this last year, another Scot, was usually a fair woman. We had a couple of run-ins, but I think maybe she was the first teacher to notice something wasn't quite right.

Steven has remembered it exactly right here. We were already noticing that he was more anxious and 'eccentric' than usual. His teacher had spotted it too and called us in to discuss the situation. She had noticed a high level of anxiety and a certain element of isolation. We agreed that we would all keep a careful eye on Steven and respond to developments.

I stuck out as a bit of an eccentric. It was general knowledge that I was now actively collecting street lighting equipment. These were bought new or donated by the manager of the council scrap yard. My dad persuaded him to exchange old equipment for a couple of his cigars. This strange hobby didn't help people understand me any better.

I became interested in the Goon Show for the first time after my mother's friend lent me a few LPs, and I became an instant fan. Then I started reading Spike Milligan's poetry and loved it. One future day I came across a poem of his about manic depression. I knew he suffered from it, but I didn't know what the 'manic' part meant. I thought it just meant severe depression, not the high flying, grandiose, psychotic and irritable mess waiting for me. I fell totally into Spike's world; I could picture each character that he had invented. At that time, it was my only solace, and supported me through the horrors to come.

I arrived home from school on 21st February 1991 to the news that a family we were close to had died when their home burned down in the night. The mother, a nurse, used to call me 'unique', with genuine fondness. If she had lived she might have changed her view to 'utterly insane' with time.

Steven is just 11 at this time and in his last year at junior school. Our friends died in a house fire, parents and three children including the 6 week old baby. Steven had formed a strong relationship with the twin girls aged 8. It was devastating news. We had met the family through my connection with the local St John Ambulance Brigade. I was traumatised by the event and maybe that's why I didn't pay enough attention to how my son was feeling. I played an active part in the funeral, which was an official St John Ambulance affair, with the local brigade in full uniform. A colleague and I had agreed to carry the tiny white coffin that held the remains of the baby girl. It was shockingly heavy and even though we carried it with a strap and not on our shoulders, it was a trial of endurance. Dr Bach Rescue Remedy helped us through.

The effect on Steven was profound. He asked me many times if I thought that the family had been frightened, had they been in pain, had they felt the fire burning them? I reassured him as best I could. I told him what I believed – that the smoke would have rendered them all unconscious and oblivious to the heat and fire. The only other comfort that I could give to him and to myself is that wherever they were, they were all together. He cut the photograph of the three girls out of the local paper and kept it for years. Perhaps this is another trauma that contributed to the one of his diagnoses of personality disorder.

I'd sensed some serious darkness coming over me in the early winter 1990 and became rather shaky and nervous in general, and this news floored me. I became a paranoid wreck, terrified of fire and didn't sleep properly for about 2 months. The sound of heavy rain on the roof would shock me awake, sounding like a roaring blaze of flames.

At this point Steven was so afraid of fire that we called in the fire brigade to do a check on the house to try and reassure him. They were taken aback by the level of Steven's anxiety and the clarity with which he expressed the dangers of house fires. The result was a smoke detector in almost every room and an 'escape' window in Steven's bedroom. There is a smoke detector in his bedroom to this day.

I seemed to pick up briefly but then my mind decided to betray me yet again. I had some very good news from a lighting manufacturer. They'd invited me to come and see their factory and I was looking forward to it. I was sat in the bath that night in a very good mood indeed. For no apparent reason, I was suddenly aware that I could kill myself. This was what I now know to be a 'mixed episode' that would intensify and not stabilise for over a year. I could not think why this was in my head with so much promise from life. A mixed episode is mania spiralling into a depression and showing traits of both.

I was suddenly very agitated and could think of nothing other than suicide and how many ways there were to do it. I didn't want to do it, but everywhere I looked I could see a means, from the obvious to the utterly bizarre. I could not sleep. I didn't dare. What if I fell asleep and hung myself sleep-walker style? During this time, I became deluded that I was James Herriot, actually thought I was a vet. I have since learned that mania is a cause of, and product of a lack of sleep.

I realise on reflection that we had come to accept Steven as he was, bizarre behaviour and all. His obsession with James Herriot was one of his less obvious passions. He read and re-read every Herriot book and watched the videos of the series late into the night.

This escalation started in April 1991 and from then on, I was trying to find any project I could work on to distract my mind, all to no avail. Even the lighting factory tour didn't abate thoughts of suicide. One horrible day in mid-summer I awoke at first light, about 4 or 5 am, feeling the most all-encompassing depression. The worst that I had ever experienced. I couldn't see an end to this and wanted out, but I was so scared that I was powerless. All I did was pace about like a stereotypical mental patient. I became preoccupied with hanging. I even spent a brief time under the delusion that I had killed myself and was actually a ghost.

The worst day of my life so far was 26th August 1991 when on a family outing the depression built to a level that was equal to the worst physical pain I could imagine. With secondary school looming, I wondered what would be next.

When it came to responding, maybe we didn't get it quite right. Steven seemed to become more anxious and unhappy until one summer bedtime just a couple of months later, I was forced to realise that we had a real problem. He had been irritable and upset most of the sunny summer's day and finally came downstairs at teatime telling me he needed to talk to me. I heard him out but brushed off his upset and anxiety and didn't take him seriously. He told me that he was frightened all the time and I tried to reassure him. His level of fear and upset escalated and I really started to listen. He ended up crying hysterically.

I finally understood that his head was full of fearful thoughts and visions and he had had enough of them.

Our first trip to the doctors the next day was the official beginning of Steven's struggle with mental illness.

I have copies of reports from the educational psychologists written during his first and second year in secondary school. It is noted that he is suffering from bouts of depression, that he is anxious, friendless and the first label of Asperger's Syndrome comes up. We are given no advice on what it is or what we can do about it.

CHAPTER 2: THE NATURE OF THE BEAST

About 1% of the adult population suffers with bipolar disorder. Personally, I prefer the older term, manic depression. Depending on whether you're in the USA or European medical regime there are 4 or 5 subtypes. Type 1 is the most typical and most serious, with extreme manic phases interspersed with crippling depressions. Type 2 involves less serious highs, known as hypo mania, and less crippling depressions. Some people with type 1 only have one episode of either mood swing in their lives, but for most it is an ailment that, like diabetes, requires lifelong medication to control it. A lot of patients have long 'normal' periods between episodes, especially when medicated appropriately. In most manic-depressives, the mania precedes the depressive episode, but it can also work the other way around, depending on the subtype of your illness. It can also manifest as the dreaded 'mixed' phase. Manias tend to last from a few days in mild cases, to weeks in most other situations, but tend to burn out in a couple of months at the extreme. The typical signs are increasing agitation, sleeplessness, financial recklessness, and sexual abandon; also delusions of grandeur, obsessive creativity and unrealistic plans for the future. Some believe themselves to be someone else, either famous, known to them, or plain imaginary. Sufferers may hear 'commands' in the form of imagined voices and experience reckless impulses which they believe to be real and cannot control. Perfectly normal surroundings can suddenly become threatening, and in extreme but thankfully rare cases, visual hallucinations may be present and can be terrifying or intensely beautiful. I've never tried acid, but I bet it's close to these experiences!

Depression becomes officially clinical if it lasts more than two weeks, and severe episodes can last months, even years. Mixed phases in my experience can last several months, even up to a year. Signs include lack of appetite (both for food and sex) general malaise and lack of energy. Some patients experience a mental 'numbness', others feel so low that a desire for suicide arises. Due to their scrambled mental state they don't care by which method, as long as it gives release. It doesn't matter if it hurts like hell. Though most depressions leave you too tired to think or get out of bed, let alone act on these thoughts. But being tired does not mean you will be able to sleep the pain away. Personal hygiene may go out of the window after all you're worthless so who cares what you look like anyway? Feelings of persecution are common, and in severe cases these are backed up by hallucinatory voices telling the patient so.

Whether manic or depressed, if psychotic symptoms are present such as hallucinations, paranoia or sheer restlessness, a doctor may prescribe an anti-psychotic or sedative medication at first. These act almost straight away until any prescribed mood stabiliser or anti-depressant medication can begin to work. These can take between 4-6 weeks to take hold.

There are subtypes at each end of the spectrum that do not appear severe enough to qualify as straight 'bipolar'. There is also a condition known as Bipolar NOS (not otherwise specified), rapid cycling (hypo-manic and depressive phases pass quickly) and cyclothymia (even more rapid cycling) and not necessarily as intense mood shifts.

Manic depression can be confused with schizophrenia due to some similarities of how the two conditions may present themselves. Schizophrenics may appear to be depressed. They may hear voices, as can a severely manic or severely depressed bipolar patient. Schizophrenics may appear agitated, also a symptom of mania. Both illnesses have the chance of a sufferer becoming delusional. The best way to find out is to see a doctor, who may suggest the patient perhaps undertake a PETT (positron emission trans axial tomography) scan. Manic or hypo-manic scans show a lot of glucose being used in the brain and the scan shows it lit up like a Christmas tree. In schizophrenia the brain activity appears reduced and quite similar to a scan of a sufferer of dementia. I have not seen a scan of a brain during a period of depression but would imagine it to be similar to the latter two, which show blues and greens, instead of the reds, yellows and burning whites of mania. The other scans available include the MRI (magnetic resonance imaging) which, in a few years I would undergo myself. Apparently these also show any abnormality in the functioning of the synapses.

This refers to the scans that Prof C asked us to organise via our GP in 2008. By the time Steven was seen he was again under the care of the NHS and Prof B. Prof C had wanted to rule out epilepsy I think. Steven was never told the results, and neither were they mentioned to us, his main carers at any time. I found out later that they showed brain damage from alcohol use. This should have flagged up a treatment plan, but again we seemed to be lost in a system that was not co-ordinated or holistic. If there had been a robust intervention at this point Steven may have been saved from himself.

What exactly causes bipolar is unproven, but it seems to be genetic. It is a definite chemical imbalance in the brain and can be passed on genetically. It may skip a generation now and then like diabetes, but the chances are higher for the child of a bipolar parent inheriting the disorder. Yet sometimes it comes out of nowhere.

There are no bipolar cases in my family line, but several cases of clinical depression, one 'nervous breakdown' as they used to call things they couldn't 'label', a couple of cases of Alzheimer's but as far as I am aware, no manic sufferers. Apart from myself.

We later discover that my paternal great grandmother murdered my great grandfather. The family story was that she was defending herself from domestic abuse. The real story is much sadder. Apparently after she murdered him she was judged to be criminally insane and she was committed to a mental hospital where she died many years later.

There are some people who only suffer highs without the depression, just as some become clinically depressed without ever getting high. This is what is known as 'unipolar mood disorder'.

Also well documented is seasonal affective disorder, or S.A.D, in which sufferers become depressed in the winter months when the days are dark and the nights long. They usually feel perfectly normal all year until the nights draw in. Many benefit from light boxes which distribute the colour temperature of daylight (6400-6700 degrees Kelvin, or think of it as you might a 'grow-light') with an ultraviolet component to make up for the lack of real sunlight. Ordinary light bulbs and fluorescent strips usually only provide a spectrum of 2700-4000 Kelvin and do not give enough light output for these sufferers.

Many bipolar patients (myself included) who don't have S.A.D. find that whilst they may become high or low at any time, should any mood shift occur, depressions become deeper in the winter months and manias more intense during spring and summer. I know first-hand that seasons do affect moods.

Steven hated bright sunny days in summer and would stay indoors. I believe that this is what started his trademark look of always wearing sunglasses when outdoors.

The biggest problem is diagnosis, as I am about to show. Most people start with symptoms in their late teens or early twenties. I was an early starter, but it wasn't until I was 19 or 20 that I completely lost it. After that awful day in August 1991, when I was nearly 12 years old, my parents realised I was seriously disturbed about something. I told my parents about my depression and that I didn't understand what was going on. My mother would say "it'll pass", but it didn't. Next stop, child psychologist.

We were referred as a family to Dr PJ and CAMHS for family psychology. We had a couple of sessions as mum, dad and child, then Steven would be seen on his own. Unsurprisingly some of our own 'stuff' surfaced and it came to light that Ian and I were not happy with the strong influence of his father on our little family. However, his influence was because he loved us too much, now being a widower. Without granddad Ed's help we could not have continued Steven's therapy as he transported and accompanied him when Ian and I were both at work. A living still must be earned even when your child is unwell. At this time Steven was so distressed that he would often come into our room at night and lie down on a mattress on the floor. It was like having a toddler again, but this way we at least we all got some sleep.

A very well-meaning woman doctor saw me for quite a while but it made no difference. She made no diagnosis and as my mood lifted naturally during the time I was visiting her, she presumed it was just a phase. It wasn't. I had another major depressive episode within the year. This time more a mixed phase, as I was down on myself, doing a lot of random, manic type things, becoming obsessed with bizarre activities. This included the classic outcry of setting fires. No longer afraid of flame I would have a bonfire at least once a week in the garden. Pyromania. I saw the lady doctor again, and once more undiagnosed, she referred me to a colleague who basically looked straight through me and his genius advice to my parents was to tell them to tell me to shut up about my 'problems'. Rightly, they walked away.

This must be Dr NK, who I have little memory of. I don't remember him engaging with myself or Ian. I accept that that doesn't mean he didn't, but I remember nothing of significance about him. In the notes it says that Steven didn't want to come any more – what happened? It does seem that the therapeutic relationship broke down, but we were not involved with this, in fact we were excluded. Our understanding was that Steven had been discharged and was therefore 'cured'. Nothing could be further from the truth. So why the discharge with no follow up care?

At the beginning of 1992 I began self-harming, but no one knew at that time. Even the doctors who saw my wounds thought it was an infection or an allergy. I was ulcerating myself by attacking my skin with rough objects, as opposed to the blades that I would use in the future. I really don't know why I did it. It wasn't the same degree of harm that I would do later, when I made attempts to end my life.

Steven began this behaviour earlier than he remembers. I think he was about 8 years old when I first took him to the GP. He had strange raw and weeping areas on his shins. The GP decided that he had been bitten by fleas! Almost as unbelievable as the truth which he shared with me later when a young man. He had regularly taken sandpaper to his shins and abraded the flesh, causing long term wounds that took ages to heal. None of us got to the truth at that time.

In the autumn of 1992 Steven visited a lighting factory on a local industrial estate as part of his school work experience. He was accompanied by a school friend. His obsessive passion for all things lighting won him a few friends and a couple of doubters. The boys visited and engaged with the staff in the technology centre and the manufacturing area. Most were impressed by Steven's knowledge and interest, but one person noted that Steven "was irritating and did not listen" and another noted "an experimenter, a whiz kid, unique." His guide for the day noted in his report that "Steven was very attentive, very keen and has a very enquiring mind. His manner was very confident and self-assured. In some instances, I feel that his enthusiasm and display of knowledge may have been mistaken for arrogance, which is unfortunate but, perhaps, to be expected."

1993 began terribly. Every time something that I did went wrong, I hated myself for my incompetence I thought I should be better. I was 'the best' in my head, so how could I fail? Even simple things had me literally beating myself up.

Mid-year the manic desire for all things lighting got me a tour of the commercial exhibitions of various lighting companies. Later, I had a tour of two major manufacturer's offices, and the year ended reasonably well. In early 1994, just having turned 14 in the previous December, something went very wrong indeed.

I thought (or at least felt) that I'd grown up overnight and could feel darkness rushing into my mind. I was preoccupied with death, it was all that I could think about. I began experimenting a lot with high voltage transformers and created weird electrical experiments. Mania does have a plus side when it comes to creativity. In the last year I'd made many electrical gadgets; a light bulb, an arc welder and an electric cigarette lighter. The down side is that I managed to blow myself across the garden using mains voltage on wet grass. I went flying, but the innovative lighter that I was working on did light my cigarette! Understandably, my parents had noticed I was not your average teenager and became used to patching me up. I was so anxious and depressed that I wished that I had never been born. Or if I must be born, could I not go back to a time in my life before all this happened?

This was a busy year. We had regular appointments with the Family Psychology team and had visits to Croydon and Glasgow to visit lighting manufacturers. Steven was well received at Phillips in Croydon. He disappeared with the sales manager to be 'tested' on his knowledge. This had been a request made by the educational psychologist. She needed to know if his apparent knowledge and understanding of all things pertaining to lighting had been learned parrot fashion from catalogues and stock lists, or if he had an actual understanding of the subject. It came back that he understood it all and his grasp of the subject was on a par with an experienced salesman. A budding career as a lighting engineer beckoned.

The visit to Glasgow was equally 'enlightening' and the lighting engineers whisked him away to talk about all things lighting whilst we wandered about a Glasgow business park in the rain. Steven was presented with a beautiful book about the Mackintosh collection and lots of spare parts of lights for his collection of lamps and bulbs.

A couple of years previously I had been shooting clay pigeons with my dad, using a 12-bore shotgun. Skills I would find useful later in life, though not on any clay shooting range. I had also done some target shooting with my trusty old BSA air rifle. One bad day, I found myself with the rifle in my mouth, finger on trigger. I knew it could kill me, but it wasn't powerful enough to guarantee instant death. I am a major coward when it comes to physical pain, so I put it away again. I later heard a friend of mine had gone through the same ritual with a 410 shotgun, and had also thought better of it. His chances would have been better for a kill shot than mine, but thankfully he also put down the gun.

I was hanging around with good friends but still couldn't shake the downer. One night I decided to put myself on to the railway lines. On my way to end it all one of my friends intercepted me. We started drinking socially and that temporarily blocked the nastiness from my mind. I also dabbled with marijuana. It didn't do anything but augment my feelings of paranoia and anxiety, so I tended to leave it alone.

On my depressed wanders over the next year, I frequented an abandoned warehouse on a derelict site. It seemed to me like a by-product of Armageddon. Sometimes I would go alone or sometimes I'd take a friend or two. We would sit and smoke a pack of cigarettes listening to the rain beat upon the roof. All of us thought that it would make a great practice space for a band if it only had a power supply.

These 'wanders' are relived in Steven's poetry. As parents we don't remember any concerns at this time about drink or drugs.

At the end of the year a friend and I set fire to a skip outside the warehouse and watched it burn. There was no damage done to anything. When we lost interest, a couple of younger kids took over stoking the blaze, throwing old wooden pallets on to it. We decided to split. The fire bug would later extend to home-made fireworks, but no harm ever came of it. It easily could have and I am not proud of these actions.

Steven seemed truly ashamed of this act and talked about it in later life. It seems that parents never really know what their progeny are up to – nothing changes.

By Christmas 1994 I was experiencing a definite 'mixed' state of mind. I was down on myself and drinking too much. My electrical experiments were becoming even more bizarre and it's a wonder I didn't burn the house down. Anyone who puts 10 amps of current at 30 volts though a pencil will find out why! The wood burns off and the graphite core glows red hot like an element. Scarily impressive!

I suddenly became interested in music again. I decided the only way forward was to buy an electric bass guitar and join my first band. Obviously, we were awful, and we didn't even have a singer. Experiencing and playing the grunge music popular at the time was a good way to let out rage. So was 'guitar cricket'. My friend Simon would hold his guitar up like a bat and I would bounce my heavier bass off it like a ball. They got dented but never broken. We rehearsed our music endlessly. Simon's cousin Jon was the drummer, Simon was on guitar and I was playing bass. Jon's dad had converted his garage and decorated it to become a vast fully functioning bar. This was our rehearsal room and we spent as much time drinking beer and smoking as we did rehearsing. We entered a local school competition and surprisingly we managed to beat the house band on the number of tape sales that we made!

Steven seemed happier and creating music became a huge part of his identity. The obsession with lamps and lighting moved into the background to make way for music and electronic instruments.

Then, after a particular evening of partying, I remembered why I'd given up pot smoking. I had a massive panic attack with visual hallucinations after not using for a long while. I used to play a bit of 'pass the joint' every few weeks in the past; this night I rather overdid it and vowed never again. Despite this vow I would later use it again for pain relief. Not enough to get stoned, but it would ease physical pain. When used sporadically, it is better than any analgesic. It is of course not recommended. My head is messed up enough without adding to the mix a drug known for destroying sanity. The destruction of my sanity was still some time away, and no, I'm not a pothead today.

During 1995 I suffered a year of crippling depression. It started off as a very bleak spring. By the summer, the persistent black thoughts of suicide, visions of grisly murders and death were tortuous. Everything seemed to be rotting and strange. Images of executions tormented me. I was aware that I was becoming 'something else' but nothing good. The only thing that penetrated the blackness that year was the acquisition of my first Hammond organ. It may have been small, but others like it have produced the distinctive sound that can be heard on many blues, jazz and rock standards. I was so depressed that I didn't have the concentration to play it.

Steven couldn't attend school on a regular basis over the last 18 months of his education. He was still developing his musical skills and this interest seemed to be the only salvation from his painful mental state. I struggled with the mechanics of a child not attending school, but Steven's GP provided a medical note that stated that he was suffering from depression and would often not be able to attend. There were mornings when Steven put on his uniform and tried to walk out of the front door. The times he actually reached school were few and far between and he would panic as soon as he stepped outside. At first, I tried to force him and would threaten him with God knows what, but in the end, I gave up trying. His distress was painful to observe and affected us profoundly. Better safe up in his bedroom than out in the world and at risk because of his mental state. I felt very alone in dealing with this and did the best I could at that time. The GP offered nothing else other than the medical note. Ian and I were so ignorant that we did not question this.

This deterioration in Steven's health coincided with me leaving my part-time job in banking in June 1995. It did mean that I was at home a lot of the time which is where I needed to be. I did manage to enrol at college and began to train as a clinical reflexologist with a view to starting my own complementary health business

By the end of 1995 I cracked, and developed a full-on depressive breakdown. I was sitting at home crying, paranoid and terrified to go out. The winter fogs were oppressive and added even more darkness to my world. I was further saddened by the state of health of my maternal grandfather. He was now confused and disorientated by dementia, and in an old folk's home. This upset me and made my life even grimmer. I last went to school in the November of 1995, just before my 16th birthday.

Christmas 1995 brought me a break. My mood lifted just a little when I received the best present I could have wished for. My parents gave me a proper, brand new Fender Jazz Bass. I'd wanted this Fender since the first time I'd set eyes on it. I was understandably grateful to them for the gift. Even though I was blown away by my luck, I still felt miserable. The Bass was to get plenty of use in the next year when mania hit me again. I still have it today, now tastefully customised. No playing cricket with this baby!

I did manage to go back for my final exams in the May of 1996, the same month in which my grandfather died.

Steven had a strong relationship with his granddad (my father) and the two of them shared a quirky sense of humour. Granddad Charles had been one of the main carers for Steven from a young age, stepping in when Ian or I were working and when his other granddad Ed wasn't available. Steven generally felt safe with both of them and they contributed to his wellbeing.

Daft as it seems, I started thinking that the chimneys, which I could see from my bedroom window, were trying to send me messages. My biggest fear at that time was that I might have schizophrenia, and this is what the messages were saying to me. I did not know it then, but experience has since taught me that severe depression can bring on psychotic symptoms like this, just as much as mania or the dreaded schizophrenia can.

Desperate for help, I agreed to try a course of homoeopathy. Dick, our homoeopath, shared the same birthday as me and I was able to talk to him sometimes about things I couldn't share with any of my family. This helped me a little but was never going to cure my madness.

Steven was resisting seeing a GP but was willing to talk to our homoeopath, a mature and kind man with experience of mental health illness. The talking and the remedies did help but we needed more. Steven had spent most of Christmas 1995 in bed in a state of deep depression. We finally persuaded him to trust his GP.

Christmas was over, and I had given up all hope of feeling better. I was completely broken. I spent my 16th birthday wishing that I was dead. I spent New Year's Day '96 in tears. Early in January, I bit the bullet and went to my GP who had no hesitation at all in prescribing me Prozac. Nowadays, it is recommended that these drugs should not be given to under 18s, at least in the UK. Maybe I wouldn't have to die if the Prozac would work. Initially, it did. The three months I spent on the drug pulled me out of my black pit. I still had the odd intrusive thought but overall my mood improved. The GP was able to reassure me that I wasn't schizophrenic, and that the persecutory voices, especially any suggesting suicide, are common in severe depressive states. Unfortunately, the manic side hadn't been noticed or investigated yet. Some types of bipolar disorder are sensitive to the use of an anti-depressant without a mood stabilizer. Although the depression will be treated they can send you on an ever-upward spiral and trigger an attack of mania. When I came off Prozac, I soared again into hypo-mania. At this point no one had explained to me (and I hadn't asked) what 'manic' meant. Most of the time when I was high, I felt good. I only went to the GP when deeply depressed. It would be another four years before someone medical would notice the highs and formally diagnose me as bipolar.

I have no idea or memory of why Steven stopped taking Prozac. However, this is a feature of bipolar. People think that they are alright and well, so they stop taking the medication. Why did this happen? Should a GP or someone from the medical fraternity have been keeping an eye on Steven? Ian and I were still ignorant of mental health illness but were trying to learn more about clinical depression. Steven is old enough to exclude us from his appointments and to refuse medication, so we didn't really know how to support him with this. For those of you who think we were negligent parents please consider how you make a teenager take medication that he doesn't want to. Neither of us had considered bipolar as a diagnosis. Our struggle to find out what was 'wrong' with Steven and how to help him began to escalate. No medical person informed, or supported, us as his parents or carers.

I went on a wild spending spree with my trust fund. I felt guilty about the fact that I was doing this when there were so many starving orphans in the world. I sold my little Hammond organ and bought the godfather of all Hammonds, a full console C3 and a valve-driven Leslie tone cabinet 147. These were the types which were used by bands such as Deep Purple and the masters Keith Emerson and Rick Wakeman. My appetite for vintage electrical instruments was well and truly whetted. Later on, I would buy a classic Fender Rhodes electric piano and quite a lot more besides.

Responding to an advert, Steven found this C3 languishing in a Working Man's Club in a coastal town nearby. As a well-used 'big club' organ, it was filthy and rather battered. Accompanied by his father, as bodyguard and roady, he managed to achieve a bargain price of just £400. It was transported to our home in a rented van with Simon and another friend helping out. The Hammond and the Leslie speaker took up residence in our large front hall. Steven spent a very long time cleaning away the years of dust and nicotine. The hours he put into refurbishing this organ were worth the effort. It played beautifully and we all grew to love it.

1996 was a difficult year for our family. My father died in the May and Ian's grandmother in the November. I had also started my own business, having left the bank the year before. This suited our now fragmented lifestyle. I was able to work for myself from home and part time, so felt that I could be available to troubleshoot the difficult days with Steven – and there were a lot of them.

I took myself to out of town places, not a soul or even a building around. I walked in a vast landscape of uneven and broken rocks. It seemed to me as if every living thing had been eradicated from the earth. One favourite haunt of mine was a dilapidated bit of old farm land, barren and craggy. It seemed like a strange desert, the surface of the moon or another planet. I would spend many hours there brooding and alone. The world was mine for a short while. I would stay out until dark, on edge and ready to run from the dangers I believed to be waiting for me. I was sure that everyone was looking at me, and my mind was racing. It felt strange having to come back to earth again.

I would spend night after night wide awake. I saw visions in everything I looked at, some were terrifying. I would have to move pictures and ornaments out of sight, because I could see nothing but death in them. I was designing strange electronic equipment until the early hours; most never got beyond the drawing board, yet some would prove to be workable a few years later. I began carrying out pointless experiments that were frankly dangerous, but I knew no bounds. Accompanied by friends I carried out controlled explosions using various chemicals. These happened in the middle of nowhere and were just for 'laughs'. I accidentally discovered a compound that could dissolve aluminium using a mix of random cleaning products. A further advantage was that it got hot enough to blow apart glass jars without an ignition source. I did not recognise the early onset of mania.

I have often wondered what Steven's friends thought of his behaviour. Did they think he WAS mad, bad or just stupid? Did they feel uneasy or frightened or was it all just a laugh for teenagers? As parents we didn't have any idea what he got up to outside. He always told us where he was, and what time he would be back and never caused us any worry other than his obvious unhappiness. The fact that he was with friends was reassuring and it did seem to lift his mood. His friends often came to the house and were always welcome. This just demonstrates the secret world of teenagers that parents are oblivious to.

Later, I started getting serious panic attacks and went completely nuts. By then I was so manic I did things that were ridiculous, quirky and even unspeakable. I researched schizophrenia, and satisfied myself that I didn't have it. I then researched depression which I immediately recognised. I then cross-referenced depression with manic-depression. A bell rang for me at this point, but I shrugged it off, it couldn't be that.

It was at this point we went to the GP again. I think it was the summer of 1996. Steven and I went together, and he was keen to find some relief. We were advised that a referral to psychiatric services could take as long as 6 months. We were given the explanation that services were extremely stretched. No local services were available, and another area might or might not agree to assess Steven, giving priority to their own patients. At that time, I was not aware that I could even query this, let alone kick up a fuss! Uneasy at the situation, I asked for a private referral and Steven and I paid a visit by train to Yorkvale, a private clinic, a few weeks later. Ian and I had agreed that the fee of £200 was irrelevant when balanced against the urgent need for help and support for Steven. This is one of the points where Steven could have been helped by the NHS, and wasn't even though he was just 16 years old.

I then saw a private psychiatrist who prescribed Tofranil, a tricyclic anti-depressant useful in depressives suffering anxiety, believing it would help. After one dose I had a serious manic attack with visual hallucinations and was taken to hospital by my parents.

I ended up numb down the left-hand side for two weeks afterwards.

This is exactly as it happened. Steven was told at hospital to stop taking the medication immediately, and we did not know what else to do. I have since seen the correspondence from Yorkvale that suggests that Steven should have been started on a much lower dose. This was not communicated to us as a family and understandably Steven was now terrified of taking any of it at all. Neither were we advised that we could, or should, go back for further help. Looking back on this I'm shocked at my naivety and my lack of awareness. We had assumed that our GP would be aware and look after Steven. Who was looking out for my son or for our family? At this time, we did not have any more money for private healthcare, so we were in a cleft stick.

This drug reaction was one of the first seeds of mistrust that grew in Steven's psyche and was to hinder his recovery. So now he is back under the care of his GP with no psychiatric support.

By December 1996 I was re-medicated with Seroxat, which seemed to calm me down. I will explain later in my story why this was a very bad move. Soon I was in a mixed, numb state again, doing everything but feeling nothing. Seroxat saw me back on an even keel feeling surprisingly 'normal' which was abnormal to me. I even got the courage up to go after my first serious girlfriend. Previous one night stands don't really count. This relationship would in time prove to be a train wreck, but for now I was happy.

Steven was now receiving severe disablement benefit and I had applied for this when he left school. I had taken advice from the benefits help line realising that he must be entitled to something if he was too ill to work. No one bothered to tell us about Carers

Allowance at that time as it would have helped us greatly. My working ability was severely restricted by Steven's illness and needs. He would become very distressed and wound up if he was left alone for any length of time. Hoping to get him into work and out in to the world we asked the GP about therapeutic work which is allowed on some benefits. Again, this is something that I found out for myself. The GP was supportive. I can't remember how we found out about the part time work in a music shop in a town close to us, but it was an ideal starting point for Steven. Transport was a problem, but his granddad Ed and Ian took turns with driving him there, and I do think that once or twice Steven was brave enough to go by bus on his own.

1997 I got my first part time job in a music shop. After a while I realised that the customer turnover wasn't exactly massive. Some days just an odd one or two people came in for sheet music, guitar strings or a saxophone reed. I had nothing much to do but play with a wild variety of expensive Fender guitars. I could of course alternate with very attractive 'sparkle painted' Les Paul guitars or a range of keyboards and digital pianos. I also had the use of a whole cabinet of effects units. Added to this intoxicating mixture were a whole heap of amplifiers. Some were not particularly good, but I had to pretend that they were in order to sell them. There were a couple of wonderful valve-driven Fender beauties in there that sounded orgasmic and I was in heaven! Getting paid for playing with excellent things seemed like an ideal job, but it was only a temporary contract. However, after my first three months, I got given an extra month, which would prove to be fate working for me rather than against for once.

Steven seemed much happier over this period and his musical ability and his confidence grew.

One day I just happened to be strumming on my favourite shop-owned Fender Stratocaster, a lake placid blue 1962 reissue playing an ELO song through one of my favourite valve amps, just to pass the time when into the shop walked a man who was the spitting image of ELO's Jeff Lynne. He was accompanied by a bloke that looked a lot like ELO's bass player. They weren't of course from ELO, but the Jeff look-alike recognised the tune and we started up a conversation about the band. It turned out we were both completely nuts about The Electric Light Orchestra. He introduced himself as Drew and said "I'm going to France for a few months when I get back would you be interested in putting a band together?" Would I? Sure! So 'Afterglow' was born. Drew became a friend and after all these years still is. In fact, he's like a brother to me. He and his wife Sindy deserve medals for helping me later when I was more seriously ill.

After a few months of 'normality', something began to go wrong again. I had a party one night and thought it would be funny to pull a hilarious stunt, in which I broke two of my fingers. Whilst this was going on the party was gate-crashed. In the morning I had to literally rebuild the house with just one usable hand. Luckily two friends joined in to help me and they had a neighbour drive me to hospital. I was reluctant to go but the extent of the injury had become apparent when I woke up that morning. I was in great pain and my hand was black and blue. The x-rays showed one finger in seven pieces, the other cracked vertically. I was lucky I didn't need pins, but I spent six weeks with my hand and wrist in a cast. After the cast was removed it took a long time before I could play an instrument again. By the time I got myself sorted, Drew was home from France and we started rehearsing and recording, just the two of us together.

This event took place when we were away on a short break in August 1997. It set the pattern for every holiday or break that we took from that point on. I have no idea if Steven was drunk, manic or both. He had crushed his hand trying to throw a metal lamp post about, a souvenir from his lighting days. When we talked the incident over later he didn't have much recall. He confessed about the party and was devastated to find that some money belonging to my business had gone missing. He learned a lot about human nature because of the gate-crashing. Once again, I wonder what his friends thought about his behaviour. It became obvious that we could not leave him in the 'care' of friends. It is not fair on the friends or on Steven.

After one of our first practice sessions I returned from Drew's late at night, and was invited to a party at my friend Simon's place. I spoke of the evening's recording, and was by then pretty drunk. Simon expressed an interest in the project. As we walked to his house to discuss it, we were 'jumped' by a bunch of soldiers much older than us. They had us pegged as 'faggots' because of our long hair and my loud shirt. I simply, politely assured them I wasn't gay, and neither was Simon, not that it's anybody's business to ask, or even care. The response was to call me a cheeky bastard, and proceed to kick my head in until I was a bloody pulp. We were outnumbered, save for a bunch of unresponsive onlookers. Simon made a break for it and got away, after a less violent kicking. I was too drunk to think or feel it, as someone at the party we'd just left had dared me to down a half pint of gin. The squaddies stamped on my head and left me in a heap. I dragged myself away from the scene to go and find Simon. Unlike me he was okay.

September 1997 Steven arrived home in the early hours. We were laid awake listening for him as worried parents do. He crashed through the door and fell into the hall. He was covered in blood and mud and extremely distressed. Evidently beaten up and incoherent, we realised that he was afraid for Simon's safety. After phoning the police and various other parents we ascertained that Simon and the others were safe. It was Steven who didn't run fast enough. Ian took him off to hospital to be checked over. I have no idea if the reference to huge amounts of alcohol is true or just bravado. It is about now that we begin to realise that Steven drinks. At this time, we are not able to do anything about it other than talk to him about safe levels. We begin to link it to his mental health, but alarm bells have not yet sounded. We were ignorant, and Steven was very good at hiding the truth.

The next day the boys all sat in a group in our home reliving the event. It was evident that they were in shock and distressed. After debating the incident, it was apparent that they believed that the police were not much interested.

The next day at home my head was glued to the pillow with blood where my mouth had exploded. The hospital had let me go home at about 4.30am. On waking that day, I went to the law. Despite me being able to give a name, and the event having taken place under a CCTV camera, they were bloody useless. Simon came as a witness, but he was okay. They said that they could photograph my injuries, but suggested I don't press charges, because the guy would be back to get me, and they didn't know who he was anyway. Terrific! So, imagine my glee when I heard the ringleader's father in law gave him a damn good kicking and put him in hospital. The dad-in-law had been with his daughter, who was giving birth to this bloke's kid. Outraged to find that baby's father was out drinking and fighting instead of being at the hospital that night, he sorted him out. Karma. And my name isn't Earl.

This refers to a character in an American TV show who is one of life's hapless victims.

After healing from the beating, I brought Simon into the group to make a decent live show. One night at my house, Drew and Simon were recording upstairs. They peered out of the window in to the garden, and saw a very manic me and a drunken friend jumping through the flames of a kerosene soaked cardboard box. We were throwing anything combustible that could be found onto the pyre. When clothing began to be thrown on, Drew and Simon, laughing hysterically at the foolish spectacle, leaned out of the window and reminded me I was needed in a recording session. I'd taken a rather longer 'smoke' break than they were expecting.

I attach no blame or responsibility to Steven's friends, but I do wonder what they thought? What is normal? What is acceptable? What is being passed off as just drunken behaviour? Do they recognise abnormal behaviour or mania? And where were the other parents! Does anyone looking in from the outside have any concerns about Steven's mental state and behaviour?

The Seroxat had obviously stopped being of any benefit. I started getting white-outs, sweats, nightmares and tingling sensations, plus the depression seemed to be creeping in again slowly. I ditched the pills and the symptoms vanished immediately but the withdrawals were terrible. I was awake for a fortnight, visually hallucinating, shaking and sweating like I was in hell. After a fortnight of that I had to have a drink to get some sleep. Believe me, detoxing from prescription medication is worse than detoxing from alcohol addiction. I've done both.

It was during this period that Steven brought home two young girls aged 13 and 15. "Their mother has thrown them out and they can't get back in." We had been on an extremely rare night out to a Phil Collins concert in a nearby city and arrived home at half past midnight to find a 'fait-accompli'. "Can they stay the night?" We phone the mum who is incoherent with drink or drugs and not interested. We put the girls to bed in our tiny third bedroom and await the dawn. They stay with us for a further 9 months…

From then on, I pretty much put up with my odd thoughts for a bit. Relationships came and went and good old Mr. Alcohol was always there if I felt I was too troubled to sleep. Evidently, this eventually leads to addiction but it's my choice and I don't now drink anywhere near as much as I did when my illness went full blown. I continued to have my moods and odd feelings for most of 1998. In February, after much rehearsal in Drew's mother's kitchen, we launched Afterglow as a live band. Drew on drums, my genius friend Simon on guitar and I played my ass off as chief keyboard player and bassist.

On Easter Monday 1998 Afterglow played in the local pub, The Tree to a packed audience. I wrote the press release for a local music magazine. I also note that they are due to play at our Civic Hall on Friday 19th June 1998.

I felt great playing before hundreds after the initial nerves wore off. My girlfriend had recently confessed to cheating on me and I got my revenge at this concert, by going home with one of the female support duo. I didn't find her attractive but did the deed and it satisfied my desire for revenge. Morning came and having had too many after show drinks I didn't know where I was. I called Drew in a panic. He was like a homing pigeon, so he must know where he had dropped me off. The phone call was simple; Me: "HELP!" Drew: "I'm on my way!"

Steven's use of a willing girl for casual 'revenge' sex disturbs me. It is out of character, but I believe this is where we begin to see the real damage being done by alcohol and untreated bipolar. I don't think the concert mentioned was in front of 'hundreds', but it was very successful, and Ian had acted as roady and then left them to it at the end of the event. The mention of alcohol when he can't sleep is significant.

The guilt boiled inside me for three days until I had to confess what I'd done, and even though she'd done it first, my girlfriend dumped me. But only for a fortnight, we had the rest of the year together before she started playing around again and I left for good. But that wasn't the complete end, as we will see later.

The gig at the Civic Hall went down well and between us we sold over 100 tickets for charity. I cried into my brandy when I saw Steven performing on stage. I had believed that he would have killed himself before this moment and I was very proud of his achievement. It gave me hope for the future.

We played quite a few gigs and went down well, often being asked back. It felt great again to be getting paid for something you love doing. I realised another dream the month after the gig. I found myself a Wurlitzer EP 200 electric piano, for which I had been searching for two years. This is the piano used on 'You're My Best Friend' by Queen and many others, including Supertramp and ELO. I found myself dipping into another bit of my trust fund and went crazy kitting out my first workable multi-track recording studio. The next year 1999 was the same. I had come into more money, thousands. I went on a spending spree for a fortnight, buying practically anything that caught my eye, including a beautiful 1957 reissue Fender Stratocaster, PA equipment and speakers.

To help Steven mature and become more responsible, we allowed him to control money that had been given to him from his deceased grandmother's estate. It certainly wasn't thousands in the sense of unlimited funds. I believe that it was five thousand in all. He had used this sensibly over the past couple of years to buy musical equipment and the kit that he needed to be able to play at a concert and rehearse at home. He generally managed his money well and his spending did not give us any cause for concern at the time.

Soon I would meet a girl who was into some of the same music as me. She really could sing and was for a time Simon's girlfriend. We put together a side project to Afterglow, with her singing, and me on harmonies. We concentrated on Fleetwood Mac covers and other rock songs. We called the project Fusion.

I hadn't seen Drew for months. I'd split with my girlfriend, he'd been going out with her mother, and then they had also broken up. Both women had tried to break Drew and me up as friends, and he just vanished, believing their slander as much as I did. Time passed and one day I found him at my door. He explained that he'd had a massive depressive episode and had spent weeks and weeks on his couch. He occasionally rose to record a new track during sudden bursts of high spirits. Unsurprisingly he was put on antidepressants. Two and a half years later, we were both to be diagnosed bipolar and put on mood stabilizers, within weeks of each other. His stint on them would turn out to be only short term. When we were reunited, things rubbed along as usual with friendship and music, but Drew wasn't buying into Fusion. He didn't like Fleetwood Mac, so he wasn't interested, but he would come to rehearsal to laugh and muck about.

I should have seen my mania developing. I wasn't sleeping and was rehearsing all the time I could. One morning a friend of mine called me at 5am (he'd been up all night working on a university project) and was surprised that I was awake. He was about to crash through fatigue. He wanted me to accompany him to university, so he didn't fall asleep on the way. He needed to get his essay there in time for the deadline. He shouldn't have been driving but wanted me to keep talking to him to keep him awake. I was a maniac to go and to let him do it. (No pun intended). On the way home, I flicked a cigarette out of the passenger window. It just happened to sail through the open window of an unlucky woman's car. I remember seeing it explode in a shower of sparks all over the poor woman's dashboard as we set off at speed. It was a complete accident but for some reason I found it hilarious. I think I know what that reason was. Horrible things seem funny sometimes when you're going barking mad. At least she didn't crash. I wouldn't have found that remotely funny unless she was my worst enemy.

Once again, true to his character Steven is upset by things that happen that hurt people.

Fusion never really got off the ground. Just as well, because shortly, due to flu and working myself too hard, I would have 3 heart attacks as the result of myocarditis, and not notice until the last one hit. I thought it was indigestion. I spent a few days in hospital but was so agitated and impatient that I discharged myself against advice. Nurses told me that severe cases of flu, plus serious overwork, often lead to this. I was part of my own road crew and trying to sing with a throat infection.

Steven either does not remember accurately or is skating over the truth. On 22nd February 1999 he wakes me in the early hours. He has chest pain and is finding it hard to breathe. I struggle to get him dressed, throw on my clothes and get him down to the surgery as the doors open. After examination, the GP tells me to take Steven straight to Accident and Emergency and he phones ahead. What I thought might be pleurisy was myocarditis and Steven is very unwell. Many years later I find out that this could be because of heavy drinking yet no one flagged this up to us.

After a couple of days, we have to bring him home because of his distress in hospital. I check what they are doing for him – nothing but anti-inflammatories and bed rest so we bring him home. Yet another pattern, being painted for the future. He did not receive any further checks on his heart and I do not know if this is because we brought him home. Steven is obliged to hold off beginning his first proper job whilst he recuperates.

I began work at a mobile phone call centre after a couple weeks recuperation. It was simply insane. Each team of operators was like a little family. And just as it is with a real family, some get on like a house on fire, others hate each other. We would laugh at some of the crank callers, some were in it for laughs, some seriously disturbed. One man had notes on his account stating that he'd called to say "I'm not human but what I'm wearing is." He had a ream of bizarre notes like this. His occupation was listed as 'writer'. He was in my opinion a prime candidate for being a bipolar patient, after having spoken to him myself. He would call repeatedly within seconds of a previous call to harass another member of the team. Once I listened in when a colleague got a call and, stupidly, uttered under my breath as I walked away from the phone, "Jesus, get medical help!" The man heard this somehow and my unfortunate colleague, trying not to laugh, was left trying to reassure this person that he must be hearing things again, as was documented in his notes. We had many schizophrenic clients also, one of whom, before my time in the job, was banned from calling us and was told to communicate with the company by letter. Another thought our corporate logo of the time was stalking him. What it was I can't say without naming the company.

I do wonder if the staff had proper training in how to handle disturbed or distressed people? Steven seems quite blasé about the prevailing attitude. It bodes ill for his future when he experiences prejudice and discrimination himself.

All was well until mid-summer 1999 when the dark thoughts began returning. It was shortly after this that I met my first wife.

Acting as deputy supervisor, I was unexpectedly attracted to a somewhat naïve but essentially harmless young girl working in the call centre. She decided after a week of dating that we should marry. Feeling a bit high and not taking it at the level of seriousness required by such a premise, I agreed. Ten months later, this would happen, but for now we just spent most of the week swapping between one and the other's home. It all went well for a few weeks until I started feeling strange again.

During the summer of 1999 and over the next few months the relationship is full on. He spends a lot of time at this girl's flat in a rural village. We are relieved that he seems to have found some normality and a relationship that makes him happy. When he is at home with us we rarely see him. He works 12 hour shifts and is either at work or in bed. The young woman gradually begins to spend time at our house. We discover that this is because the heating bills have not been paid, she doesn't cook and it is a very cold autumn.

CHAPTER 3: THE STORM BREAKS

Late 1999 I thought I was doing fine. But the thoughts in my head were making me drink just to tread water. At first, I lived with my intended at her ice-cold, middle of winter, no heating flat. Then she lost her tenancy, and through her own fault, her job. So, she came to live with me at my parents' house.

They arrive together just before Christmas 1999 and she has a suitcase. Both are loaded with flu and unable to work. They don't tell us at first that the flat is no longer a home. No one asks us if we will take her in, but we were always a soft touch. Christmas and New Year go along okay but we all need some space. I am not happy listening to sounds of vigorous lovemaking. I have never been a prude, but sexual gymnastics should be a private matter. During her stay with us, she lost her job for breaking a financial rule. Not embezzlement, but something very silly and unnecessary. She is a gentle, kind and quiet girl but seems to be very naive and not very street wise. Regardless of what Steven writes about her, he really loved her. I think it is regret and guilt that colours his words here.

I began to feel paranoid about the impending Millennium. Surely, I should be feeling different on the morning of 1st January 2000? I was cracking again. We both decided to quit smoking to save money. We are both 20 and stupid and thought the world was our oyster. We stayed awhile with my parents as we planned to buy a house before we got spliced. We moved into our new home at the beginning of May 2000 with the wedding set for the September. It was a simple house, but nice, just needed the décor updating. I got the mortgage as the only one currently working, she put down the deposit.

The first night in the house she started to cry saying her parents hadn't done enough for her. I think that they had, but my words meant nothing. Shortly after, it was me that was crying. My cat, who was a bit too old to move, and a bit of a nutter himself had been left at my parents' house. He died of Feline Aids whilst I was at work. Three days later, mid May 2000 we went and got a cat from the Cats Protection League. This is Kia who still loves her adoptive dad today.

This is our grand old lady, black and white Kia, still alive whilst writing this but put to sleep 9th Dec 2016 aged about 19.

We were okay in our new home but things from the past kept getting in the way. In the February of that year my wife crashed her car whilst driving me and a friend home. I was injured and off sick for two weeks. The friend who was already fragile from a previous physical injury was also hurt. Ironically, we were returning from said friend's hospital check-up. She tried to overtake a 40 foot length of traffic in a no overtaking zone. The friend sued for injury caused and won damages. I did not see the court case as I was working and not a plaintiff. But the stress drove me bonkers. When I found out that my soon-to-be wife had lost her license and been heavily fined I was sad for her. It would be my money of course and I wondered where I would find it. Her parents paid the bill as it turns out, but I lost the plot. I felt so useless working in a call centre when my partner needed me.

I am confused here. I know that she was sued by the other passenger, but I didn't know that her parents footed the bill. I took her to the local court for another traffic offence and gave her moral support. I had to help her sort out her documents for the case and it did become apparent that she was not one of life's copers. So not only was she without a job, but she was fined, lost her license and had to pay damages to the injured passenger.

On a stressful day at work I had a call from a particularly nasty customer and my blood boiled. I ended the call and started shaking and cursing uncontrollably. My chief sent me home with pay for a few days. I arrived home, totally manic, cursing the bus service that hadn't delivered. I ended up in a taxi and was very worried about the expense. I remember it vividly, 25th July 2000 the day that Air France Concorde caught fire. I paced around at home like a nutter until a couple of vodkas kicked in. I woke up in the middle of the night thinking someone was sending text messages directly to my brain. The spooky thing is that I got real text messages of similar content several minutes later to my phone. A few days later I'd decide to have my trademark long hair shaved off.

This random amount of information, including the hair cut seems to reflect a truly unbalanced state of mind. We did not immediately know about Steven being sent home or that there was a problem. We had tried to leave them both well alone in the hope that they would sort out their own issues. Again, we have the upfront admission that Steven needs a drink to calm down. His recall of dates may not be accurate as I have evidence that he was already 'signed off' work on 17th April 2000.This could have referred to the car accident.

I felt that I couldn't go back to work, but I had to make up the time I'd reneged on which was fine. It was a mission that took me two pints to face. My chief said, don't sweat about it, but I was manic as hell and got through a half shift by the skin of my teeth, then went home for good. I stayed on the payroll for over a year, causing problems with disability claims. That last day I was on the works floor I was laughing insanely at anything and everything. I was terrified of the simplest things. Still am.

I went to the local shop and saw that although the sky was cloudless, and the sun was shining over the horizon, a strange haze had gathered around far-off buildings. Something was coming. I was right it thundered none stop for about 3 days. In an excitable state I hooked up my recording gear and leaned out of the window with a metal boom microphone to record the cacophony. Pretty brave considering the violence of the storm and the many lightning strikes that blew up a chemical plant and a few other properties that night.

I am not editing all of Steven's writing as the phrasing shows to me that he is in a state of emotional arousal. It is unrealistic to think that his story was written only when he was well and functioning normally. His reference to the storm is a little overblown, but a lightning strike to a tower at a large chemical factory on the nearby trading estate did result in a spectacular fire and a lot of disruption.

The rest of the year 2000 I spent writing songs, just as I had been doing for years. Now I had my own home and studio. It was fully kitted out by my manic spending on musical equipment. I had procured a Moog synthesizer for a reasonable price bringing my studio up to full specification. Just before we moved into our new house my lady and I had a little holiday. We went to visit Drew in France, he had moved over there for a while in late 1999. We started making spoof recordings together, working each side of the channel and exchanging content by return of post. It was all built around a delusional idea about the world being taken over by bathmats, but it wasn't actual madness, just fun. Just take a classic recording, rewrite it to be about bathmats, throw in a few private jokes and you can give a mate a laugh.

We were thrilled to bits when Steven, with his fiancée managed the trip to France in April 2000. We deluded ourselves into thinking that this was a turning point and that he was becoming more confident and more independent. He couldn't have managed it without his fiancée's help and they muddled through the journey together. There were many times that Steven didn't manage to walk along the street or even go to the pub, so this holiday trip was a real achievement. And he missed Drew so very much – his 'blood brother'. The reference to the 'Bathmats' relates to comedy recordings that are hilarious and creative.

September 2000

By now I was married, yet my wife did not share my interests. She would live her life, I mine. Sad really and I found myself drifting more towards my music, my beautiful adopted cat girl and getting sloshed when the wife went out with the girls. My only visions as the year swung around to autumn happened on my visits to buy something from the shop, under grey skies and high winds. I would not go back and 'weather the storm', but continue walking forever. But this was only a vision, and the practical part of me managed to stop that from happening. Christmas went okay that year, a good dose of tryptophan (from the turkey dinner) plus a few G and T's made me sleep like a baby. It was the last bit of peace before total meltdown.

Steven has hardly mentioned his marriage and wedding in September 2000. It was a very strange affair, a weird mix of traditional and doing their own thing and interaction with the bride's parents was difficult. I believe that they knew the marriage was not a good idea. When I realised that Steven was really going through with it I attempted a serious talk with his bride to be. "He is not well, and he drinks because we can't seem to get any help. He has some kind of mental health problem. Are you sure that this is what you want and that you can cope with it? Can you look after each other?" She gazed blankly at me and on reflection I realise that she had no concept of what was really going on with Steven. I should have tried harder to dissuade them, but they were set on the idea of marriage and happily ever after. I think it is significant that Steven does not say much about his wedding or his marriage. He later told me that he married to stop the nagging and because he didn't want to be a 'sad bastard sitting on his own'. This is not the total truth. At the time of marriage, he loved this lady and later wrote her a special song for her 21st Birthday 'It'sYou'.

Early 2001 saw me manic again, back at the doctors. My doctor had already signed me a permanent sick note before he retired. My new doctor prescribed me Lustral. It helped with the depression but not the dark thoughts. When I reported this, he doubled the dose and I went off the scale with mania. I felt lethal. Even the house plants seemed sinister. I would encourage friends to visit lest I do mischief to my wife. I could not sleep. The living room seemed to morph into strange shapes. I started drinking 6-8 cans of cider, plus a bottle of schnapps and a litre of vodka just to have a nap. I was seriously unnerved by this. I developed a delusion that I could persuade Roy Wood of Wizzard fame, formerly of ELO and the Move, to record a charity single with me. He could even come over and sleep on the couch! Obviously, it didn't happen, but the next best thing did when I went to see him in concert some time later.

The reference here is to the visit to a concert that Steven and Drew made. Again, I was amazed that Steven managed the journey but with Drew to bolster his courage (and probably a lot of booze) they got to the concert in Birmingham, got the autograph, the photo and the t-shirt!

In the spring of 2001, I continued to renovate the décor of the house. One day I was about to start and had a full blown panic attack. I was physically sick and fell over with no apparent cause on a trip to the local shop and felt damn stupid as a result.

Is this how Steven really saw it? Or is it the sanitised version of a prolonged binge? Steven was drinking so much now that his wife and her mother came to see me to discuss it. "He stays up all night drinking and I find him spark out on the couch in the morning with his booze spilled all over. He won't listen to me. I don't know what to do. Can you have a word with him please?"

I was only too happy to have a word but on reflection, maybe we had become blasé about his habit. I did 'have a word' but of course it fell on deaf ears. If I had known more at the time, I would have dragged him back to the GP then and there.

On 18th January 2001 I sat with Steven whilst the occupational health service for his place of work interviewed him at home. He was too unwell to go to them.

I was overspending everywhere. The internet offered everything, and I wanted it all and through the easy availability of credit, bought it. I also found another classic manic symptom that turns up in many a description of manic depression; sex addiction. I was never unfaithful but never satisfied, much to the disdain of my wife who must have been completely exhausted. It became too intense. It was time to call in the big guns.

Steven wanted help and asked for our support. On the 24th April 2001 he was referred to the local Community Mental Health Team and prescribed Sertraline whilst he waited. It was a lengthy process. Three months later on 2nd July 2001 is the day of the first appointment to see a psychiatrist. Steven was unable to get out of the door and was distressed and agitated. I encouraged him to write a letter which was hand delivered to his appointment by his wife and me. This was probably the only time we managed to work as a team. Prof A agreed to come out to the house to assess Steven on 13th July 2001 and we eventually all met together, me, my husband and Steven and his wife. The process was a revelation. Prof A was positive that Steven had bipolar and prescribed him appropriate medication. He also set the wheels in motion to get Steven 'dried out'. It would take months to get a bed to do this. We foolishly thought the problem was solved and all would be well.

With help from my parents I managed to get an appointment with a professor of psychiatry, we'll call him Prof A, now retired. He immediately noticed what a head case I was, except he put it a bit more delicately in his report. In his opinion, and that of his colleagues, I definitely had bipolar disorder and was one of the strangest patients he'd ever met (in a kind way).

I said, "Oh hell, does that mean I'm going to get put on Haloperidol?" (An anti-psychotic often used to calm manic and other psychotic symptoms.) He responded, "Well, maybe if you were my worst enemy, but as it is, no."

People I would meet later would give me the horror stories of their experience of this early 1960's drug, whereas others tolerated it well, even if it meant spending two-thirds of the week asleep.

He took me off the Lustral, and put me on valproate semi-sodium (a modern version of lithium) which slowly levelled my mood back to the ground. And what fun it was coming down. The delicious state of hypo-mania is intoxicating and causes many to avoid medication. I saw some beautiful visions as I came back to earth and wrote some songs like a man possessed. I emphasise the word 'visions', not the full-on hallucinations that can accompany full-on psychosis in mania or schizophrenia.

I don't remember what support Steven was offered. He was given medication to stabilise his mood whilst he waited for a bed in hospital to be 'dried out'. He suffered on his own and channelled his fear and distress into music and writing. On checking medical records, it seems that he was to attend the Community Mental Health clinic, but I don't know what support he received. He was often too anxious to leave the house, he was frightened and agoraphobic. There is a note in the records that says Steven was observed having real difficulty climbing the stairs to the room where the Community Mental Health Team hung out.

My wife got a new job, leaving me alone all day. I went insane when she left on a morning. Being left to an empty house didn't do me any good at all. I would do all the housework, then if no friends were available I would have a brief chat with my cat, then pace madly around the living room giving myself a thorough telling off for all the wicked things I thought I would go to hell for. I became obsessed with death, my greatest fear. All I could envisage was the sight of decomposing bodies. Thoughts of them under the floorboards plagued me. I could not shake off the image of myself rotting away.

There was a plus side. Trying to put my mind elsewhere, I came up with some wild inventions during this time. I successfully built from scratch an electronic speed switcher for the Leslie rotating speaker that I used with my Hammond organ. I had designed a circuit when I was aged 16, and had forgotten about it until now. I etched it in a washing up bowl full of ferric chloride in my front yard. Anyone familiar with Leslies will know you can get an audible 'pop' through the speaker when you switch from slow to fast with the original mechanical relay. My solid-state circuit eradicated that, plus offered a stationary setting, meaning no need for an additional tone cabinet when you didn't want the sound to be animated. I also had a foot pedal welded up to enable the player to switch speeds without taking his hands off the keyboards. I was working on plans for a Leslie simulator for use with guitars. I had the circuit plan, but it never got past the basic on-paper design, plus it had been already done. Mine was just a bit more intense. I've always been good with electronics; some classmate when I was 16 had asked me to make him a taser, and whilst I could have easily done so, I didn't, on moral grounds. Then I made the legendary 'beer guitar', starting with my beat-up classical that had some damage to the front. I filled in the chips in the wood and covered the top with every beer, wine or liquor label I could get my hands on. I made a perfect collage right up to the instruments binding, and then painted over it with clear matt sealant. Lots of people have offered to buy it on sight.

I also began writing an instrumental album in the style of Jean-Michel Jarre. I spent hours each day occupying my mind whilst alone, and used every single synthesiser I owned to get the tracks down. Then I would have a few drinks and relax until my partner got home.

I have left Steven's phrasing here, it reflects how he was functioning at the time.

I became incredibly impatient at home, with the slowness of everything. My mind wanted everything done yesterday. A printer that refused to print got launched down the stairs and smashed to kingdom come. Too impatient to wait for a bus I called a cab to take me the £15 worth of distance to buy a new one. Then I got another cab home. A violin, that nearly had my eye out when a string broke, got ceremonially burned in the barbecue. I danced around the fire in a manic rage. I was up at the break of dawn cleaning the house. I was so wired I had to do something; I probably had the cleanest house going back then. But I could not yet see that things were getting a bit too heavy.

I do recall a few magic moments that my wife and I experienced together. There was the time that I took her to a nearby town, some 20 minutes in a taxi from home, where we had lunch. We then took advantage of the good summer weather and walked back, stopping for a pint halfway home. And the time I took her to a local village, which is mentioned in the Doomsday book, and had gallows on the village green until the 17th or 18th century. We ate dinner in the 17th century inn by the green. I was still slightly manic, and I felt bit self-conscious popping mood stabilizers in public, but I had to do it. I decided to give her a tour of the village as I knew it well as my grandfather had lived there.

She must have thought I was barking mad as I led her at lightning speed through every street of a village she didn't know. I probably was on the comedown of mania. While I was eating my steak at dinner in the snug of the inn, I got a sense of chain mailed soldiers of yore standing at the bar with pewter tankards laughing and cajoling each other. I knew no one else would have seen this, so I just smiled to myself, paid up, and went on my mad little tour.

The upshot of this was a song that came out of nowhere the next day. Unsurprisingly I called it 'Mediaeval Dream'. Whilst sat in the living room one afternoon, I had a vision of climbing stairs in a romantic Venetian building to watch a sunset. I asked my wife to 'climb' the stairs with me. She must have thought I was putting her on as we ran around the 'spiral staircase' that I envisioned in our living room. She couldn't see it, but I could. The next day I used the image to write her a song called simply 'It's You'. This was for her 21st birthday. Despite usually being too frightened to leave the house at this point, I organised a venue for her party and acted as DJ for the night. The mood stabiliser had brought me down from the clouds nicely, and I'd envisioned some wonderful things. Now I thought I could do without it. I would later regret choosing to stop my medication when my world blew to hell.

During the summer I had, as an electrical enthusiast, been handed a newspaper story about the plans in the USA to shut down the electric chair for good. I read it with interest and then forgot about it. I even watched the film the Green Mile. Then the mood stabiliser wore off, and just before hospitalisation in September 2001 (to be 'dried out') I couldn't even look at a regular chair without going nuts and I developed a morbid fear of the device.

This was a severe obsession and some chairs were moved or covered in our home whilst Steven was with us. It was distressing for us all. Gradually I managed to work with the fear and Steven began to read more about the actual history of the Electric Chair in the USA. As a result, the anxiety faded a little.

As my mania fell away, and exhausted from staying up for days I started passing out on the couch for a random couple of hours. I would wake up and be unable to get back to sleep. Sometimes I stayed up until 4 or 5 in the morning watching TV, before creeping up to bed without waking my wife. I didn't manage to do this very successfully and soon I thought it might be best if I gave her some space.

I ended up first living with my parents again, visited by my wife who could not understand my condition, with me pacing around in a great state of agitation. Then I was institutionalised for a month.

This reference to being institutionalised is when Steven went in to a specialist mental health unit at our local hospital to be 'dried out' in September 2001. As parents we were not given access to information and we were not aware that he would be reassessed re his mental health. His wife was the next of kin now and had to cope on her own. She chose not to share any information with us, and it seems that she did not ask or wasn't included in any discussions about Steven's mental health or care plan.

My psychiatrist Prof A had retired, and I was given in his stead a jumped-up arrogant, ex-military doctor who took an instant dislike to me. He gave me Librium, which helped, but he also put me back on the dreaded Seroxat. Mania didn't concern him, and he disputed Professor A's findings. Then he ignored me.

Whilst in hospital I met a man my own age called Rob, who was to become a life-long friend. He also had experienced a breakdown, though in his case it was related to drug use. He still seemed to be the only one in there talking any sense. We've been good friends ever since, and although he's no longer doing drugs, he is like me, stuck with medication in case of psychotic relapse. We had a good time in that dated and archaic hospital. When my mood began to lift, I had my 'beer guitar' brought in. I would sit in the first floor lobby strumming away to ease the boredom. As a non-smoker at the time, I found the depressing television room boring. It was filled with patients drugged into what is probably the closest thing to a coma state I have seen. Alternatively, there was always a party in the smoke room. It had a stereo which I would sometimes commandeer. Everyone got a turn. Some nights I would bring my guitar in and we'd have a sing-along. Fast food would be ordered after lockdown. We'd send the cash down in the lift and Security would send up the food.

Steven learned a lot in hospital, both good and bad.

In there I met a woman who'd been sectioned because she believed that she had been ordered by Jesus to go to London. Halfway there the devil had made her turn back. She was convinced of this fact but seemed utterly normal to me. I met a man who believed that his friends were sneaking into his house and placing LSD in his water tank. There was a woman who, despite being on the highest dose of Lithium allowed, was uncontrollable. Unlike the rest of us in dormitories, she had to have her own room. Another was a Seroxat victim who couldn't get off the stuff and was also taking Haloperidol for her mania. This was helped along by the fact that she was also smuggling vodka inside soft drinks bottles. She was very intelligent and knew the British Medical Association Guide to Medicine and Drugs like the back of her hand. The staff didn't like it. She made an enemy of a nurse who almost gave her the wrong medication. She had a great knowledge of pharmaceuticals, as did I. A few days later she was found unconscious and bleeding, having slashed her wrists with a smuggled blade. There was an old man, who thought he was in a prisoner of war camp or something, and kept telling me to be careful, "they're on to us". He would ask constantly "when are we going to make our breakout?" The wards were peopled with a myriad of colourful characters, including one very attractive young lady. She would offer sex to anything in trousers, if they would just like to venture into the linen cupboard. We all knew she was getting regular check-ups at the GUM clinic, so there were no takers. I was to meet her in another hospital several years later.

She would be much shyer and much heavier due to medication and she would apologise for her earlier behaviour as soon as she saw me, although of course there was no need.

Another patient, a young man a bit older than me, had tried to kill his parents. On the ward he would constantly burn himself with lighters and cut himself open with stashed blades. He was on the maximum dose of Clozaril, a powerful anti-psychotic that caused him to sleep all day. Then he would play death metal CDs all night.

I found all the horror stories about Electro Convulsive Therapy to be true. One female patient would go weekly for a session, and return from the sessions terrified and with no memory of her name, her whereabouts or indeed anything else. She would be seemingly fine beforehand. Some patients were incredibly open about their conditions, others deeply ashamed.

My wife did visit me in hospital, and when I was allowed off the ward I took her to the main hospital building. For reasons of frustration if not mania, I encouraged her to run with me up the spiral stairwell (no imaginary ones this time) from the basement to the fourth floor. Then we got in the lift and went down again. She probably was glad that I was in the right place.

I was working at the time of Steven's stay, but sometimes managed to give some support by taking his wife to visit by car. I would greet Steven and make small talk and then discreetly distance myself so that they could have some time alone. From what I could make out they only ever talked about Kia the cat. No discussion on treatment, life plans, finances or love and sorrow. Maybe cat talk was the only safe and common ground left to them.

One time, just back from a visit on my own, I got a panic-stricken phone call from his wife. In a distressed state she told me that the cat had been attacked and shaken by two lurchers, and was now up a tree in the back garden. I hastily collected the cat carrier and drove to their house.

I find her in tears and covered in mud. She has been trying to retrieve Kia from the tree. I calm her and suggest that she leaves the patio window open whilst we wait quietly together. Eventually the cat slinks into the room and heads upstairs. She is streaked with grass stains where the dogs have literally wiped the floor with her and is limping. I am relieved that there is no visible bleeding. I follow her quietly and scoop her up into the carrier. We head for the vets where Kia is examined and suspected of having internal injuries. We leave her and return home. Unfortunately, whilst trying to phone me for help, she has also called Steven who is now distressed, agitated and threatening to leave hospital. I reassure both of them and I deal with the vets and the cat. Kia has surgery for ripped bowels. She has been shaken so hard that she has literally 'bust a gut'. She has been repaired and is returned to us that day with stitches from 'armpit' to groin. I glean from the vet that she is not really expected to survive.

Knowing how much the cat means to them both I instruct Steven's wife on her care. I teach her how to dose her with water and Rescue Remedy every hour from a dropper. Over the next two days the cat does not get up, urinate or eat. She is nursed with care and having her drops administered every hour. We are relieved when the cat struggles to her feet, wees in her tray and drinks from a bowl. She is on the mend. I congratulate Steven's wife on her dedication. Steven is not told of the seriousness of the situation.

Rob became enthralled by my guitar. He wasn't allowed off the ward yet and I was. He asked if I would go out and buy him a cheap guitar so that he could learn. He handed me some money and I brought back a decent starter acoustic. He's moved on to much finer instruments since then.

When alone and bored I would gaze out of the suicide-proof and sealed first story windows. I could either gaze down to the grim looking lock-up ward, or over to the church steeple in the distance, contemplating either freedom or death. That's weird from a guy about to try and kill himself as 2002's New Year resolution. I'd lasted about a fortnight after leaving the hospital on a high dose of Seroxat - should have known better.

Steven was in hospital for about 6 weeks and was discharged 'dry' and on antidepressants with no other backup that I am aware of. Unknown to us, he had been reassessed as 'just an alcoholic'. We were all left to get on with it. We were unaware of this at the time and had assumed that Steven was still on the medication and mood stabilisers that Prof A had originally prescribed. As Steven was a married man with his wife as next of kin, we were not privy to this information.

This is what happened next. After 18 months without nicotine, I had given in to smoking after a friend had offered me a roll up and of course I had accepted. I couldn't lie to my wife, it's not in me, so I confessed and bought a packet of 20 for us both. She said she'd never really wanted to quit anyway. We smoked ourselves stupid, and with the help of a bottle of brandy, a fight ensued that made us both see we were no good for each other. We have a blazing row. I can't remember who started it, or what it was about. I turned on my heel and left my wife on the 1st December 2001.

This was much sadder and messier than Steven has remembered here. I'm not surprised that he hasn't got the full details. He was either manic, roaring drunk or both. His wife called us and said that Steven was running about with a knife and to come quickly. Ian and I arrived to find Steven racing up and down the stairs, carving knife in hand and tears streaming down his face. His wife was in a state of shock and seemed to be tidying up. It took me a while to realise that she was gathering clothes together. We did our best to calm Steven down. His threats to kill or cut himself with the knife seemed to be genuine. Ian took it off him as he tried to saw at his wrists. Luckily the knife was incredibly blunt.

I quickly realised that we needed help and knew that Steven might end up in hospital again. I asked his wife to pack a bag for him. I didn't want to do it myself as it felt intrusive to go in to their bedroom and rummage. She just stared at me and said, "I am busy doing this..." I explained that I thought Steven might need to go to hospital, or at least it would be best if he stayed with us for a while. She nodded dumbly. I asked who we could get to support her, thinking she would be home alone. "My dad is coming to get me. I am going to stay with them."

I agreed that was a good idea, not realising that she meant she was leaving Steven. This is the last time that they saw each other in the flesh, and was the breakup of their marriage. His wife only became animated when she realised that Kia the cat would be on her own, no discussion about what would happen to Steven at all. I smoothed over the distress by saying that I would look after the cat and visit daily until things were sorted out. We took Steven away and called the doctor. After a tedious visit to Accident and Emergency and a promise of a psychiatric assessment the next day, we took Steven home with us.

The interview the next day with a psychiatrist at the hospital was soothing and reassuring. He was big and black and very human. However, no solutions were put in place for community care and nothing changed. As was to become the norm, we seemed to get through this with very little support even when the chair phobia returned.

For a while after my return, I couldn't even look at a regular chair without going nuts and I developed a morbid fear of the device. I'm fine with it now, even interested in the subject! I even asked Drew who's a carpenter, as well as a manic musician, to make me one for a stage prop. If that sounds strange, take a look at ELO's 1975 album 'Face the music' which has such a chair as its focus point on the sleeve. Obviously, there will be no current connected to mine. I don't agree with it as a method of execution, but as it is no longer the standard approach to the death penalty, it will only come to those who choose it in the American states that still offer the option.

Within three weeks, on my 22nd birthday, 27th December 2001 I found myself in bed with a mate's ex for 6 hours. Manic, drunk and lonely, it seemed like a good idea at the time. She understood our mistake before I did, and after a long chat next day to clear the air, we have remained friends ever since.

I hear a woman's voice talking quietly, but surprisingly it is coming from Steven's room. I get up, and realise it is about 4.00am. I knock on the door and walk in (maybe I shouldn't have but I wanted to know who was in my house without my knowledge in the middle of the night). I recognise the girl lying beside Steven, and she is someone I know and respect, but I get a bit of a shock. I am also relieved that it is not a stranger. I excuse myself and explain that their voices had woken me up. I go back to bed knowing that they realise the game is up. Steven takes his lady downstairs and calls a taxi, and waits with her until she leaves. He gets an earful from me, not about sex, but for inviting people into the house in the middle of the night.

January 2002

I am sat in my bed at my parents' home, having drunk a litre of scotch; on Seroxat yet again. I'm getting divorced. I hate my life. I'm watching Stanley Kubrick's 'A Clockwork Orange', one of my favourite films. I vomit into a nearby bucket, reach for my utility knife, and then open my arm from wrist to shoulder. Blood wrecks the carpet. I realise that I didn't go deep enough, but the pain kicks in. I wake my parents. They can't believe it and nor can I. No real harm done (except the carpet). A few scars for a few weeks, so what? Worse was yet to come.

Steven politely knocks on our bedroom door and says, "I've done something silly." He is holding his forearm tightly and blood is dripping through his fingers on to the carpet. I get out of bed, usher him to his room and find the first aid kit. I know it is pointless taking him to Accident and Emergency. They will turn him away because he is apparently drunk. I phone NHS Direct as I feel it is important to record the incident whilst Ian holds a pad to Steven's bleeding arm. They get a GP to call me back. "Can you cope?" he asks. Why did we say yes, had we already learned that we were bottom of the heap? I deal with the wounds and bandage Steven up, and by this time he is ready for 'sleep', passing out without complaint in the correct recovery position in his bed. Roll on tomorrow.

The scars were healing, I became less of a drinker and then the tablets drove me manic again. I put on weight, became a shameless flirt, spent too much money, and got fleeced by opportunists who must have had 'manic idiot' radars. I found myself in a pub, somewhat hypo-manic, and lonely. A bunch of young 'ladies', to be polite only, as they don't deserve the title, conned me into buying them £150 worth of clothes and rubbish like that. Being manic I couldn't see that I was being taken. One girl did have an attack of conscience and coughed up some money but not the rest of them. I spent another £150 which I did not have, in one day on myself buying daft t-shirts. Ironically, despite my high and pixelated mood, one was a t-shirt reading 'I'm only wearing black until they invent a darker colour'. Numerous pairs of jeans and leather trousers followed too, along with a load of sunglasses. A shed load of albums followed, on CD and vinyl, extra volume on the stereo, more upgrades on the mobile phone all calling for cash that I didn't have.

When mania calls, all rules leave via the nearest window. For some reason I bought a shirt that was emblazoned 'Dead girls don't say no', I got a lot of weird looks from the public as you can understand, and I wondered in my zoned-out state why my friends all walked behind me when out in the street. In retrospect, I can see how distasteful it must have seemed, but thought to myself, unbalanced as I was, that it was incredibly witty.

So now I am sat with my parents, taking stock of my debts and they mercifully bailed me out to the tune of a good few thousand. I will never to be able to repay the gesture, even if I can the money. Lucky for me my mother is an ex-banker and understood the ins and outs of personal finance.

This first bail out used up our savings and on reflection we should have insisted that he declare himself bankrupt then. I do remember going to his bank (where I used to work) and sitting down with an ex-colleague. I pointed out that Steven should never have been given the loan that was a major part of his debt due to his lack of earnings. Also, that he had been paying for employment protection insurance when he was not working at the time of the loan. No wonder the next 10 years would see a backlash against the banks and a tide of claims for mis-selling. I managed to recover the insurance fees but the rest was paid for by us.

With my wife out of the picture I still had my empty house to sell. I took all my instruments and what was mine and left her the rest. When she moved out I set my drums up in the empty lounge.

Part of clearing Steven's debts meant his mortgage had to go. There was no equity in the house and the utility bills were still stacking up. We were not in a position to pay, so up for sale it went. None of us envisaged him, in his current state, being able to live alone in the house. We paid the water rates, the fuel, the community charge and the estate agent's fees. His wife had disappeared and we now had no forwarding address.

Steven makes no mention here of a period of time that was even more difficult for me as his mother. He eventually is able to express what is distressing him. He is very much afraid of hurting me and his father. "My dad is a big man and if I try to hurt him he will easily 'deck' me. But what about you mam, you won't be able to fight me off." He became very frightened of being left alone with me and also just of being left alone without company. This left us in a quandary. I solved it by asking one of his friends, who was also ill with mental health problems at that time, to come and spend time with Steven. Strangely, he was not fearful that he would hurt anyone else. So, every day as I go out to teach in a local college Steven and his friend sit together and the relationship is mutually supportive. Their conversation does remind me of the film 'One Flew Over the Cuckoo's Nest'. And of course, if I am not watching then they can drink as much as they like. His friend goes back to his own house each day when Ian comes in from work. Looking back at this time I once again wonder where our support was. Steven was so obviously ill, yet we deal with it on our own to the best of our ability. This was probably not the best way forward for Steven at this time, but we had nothing else.

At about this time Drew found himself homeless after his girlfriend caused trouble for him. I let him move into my house while he was waiting for his new place. It was Drew who sold the house for me. I was too ill to turn up to show potential buyers around. Drew did this for me very successfully and the house was sold relatively quickly.

The quick sale meant that Ian and I had to find Steven's wife so that she could sign the documents, or no deal. I remember the uncomfortable phone call that I had with her mother, trying to persuade her to get her daughter to call me. Eventually she did. I explained that the house was sold and that there might be some money in it for her, but she had to agree to sell. She saw sense and gave us her address. Ian drove, and we went to an area of the county that I did not know. It was a cold and blustery night and we got lost a couple of times. Satellite navigation was not the fashion then. We eventually found her new abode – a renovated 'pensioners' bungalow in the middle of a vast sixties housing estate, flanked by a very busy road. No shops, no pub, nothing.

Inside was cluttered and very small. It was emotionally challenging for me to see the physical remains of their marriage furnishing this tiny and lonely house. She was nervous but welcoming and proudly showed us around. She asked after the cat but not Steven. She told us that she was well, and working, not too far away and that she liked her little bungalow. I am not sure that she was telling the truth. I hope that she was.

She signed the sale deeds and I promised to let her know if she was due to any cash. I did not have the guts to remind her that she had left all the bills to Steven with no forwarding address other than her parents. I already knew that after agents' and solicitors fees, the equity amounted to just £800 between them. Needless to say, she saw none of it.

I was flying high and put together a new band, 'Central Locking', as a tribute to the Doors. It consisted of me, playing the role of both Jim Morrison on vocals and simultaneously playing organ and keyboard bass à la Ray Manzerek, Simon on guitar à la Robby Krieger, and Drew playing drums, à la John Densmore. We needed to find somewhere to rehearse. Drew kept his carpentry equipment in his mother's cavernous cellar. There was also room for 'Central Locking' and we rehearsed endlessly. How she put up with it I'll never know but she was very kind. We also rehearsed on the stage of a local school during the holidays.

On the nights when we were both manic and couldn't sleep, Drew and I would call one another. At silly o'clock in the morning Drew would turn up outside my home in his converted Ford minibus. He had removed the majority of the seats and replaced them with benches. We'd sit in the parked van with a guitar and a notebook, passing a bottle of something suitably lethal back and forth until the sun came up. We bothered nobody, apart from a few passing nightclub patrons returning home. We would bid them a manic good morning as first light broke.

We concentrated on music practice, poetry and scribbling down a lot of silly cartoons. We were a bit like Spike Milligan and Peter Sellers on speed, except we didn't need any speed. Neither did they, apparently, it would have been lethal in both cases.

We only played one gig and it went well. Ironically, we raised money for the mental health charity 'Mind'. I thought it was hilarious seeing my former CPN rolling joints and obviously stoned out of his brains, a degrading spectacle. This was the man who had told me alcohol was dangerous in bipolar and was to be avoided, along with other noxious substances. Having had only 2 or 3 beers all night myself, I thought this was hypocritical bullshit but very amusing.

This was on the 20th July 2002 and was a true and sad observation made by Steven and witnessed by all of us.

I had been spending most of that year writing a very strange journal of poetry and it perfectly illustrates my shifting moods. Manic writings tend to be of a grandiose nature and written in unnecessarily large letters. Depressive entries are bleak and written in small neat text. Some of the really manic entries are written in blood, but don't be alarmed. I was sharpening my pencil with my knife and had accidentally nicked my finger, making it bleed. In my odd state of mind, I thought that it would be a shame to waste the blood, plus it would have a certain impact! My mood levelled out later in the year when I gave up the Seroxat, this time without withdrawals.

September 2002 saw my fine friend Drew surprise me with a visit to Wolverhampton to see Roy Wood of Wizzard fame play. Just over a year ago I had been in touch with a friend of Roy's asking if he would record a charity record with me. Drew, also a big fan of Roy's, had spoken to this friend and got us into the concert before anything was set up. We also got backstage to meet the man himself. The gig was brilliant and we both had photos taken with him and worked on him for a couple of cheeky autographs. Sometimes mania pays off. This time it was Drew's, even if I instigated it. His perseverance gave us a night to remember.

We were delighted that Steven felt he could make the trip and confident that Drew would keep him safe. They did meet the man himself and we have the photos to prove it!

Things were generally okay except when another manic spell developed. It caused some impulse buying and I also succumbed to the advances of another mate's ex. I really regretted the latter. My divorce from my first wife came through, and a week or two before Christmas the blackness set in again. I spent a fortnight in bed as a total recluse, thinking endlessly about death. I caught a kidney infection which didn't help at all, and I was getting dark 'messages' again from household items. Luckily both cleared up of their own accord.

However, without any appropriate medication, the next shift of mood should be just around the corner – about 5 months around the corner.

CHAPTER 4: IT'S GONNA GET YOU

I was feeling okay as 2003 dawned. I was at peace with the world for a bit, at least as much as I could be. I was just keeping my head down, staying out of everybody's way so nothing would happen. Obviously, I kept in touch with friends. I had started going out a bit more, but only when I had to, or when the mood took me. Slowly, I was getting the feeling that all would be okay. I was enjoying myself as much as I could, but still feeling a little anxious. The weight that I had put on through medication had dropped off in the previous year, my hair was getting long again, and I was still writing. At first the poems and songs were not too bizarre, but this did change.

I got back into normal life. I really convinced myself I had, and was enjoying the freedom. At the close of the previous year, late December 2002, my first serious girlfriend called me at home and said "I know you probably don't want to talk to me, but I need Drew's number. I've got a door that needs fixing." I hadn't seen her since I was 19. I thought for a moment. Then I agreed I'd ring him for her. He doesn't give out his number. Then I asked how she was doing. She told me her husband had left, but that they were not yet divorced. We chatted, and I suggested that the past should be the past, and maybe we could be friends all these years later? She said "Yes, come around any time." I had a bottle of wine, so I mentioned this, and she said "Well, how about now?" That was the beginning of an on-off casual fling.

However casual Steven makes this seem I think it was much more than that. They obviously gave each other a lot of comfort and Steven seemed to improve in well-being. I had hopes that the relationship might progress. This young woman was sensible, intelligent and was making something out of her life regardless of her challenging background.

If she needed something doing, she'd get me to do it and pay me in sex. Sometimes I'd just get a call when she was plain horny and had no irons in the fire. Or she would just get lonely and cook me something, and we would have a cuddle and a fumble for dessert. I'd get text messages at 6am saying "quick, before the bairn wakes up" and I'd be round to hers despite the freezing winter snow for a bit of human warmth. Then I'd get her and the kid on the bus. She would be off to work, and the kid spent workdays with her grandmother. I had to keep my head down when her husband came to see their kid. He once claimed to have seen us doing 'you know what' on the living room floor when he brought the kid back from the park, but she swore blind I wasn't there. He wouldn't have liked the knowledge that I was often kipping on the side of the bed he'd deserted. I enjoyed the danger and the relationship, but the situation would soon become untenable. After a few months my interest began to wane as my mood spiralled downwards. It's not easy maintaining a good relationship with bipolar in the background.

I managed to keep seeing my friends. One day Simon took me out to the local town to visit the music shop where I had once worked. I bought a professional condenser microphone for recording vocals and acoustic instruments. They work better in the studio than cardioid microphones, which are best used on stage or with amplifiers. Suddenly, my great mood began to evaporate, and my anxiety levels began to climb, with no apparent cause. We decided to go for a swift pint in a pub over the road. This done, we headed home, and I set up my new toy. The rest of the day went perfectly, I saw some visiting family, and went to bed as normal.

The following morning, I awoke feeling strange. Very strange. It was late May 2003 (incidentally the peak month for suicides) and the spring was turning into summer. The blossom was shedding from the trees and the sun was shining brightly. I just felt odd. I couldn't put my finger on it but everything I knew or looked at just seemed eerie and unreal. There was no depression, just the feeling my head was running fast, and I knew I was high. I started getting 'messages' again, but this time they were firmly within my head, not extraneous. Along with these came the visions. Not the beautiful ones that had presented themselves during my previous hypo-manic episodes, but evil, nasty visions that scared me. It seemed as if the whole world was skewed and I was trapped in a strange and unfamiliar place. "Life on Mars…?"

This refers to the TV series that aired later between January 2006 and April 2007 and became an obsession for Steven.

I began to be afraid of everyday objects again. I could not stand to be alone, and did not dare go out and look for company. In the bright sunlight, trees and buildings took on unfamiliar shapes and colours. I began writing in my notebooks again, my brain and words speeding along at twenty to the dozen.

Occasionally I would venture to a friend's house armed with a bottle of Irish whiskey to keep the noise out. In the height of warm summer weather, I was dressed in a full leather suit, wraparound dark glasses and a black cowboy hat. I grew a full beard. I must have looked like a biker version of John Wayne crossed with Geordi La Forge from Star Trek. I was drinking neat spirits in the beating sun, wearing enough insulation for a greenhouse, but it didn't seem to affect me. I was comfortable in my 'disguise', much to everyone's disbelief. My paranoia grew. My parents, with whom I was still living, were going on holiday and I could not bear the thought of being alone in this state. Thankfully, Simon agreed to move into my parents' room while they were away and hopefully keep me sane.

Some nights I was the one looking after him, when he got a bit too much of my potent whiskey in to his system. I would be looking in on him in the next room every now and then, to satisfy myself that he was still breathing. Then I would retire to my own bed. As the summer wore on my anxieties grew.

It is at this point in June 2003 that I look for more help for Steven. He has been dumped from the system for some time and is getting worse. I do not know why we did not go back to the GP. Perhaps it is the fact that we keep getting told that Steven is 'just an alcoholic' and no other intervention or support is offered. I read some positive editorial about a Nuffield Hospital which is reasonably close to us. They have expertise with addictions and mental health issues. I check it out, rake around for the consultation fee of £200 and we have another attempt to improve matters. Steven is up for it and would like his misery to stop.

I saw another private psychiatrist who saw me for all of an hour, if that. She didn't listen, and was obviously useless. She tried to palm me off with the excuse that it was psychosomatic. There was no way I was going to allow her to call me a hypochondriac. I began hating all doctors, full stop. I knew what was happening was real and once more I'd just have to wait and live with it. And that little piece of wisdom cost money.

Dr AT was very professional, but her manner was clinical and cool. She talked a little with both Steven and I and then I left them for a private consultation. She decides that Steven has a personality disorder and apparently tries to explain this to him without me being present. He does not understand the term and is very upset by it, thinking that she is telling him that his illness is not real. I do not find out her diagnosis until much later and at the time, I did not understand it either. She offers a new set of medication and leaves. Steven refuses to take the medication, the name of which is now lost to me. He is horrified to find that it is on some kind of 'black flag' list that cautions about the danger of death! He flatly refuses to take it and we are once again powerless to move on, with no other support or input.

I was being pursued by the girl I mentioned earlier, the girl I'd been having a careless fling with last winter, but I just didn't answer the phone. I decided to become celibate forever if need be. You will see later that whilst that didn't happen, it should have. At the end of the year, something dark started creeping back in as the mania gradually left me, replaced by a mixed phase of depression and great unrest. I wanted to give a manic yell at the world. I was particularly incensed by articles in the news about animal cruelty and visions of the stories haunted me. The image of a kitten being microwaved drove me to despair. The blacker my mood got, the more reclusive I became. Whilst buying my dad a birthday drink on Christmas day 2003, I felt like running out of the pub. After drinking only half a pint, I did. My mind was as cold and grey as the sky that day. I holed up, decided to do nothing but continue to write the next episode was waiting to happen.

2004

On New Year's Eve 2003 the weather had changed for the worse. A brave look out to a friend's party came to a painful end when I slipped and landed on my arse. I had become almost incapable of going out and this just emphasised the feeling. January 2004 rolled in cold and bleak, with me much in the same state of mind.

There were an unusual number of blizzards, even for our part of England. The snow carried on for quite some time. I was dark and cold and brooding, but something was starting to boil within.

Over the previous year I had written a lot of poetry, gathering it in my notebooks. Most of it was black, desperate and mocking the world. One of my synapses triggered the idea that if it was put to music, I could make a rock album out of it. I had all the equipment and Simon could play lead guitar. I invited him over to talk it out. I had songs in my head ready to put down, and he was a better lead guitar player than me and I'd need his help. If you're going to do it, do it right. I knew that Simon had a load of tunes with no words. He'd tried writing lyrics and didn't get far, just frustrated. Cue my frustrated, manic ramblings. They could be chopped up and reshaped to make songs. Simon had ideas for titles for his stuff, and I'd go through my notebooks and find suitable poetry.

Raring to go, I got onto the music store and had some custom cables made. With these I could record in any room in my house without having to be in front of the recording console. The hard-drive on the console was rather noisy and would spoil an acoustic recording. Two lengths of wire later and I had Simon playing acoustic parts in the bathroom with a talk-back rigged through his headphones.

I got well into it after that. I became intoxicated by it. I would lay down a tune in a few hours, and call Simon the next day to put some solos down. Then later I'd record one of his tunes. I'd pick out some lyrics for it, and even write another tune during smoke break, using a portable tape deck so it wasn't forgotten. The next day, after a bit of padding out and manipulation, we'd be ready to put the finished article on to the main console from scratch. The first track we laid down was one of Simon's. I'd been singing for a while, but it was invigorating to learn I could scream in tune as well.

I called up Drew and we did a photo shoot with my fair hair dyed purple for the occasion and it is now my preferred colour. Drew lists photography amongst his many skills and accomplishments. I used the photos and started making album covers, burning CDs, making disc labels and generally wearing myself out. We sold over 400 units the month the project finished. It meant that I had to get up early, play all day until it was perfect, master it until silly o'clock in the morning and prepare for the next track. By the time our recording was finished in early April 2004, I was exhausted. I still managed to spend all day and every day making covers and selling them on. Even Roy Wood asked for one but obviously to him, no charge.

This photo shoot took place in a village near us, on a railway embankment and the results are surprisingly good. Mean, moody with a touch of the southern USA. They successfully produced a CD which was distributed throughout their network of friends.

Most people didn't realise that it wasn't an actual full band, and that Simon and I were playing all the parts ourselves on multi-track. I got a bit of a swollen head with pride when people commented how good the production was. Many people didn't believe I was the producer and that a lot of the acoustic guitar parts were recorded in the toilet! The room not the bowl. However, like any fair-sized project, the energy burned itself out. When we finished, I crashed to earth with a bang and put myself back into hiding. Reclusive, paranoid and tired, I'd have to be coaxed out of the house for any occasion.

The positive aspect of this project was that Steven was busy, engaged, creative and working with Simon. The focus of his work and the contact with Simon lifted him from his fears. Regrettably we had to contend with an irritable and exhausted wreck, who wouldn't eat, didn't sleep and was obsessed with perfection. We were particularly distressed as his volatile temper was directed in-over at his own failings. In the summer of 2004 I asked for a Carers Assessment for Ian and me. This didn't take place until October 2004 and it was months before we got the report. It didn't really matter. All we needed was for Steven to be properly diagnosed, treated and managed but Carers Assessments don't cover that.

My mind was turning to the occult now. I began to develop an interest in Wiccan, but did not practice anything much. Even I am not so mad as to mess over much with what you don't fully understand.

As autumn came back around, I would sit in silence at dusk and just stare into the open flame of a large candle, images forming in my dark and agitated mind. Despite my outward appearance of catatonia, my mind raced onwards. The next few months of the winter were relatively normal but in the next year I would be betrayed by a friend and later meet my Nemesis.

2005

The friend? I met her completely at random the previous year. She was maybe only 17 or 18, and quite beautiful. I got talking to her after seeing her playing guitar in her front garden. She asked me for a copy of my album and liked it. She told me she was quite experienced in Wiccan. This interested me, and we stayed in touch as friends. She would visit me at home and got chatty with my Mam. I took her to meet my friends. They got bad vibes and warned me to be careful. I thought 'each to their own'.

A year had passed since I first spoke to her in '04. She asked to borrow some of my mother's books, and she got them. She asked me for a loan to buy a train ticket to visit a 'friend' and I obliged. I then asked her if we could ever be more than friends. She said no, but was happy to carry on as we were. That was okay with me, win some, and lose some. For a while I took out my frustrations by battering my drum set or cranking up a guitar, and crashing down on various keyboards. But in the way of things, everything ticked on nicely.

My young friend took the train alright. It turned out she was a lesbian fleeing from her sexually abusive father. She ran away with my mothers' books and my cash. That just left me with a lot of time on my hands.

During this period, on a trip to the pub, I met my Nemesis, a hysterically mad woman, obviously disturbed and very drunk. I mentioned this meeting to some acquaintances and was advised to steer well clear. Supposedly she was bad news and always drunk or on drugs. I chose to ignore this. I'd seen the same woman turn up in the pub pleasant and sober. I found her to be quite a tempting 40-something with an edge about her. And it seems that she had taken a shine to me. Such a shame you can't see into the future.

The first night I met this older woman, she was loaded on vodka and had been fighting. We moved on to a house party in a group. She was so hysterical and out of control that she was ejected from the event. What a nutter, I thought. Rich coming from me I know. But what a change there was on our second meeting. She was seemingly coherent, a little shy, but I found her rather pleasant. I decided to give her the benefit of the doubt and we became friends.

I don't know at what stage in the relationship Eve first came to our home. Steven kept it all quiet but did seem a bit happier in himself. I remember being woken by voices (again!). I must have a keen ear for a random female voice in my house at night. I wake up and walk into Steven's open bedroom. I am startled by a very thin dark haired woman turning to gaze at me. She is sitting on Steven's bed whilst he is rummaging for CDs. He introduces her as Eve. A chill goes through me – in my understanding and experience an energy shift and a strong sense of foreboding as she turns away from me to gaze adoringly at Steven. This, in hindsight, was the beginning of the end.

She would come to the pub when her 'boyfriend' (no substance, no sex) let her, in the hope of finding me there. Sometimes he would follow her down. When I was there, we all did rounds of drinks and she would lavish cigarettes on me. She had a very piercing frightened look with a frozen, other earthly smile. Soon I was getting invites to the 'boyfriend's' flat which was conveniently, or maybe not in retrospect, next door to hers. The three of us would drink. I'd have two or three cans of cider; they'd have two bottles of vodka.

One night when we were drinking in her flat the boyfriend disappeared, passed out in his own abode. By about 3am we were both comatose on her couch. We were suddenly disturbed by the arrival of her 14 year old son. She had kept that a secret! It was obviously compromising, but nothing had gone on and we were fully clothed. Later, I passed the son in the street standing with a gang of his friends. They cheered as I walked by. The son said proudly, "Don't wind him up. He must be mad, he shagged my mum." I hadn't yet, but it made me grin inwardly.

I didn't find out until later that the 'boyfriend' was knocking her about, as had every other man in her life, and there was a lot more to find out as well. He became ever more jealous of me being around her, despite gathering rumours of him being homosexual. Maybe he was after me? Who knows? That's somewhere he'd never get. But she was forbidden to buy me a drink in the round, offer me a cigarette or even sit next to me. Mr.Soft here felt sorry for her.

One night we were in his flat drinking. She invited me over, so I took a few cans; they were on vodka as usual. At about 2am he announced he was so drunk he was going to sleep on the couch as he usually did (didn't get the concept of bedrooms, obviously) and would we please leave his home. If we wanted to party on, go next door to her flat, so we did just that.

I'd known her about 6 months at this point. She was in her own flat now with me, complaining she never got cuddles or encouragement from her 'boyfriend' and that they never kissed or slept together. I offered her a cuddle, saying I was good at that but you can guess where it leads. A few years of hell for yours truly.

Steven had a soft heart and certainly was a 'rescuer'. He often confused this with love and affection. He has brought many needy creatures to our door, both human and animal. This was his worst choice yet. The choice that would damage him further, corrupt him and ultimately contribute to his early death.

CHAPTER 5: IT'S GOT YOU

Still 2005

A relatively calm year was going to end rather less peacefully. At first, I was seeing this woman a few times a week. She wanted to move me in immediately. She hadn't yet told her so-called boyfriend that she wanted to leave him for fear of violence toward her. I thought things were going a bit too fast. At the end of the first week she said she had to go for some surgery, but I couldn't go with her in case it looked too suspicious. She insisted that I stayed the night because she was frightened. I said I didn't think it appropriate, considering she hadn't told her next-door neighbour it was over yet. I promised to stay in touch via the bedside phone in the hospital for the day she'd be in. At the extortionate cost of £1.50 per minute, I would talk to her the whole day if she wanted. Anyway, her son would be there surely? No, he'd just been visiting that first time I met him. He lives with his stepfather. I said I wouldn't stay the night until she'd finished with the man next door, kissed her goodnight and left, promising to call her in the morning.

Everything went fine at the hospital and then really strange things started to happen. She said she was about ready to tell said neighbour that it was over, but we were about to get found out by someone else. One evening we were doing you know what in front of the fire when suddenly I saw the face of another younger lad looking on in horror at the door, a second son who had not been mentioned. I guess he was 'visiting' too, but that didn't seem to matter much to her. He went completely insane, rushed out and started banging on the neighbour's door. Luckily the 'boyfriend' was too drunk to respond. Probably comatose as he was every night. Mother explained to son that she was in the process of splitting up with the neighbour. The lad calmed down and shook my hand. I thought this was bizarre and inappropriate and I left.

Soon my visits to the flat became noticed by 'next door' and as neither of us were having much to do with him socially any more, he was suspicious. I got a few text messages warning me to stay away. His best mate had put two and two together right away, but he'd said nothing and was quietly laughing about it to himself. What a mate. One day this 'mate' (who was also an alcoholic and usually went next door) was sat with us for an afternoon bottle of vodka (I prefer a can myself). 'Next door' heard his 'mate's' voice, walked in and was very unhappy about how cosy things looked. He glared at me for a while, sat and sulked, and angrily asked why I wouldn't take HIM out? (Explains why he didn't sleep with her much perhaps!) Before I could reply, he stormed out. Minutes later, he reappeared with a coat of hers, threw it on the couch, and stormed out again. The 'mate' with the vodka trailed after him, smiling from ear to ear.

Next, she sent a text to him that said that it was over between them, she wanted me. She said that he was dead below the waist and various other personal insults. I thought that was a bit insensitive. I started getting paranoid again, it was unkind, and should have been done properly a long time ago. Knowing that he beat the hell out of women, I wondered if he might want to try and tackle a bloke for a change, so I watched my back on each visit. I needn't have worried; he was about 6 stone wet through and a serious coward when confronted by those who could defend themselves. All bark and no bite. He gave me an 'official warning' one night when he asked me into his flat, and told me not to get in the way. His attempts to frighten me just made me laugh and I verbally flattened him without even raising my voice or even being impolite; just standing my ground. But at least now I could stay the odd night with her and he knew he had no say over it.

Both of her kids were back home and accepted me quickly. Then I learned of her three other children - a girl who died hours after birth, the eldest son who was fostered at 12 and chose not to see his mother and, finally the second eldest, the jailbird. And I do mean that literally. He was currently in prison but unfortunately not for long. Aged 19, he had spent time in prison on at least 19 occasions since he was 16. And looking into the future, during his early twenties he would do more time, longer stretches, in the big house (grown up prison with nasty men).

What has any of this to do with manic depression? I will explain. The situation that I found myself in was to lead to some of my worst breakdowns yet, with extreme depressions and acute manias. Not the nice gentle visionary type that I had sometimes experienced, but train wrecks of pure psychosis. Manic depression is aggravated by stress, as many mental illnesses are. And I was about to get a hell of a lot of stress. Normal life crises can make one depressed, this is reactive depression. Yet it can become clinical depression in those prone to it, just as a lot of stress can produce a major manic outburst. When I'm well, I'm usually fairly even tempered. When I'm not all there and I get pushed too hard, I will eventually explode.

The two kids, aged 13 and 14, were usually reasonably affable. I think they suffered from ADHD or some other emotional or mental condition. They both attended a local special school because of their difficulties. The 14 year old was very bright and had great artistic talent. The younger was not bright at all. In retrospect, I think he was in some way mentally unbalanced or stunted in his emotional maturity. I can't recall one single day on which the brothers didn't have blazing fights with each other. These could last for just an hour over who ate the last bag of crisps, or it could be a personal vendetta continuing for days or even weeks. Either way, things would be smashed and doors holed. The constant shouting and screaming permeating throughout the flat was unbearable. The boys would not listen to their mother. As a newcomer, what chance did I have? I did manage to defuse a few situations when I was well enough, even though they rarely listened to me. They were determined to defy their mother and were continually abusive to her. They stole cigarettes from us, bunked off school a lot and sometimes even refused point blank to go. Neither of us had any authority or control over them.

Things just got worse. The third son, the jailbird, was under a Criminal Behaviour Order which forbade him from being anywhere near his younger brothers. Unbeknownst to the rest of us, he had finished his sentence and the youngest had invited him home, telling him where the family now lived. He jumped train from Sheffield all the way home and walked in through the unlocked door. Jailbird seemed affable enough, apart from a sly expression which probably is learned from imprisonment.

On reflection it is probable that this son suffered from foetal alcohol syndrome and warranted empathy. His appearance was the classic change in shape of the face and some mental difficulties with stunted growth and an inability to see the consequences of his behaviour. He was emotionally needy and immature and used both alcohol and any drugs he could get his hands on. Conversely, he could be very kind and caring.

I couldn't believe he was the same person who had supposedly attempted to kill one of his mother's ex partners, thrown his mother down the stairs, and fed a block of marijuana to the cat. He would grind up and snort any medication available when the illegal stuff wasn't around, or he couldn't afford it. He'd also set fire to a bar and got his family banned from Butlins. The most shocking bit of the story was that he had taken his younger brothers, then aged 7 and 8, out to rob a bank. To further their education, he then took them to break into a rather swish house when the owners weren't there, and they trashed the place.

But here he was, shaking my hand. His mother told him that he couldn't stay, but as it was so close to Christmas she felt sorry for him. She caved in as usual. A respite until the New Year was agreed if he kept his head down and his nose clean. At first this worked. He seemed to get on well with his brothers but of course he had no intention of going as agreed, and had nowhere to go.

We all spent Christmas 2005 with my parents, which went pretty well yet there was a palpable atmosphere of something not quite right. On New Year's Eve, my woman and I visited my parents and I suddenly felt uneasy and apprehensive. I felt strange. On returning to the flat I found the jailbird rather well-oiled and all three brothers were engaged in a massive fight. Household objects were flying everywhere. My partner tried to intervene, and I looked on in horror as a mountain bike came flying down the hallway about four feet further above the ground than it should have been. My partner was drunk and hysterical. I slipped out to the next room, unnoticed by the combatants amid the chaos, and called the police. I could never have imagined how much contact I was going to have with the constabulary over the coming years.

Steven seems to have remembered most of this reasonably well. Given that he had made a choice to be with this woman, we all tried to make the best of a bad job. The two youngest boys came with Steven and Eve for Christmas dinner. All a bit strained and false but we got on with it. It was obvious that the levels of disruptive behaviour and aggression were escalating in the flat, now aggravated by the jailbird and his interactions with his mother and his brothers. I had no real knowledge or experience of the term 'dysfunctional family' until this moment and it became hell on earth for all of us. I can't remember if we banned jailbird from our Christmas table or if he turned up from prison between Christmas and New Year. I realise that I may have blotted out some of the more painful happenings over this period.

I do remember that the levels of fear and anxiety displayed by Steven and his woman were really racking up. They were obviously afraid of jailbird and his worsening behaviour. He was constantly on drugs, drunk or threatening the younger boys, desperately competing with them for any crumb of comfort from their mother. I have no comprehension about Criminal Behaviour Orders, but we could certainly see why it had been put in place. And the woman in her wisdom had been complicit in flouting it and was now reaping her just rewards.

I pretty much lived in two houses at this time, fearing my things would be destroyed if I moved them into the flat. I desperately needed time out away from the fighting kids. My daily routine was like a '9 till 5' job. I would go to my parents' house to compose and record music by day and then return at night.

This pattern of behaviour set the scene for the next couple of years. Steven wanted a relationship but couldn't cope with the standards of his readymade family. He tried very hard to be a father figure and was shocked by the behaviours and morals of the unit he had bought in to, and this included those of his woman.

Any pretence of normality that she had given Steven was now unravelling - violence, excessive drinking, misuse of medication, dishonesty, theft and gambling were the issues that he lived with now. That was on top of his own mental illness and battle with alcoholism. He didn't stand a chance and neither did she.

The jailbird wasn't fazed by the police or warrants, and we got no help from them. We had evicted him from the flat, but he just moved himself into the municipal bin shed downstairs. Much to everyone's annoyance he settled himself in, doing drink and drugs and desperately trying to get back into the family home. He would continually creep up to the letterbox, yelling through it at his brothers and mother. Sometimes the police would be called. He was usually too quick for them, and would be back in the shed before you knew it. I puzzled over his erratic behaviour, wondering why anyone would be like this. I found out that he had been assessed by many doctors as a child, and was suspected to be a paranoid schizophrenic. He also had a much lower mental age than his years of living should impart. This is not to say schizophrenics lack intelligence in general. No more does it mean manic-depressives are particularly intelligent, creative maybe, but often in very poorly-thought out and stupid ways that lead to things like World War 2...Remember Adolph?

I wonder if Steven is displaying his own prejudices here? His bipolar could give him a grandiose way of thinking. The gist of what he states is true. Jailbird definitely had some difficulties with his mental functioning and was both physically and emotionally immature. I do not know who gave Steven the information stating schizophrenia. I don't think this was true and I think the word came from his mother. Jailbird certainly had all the signs of foetal alcohol syndrome and had obviously not received the support he needed to live with this. He could be a charming and kind young man but unfortunately this feature was swamped by the effects of drink, drugs and violence, all of which he saw as normal. This was demonstrated by him walking in through my unlocked front door and into my living room uninvited, demanding that I take him to his mother. I was working with a reflexology client at the time and reacted instinctively. I stood up, excused myself to my client and bundled jailbird out. Unfortunately, his mother Eve was in the kitchen making a drink for Steven and herself. She was terrified and didn't want to talk to her son or see him, so I literally had to throw him out and lock the door after him. He didn't get the message and arrived at the front door later that night. Ian answered and was threatened with a screwdriver by the lad. Once again, he was bundled away, and the door locked on him.

The altruists amongst you could criticise us for our actions but Eve was adamant that she wouldn't see him. He was desperate for some sign of affection or attention from her. Or maybe he just wanted cash and a cigarette.

2006

Early in 2006, my partner of only 3 months starts demanding I marry her. Warning bells ring. It's too soon after the last marriage that I rushed into. She gets upset, drinks a litre of vodka in the space of 20 minutes, and then starts getting physically violent. I should have just walked then, but to placate her say I wouldn't rule out matrimony.

The issue came up again at a friend's home three months later. She again gets drunk and my friend takes me for a much-needed walk where I release my frustration by booting a sturdy and ancient electrical transmission pole in the street and do my ankle some damage.

My mood was becoming very unstable. I spent as much time as I could at my parents to keep away from the fighting kids and my woman. Her drinking bouts were horrendous, often leaving her curled up on the kitchen floor. This worried me as she drank more than I did! Then I discovered that she was also bulimic and proud of the fact. I was living in a war zone and I was sinking fast. I managed to get her to ditch the vodka and drink a bit more sensibly. I suggested that she see a doctor about the issues that were making her want to get blitzed and then binge and purge. She said it was Post Traumatic Stress Disorder.

This I can believe due to her terrible past. Some I know to be true, but she was also a good story teller. I urged her to get help, but she said she'd been on Prozac and it hadn't made any difference.

Most of the time, when she was sober, she would come to my parents with me and watch me work. Seeing a real studio and recording techniques, seemed to quieten her mind. Then we would return to chaos together.

I hated this. It felt like an invasion of our space. I was desperate to keep an eye on Steven who was obviously becoming more unwell. With the best will in the world I didn't want Eve hanging around during the day too. We had no peace or privacy. I couldn't at first get it as to why they were a couple in my space and not in the flat. I wanted Steven to decide one way or another, either live with her or don't. The half-way house solution put a huge strain on us emotionally and financially. I couldn't help but be privy to all of their differences and arguments, because they brought it all with them on their visits. The boys also regularly came looking for their mother, wanting money, food, cigarettes or just to get warm. I managed to bond a bit with the younger one, sharing baking in the kitchen or a funny story. This didn't last for long. His natural suspicion for all things 'normal' got the better of him. The answer always came back to the sons – she didn't want them, couldn't mother them and was totally dominated by them. If the boys were in the flat then she needed to be somewhere else, as did Steven. Frustrated and conditioned by their mother's lack of interest and nurturing skill, they took every opportunity to attack her, humiliate her and use what little resources she had for their own ends. And eventually they turned on Steven too.

I was pretty fraught and probably going through a mixed episode, but I managed to run the house. She didn't cook or iron, that was up to me. Her obsession was repeatedly dusting things. As my energy died out and I became more unwell nobody ate proper food anymore. The kids weren't interested in anything but junk anyway. I was too tired to cook, too tired to eat. I didn't relish the fact that after I had slaved over a hot stove, my partner would proudly announce that she was going to deliberately vomit up my fare the moment she had finished stuffing it down her neck.

It was a stark contrast to my manic days with my ex-wife when everyone I knew would invite themselves to dinner at our house. I'd gladly cook roast dinners for all. For the more adventurous, I would prepare something unbelievably spicy and my trademark Spaghetti Bolognese always went down well.

It was so very different now. The kids eating the only things they knew – pot noodles and crisps. She ate only anything that could be vomited up easily. She even scavenged and ate garbage from the bin, and she happily told me that she once ate a can of dog food. I would get something from a shop when my appetite made an appearance. That's all I could cope with now. I would hide away and strum my guitars and get everything off my chest.

At one point, I had a very bleak day and I just spontaneously erupted into tears. A doctor was called when I wouldn't stop my disjointed ramblings. This doctor gave me a dose of the anti-psychotic Chlorpromazine, which was awful. It didn't stop what was going on in my mind, but it paralysed my body for several hours. I know now why it has been nicknamed 'liquid cosh'.

I was not aware of when this happened as Steven was at the flat at the time. I have searched his medical records and cannot find any reference to this at all. It would seem inappropriate and negligent treatment just to give this medication and walk away with no other intervention. Did Steven imagine or misremember it? Was a GP called and then Eve gives Steven something?

I became so blank in my outlook on life. I felt trapped by an invisible force but at the same time I had all these intense, creative ideas in mind. I felt like that avenue had been closed to me. So, one day I thought damn the torpedoes, I'm going to go and put these ideas down. As I was doing so I had a drink and got nicely relaxed.

As usual Steven would turn up at 'home' when he needed space and access to his music. It was very hard for us to have him return just to watch him drink. Yes, judge us if you choose. We could have locked him out or banned access and left him to God and good fortune. This way at least we could monitor what was going on with a chance of intervening. We were his parents, his carers and his mental health nurses – the only ones looking out for him.

A couple of hours later my partner rang me demanding I return. I said I was nearly finished, wouldn't be much longer. She insisted that I come now. This escalated into a totally unnecessary argument which my mother overheard. Concerned, she asked me what was up. I said nothing to do with you, keep your nose out, if maybe not quite as politely. Then I snapped, and I made a phone call. As my partner walked up to the front door, she saw me getting into a taxi that had mercifully arrived lightning fast. Nobody saw me for 5 days.

This was now becoming a pattern of behaviour. When Steven couldn't cope with the demands of his relationship he would turn up back at home. Eve would give him hassle on the phone – endless texts and calls. Then as she comes to retrieve him, he would make a run for it. Thank God, he had some friends who were prepared to take him in.

I now put myself into the merciful hands of my 'blood brother' Drew and his wife. They willingly took me into their home for the best part of a week, coping with my insane ramblings and side-stepping my obviously bizarre behaviour. I may have been there 5 days, but it seemed like 5 hours to me. The hypo manic fog was lifting, and the days had all run together. I must have slept but I don't remember doing so. I can remember having a laugh and a drink with my hosts and gradually calming down. I also remember sitting on a bed playing the same Tom Petty album (Wild flowers) over and over again and on the verge of tears. When I finally returned to planet earth, it seemed like I'd just had a short nap, time all nonsense, but I knew I'd have to now go back.

After the initial welcome back, things rubbed along pretty much the same, and I got more and more depressed. I found all of my medication missing. I was not surprised, despite her denials of touching it, to hear from the kids that she had gone to bed after I left, with a waxy complexion. She had spent a few days sweating and being involuntarily (for once) sick. This ties in with her history of overdoses.

Then I started trying to escape my pain with alcohol again. We would fight, both intoxicated. She had a stash of medication prescribed for her that she had not taken regularly, and tranquillizers were her drug of choice to replace vodka. I was no better. I wasn't going to do it in front of her after I had made my fears about the vodka known. Whenever I was alone I was drinking cider or canned ready-mixed gin and tonic. Sometimes I would have miniatures of gin and vodka in the lining of my jacket. I was never drunk, but it would put a depression to bed and take the edge off a high.

Steven's statement of never being drunk notes the true alcoholic. He was usually under the influence but functioning to some level of 'normality'. When we could, we would search his pockets, and relieve him of his stash, and this caused us great stress and heated arguments. We were all lost and lonely and full of fear for the future.

I'm not entirely sure if it was now, but about this time I wrote a suicide note and took an overdose of Amitriptyline and I went to bed hoping to die. I had a change of heart and vomited up the pills. Then, a few weeks later I overdosed on other medication and went running from my parents' house determined to die, and hid from police and paramedics in a bush. They took me to a hospital that assessed me and sent me straight back home. Nothing they could hold me for, they said. I may have been hospitalised in a psychiatric unit around this time. Mania plays havoc with memory.

This is the beginning of the end – a dreadful time for all of us with many episodes and hospital admissions mostly played out between our two residences.

One night I was half dozing, half watching the TV when for no reason at all she kicked me off the bed. I thought it was a joke. I'd hit my head on the side of the bedside cabinet and it hurt somewhat. I played the same game and faked being very much more annoyed than I was whilst trying not to laugh. She panicked and called a doctor for advice. He said I should go to Accident and Emergency for a check-up. By this point I told her that I was only messing, and that it would be a waste of time. She insisted that I went anyway, and that's where I ended up. The lump on my head was enough for the doctor to want to keep me in for observation, and I got a routine blood test. She pretended she was my legal bride and found out the results of the test. This exposed the fact I'd had four cans of cider rather than the one can that she knew about. So what? But she was suddenly livid (I later found out she'd just swallowed a month's worth of sleeping pills) and arrived at my bed screaming like a banshee and trying to stuff the rings from her fingers into my mouth. Apart from half choking me she also cut my lips and gums. Security was called and she was removed.

The next day I was released with a sedative for shock. I couldn't get her on her mobile because she'd broken it in a fit of pique. I needn't have worried because she'd gone off first thing to gamble away our funds in the arcades, then returned to haunt the hospital at the exact time I was walking out of the door. After a few fractious hours we ended up separated and made separate journeys back to our homes. I was by now out of contact with the world, as my own mobile phone had irritated me to the point where, wound up and frustrated, I chucked it at a wall.

I remember this dreadful episode well and it seems that Steven doesn't. What he has written is factual but incomplete. On the evening Eve called us and said he was in hospital. We checked with the hospital and they said they would keep him overnight – we left them to it. We were exhausted and could see no point in rushing through at midnight for no purpose. On checking in the morning, I was told he would be released at lunchtime. I called Steven and told him to ring me and I would pick him up to take him home. I was working in a call centre part time, and my shift finished at noon. Unfortunately, a late call delayed me on the phone and I missed Steven's call by 30 seconds. The message that he left me disturbed me greatly. He seemed to be hysterical and talking about Eve attacking him in hospital. He said he had had enough and was going to finish with this world. I rang him back, with no answer, leaving messages telling him to come home. I got one call that he answered – he was disorientated and confused and stating that he was going to kill himself, and then eventually the phone went dead. At this point I called the police and reported him as a missing person and in a state of vulnerability. They began to look for him. A little while later, about three in the afternoon, I got a phone call from the security guard in JB Sports, a shop in the nearby town. He said that my son had asked him to call me and get me to collect him. He was apparently in a state of distress and had asked for help. I asked the guard to phone the police, as it would be quicker than me coming for him. Steven arrived back home in a police car about 30 minutes later. He was distressed and ill – drunk, manic, depressed or emotionally battered – I just didn't know.

He told me a very unpleasant story of being kicked out of bed at home, of being admitted to hospital and of Eve berating him all the time he was there. Apparently, staff had asked her to leave but she had turned up again very early the next day and had made a nuisance of herself. The continued arguing culminated in her taking off her numerous rings and stuffing them into Steven's mouth as he lay in bed. A security guard had been called and she had been obliged to leave again. It would be easy to think that this was fabrication but Eve herself rang me to check on Steven's whereabouts before he had returned home. She was angry and spiteful and took a delight in telling me what she had done. It was at this point that I began to fear that she would eventually do him serious harm.

On leaving the hospital Steven had wandered around the town. He climbed onto a roof with a view to jumping off. It was at this point that he trashed his phone. Jumping down from the roof, he was retrieved by the security guard. At this point Steven asked for help to get home. He returned to us with a cut mouth from Eve's attack on him and a damaged knee which was to trouble him for the rest of his life. We kept Steven at home with us for a couple of days, but he eventually went back to Eve as she put him under enormous pressure with constant phone calls to the house phone and visits to the front door.

When I did see her again, it was more fighting. She told me to get out of her flat and never return. When I went to do so, I got "Oh, so you would actually leave, would you?" Confusing, but she wouldn't let me go. Things did eventually calm down awhile, apart from the kids trying to kill each other.

Towards the end of the year (2006) I was feeling so unwell I decided to take a week out to pull myself around at my parents' house. I saw my GP who prescribed Valium, but this only really made me have hallucinatory dreams that scared me witless. I also vomited a lot shortly after each dose. I would wake from those strange dreams and watch TV until morning, afraid to go back to sleep. After a few days I thought the Valium was only making things worse and stopped taking it. I began to feel better, and by the end of the week I decided to go back to the flat. She'd been dropping by with apologies and what seemed to be genuine concern.

The last night I spent at my parents, I had a beer and went to bed, and then the next day I went with my partner to the GP, where the Valium prescription was changed to one of Librium which suited much, much better. My anxieties slowly lessened and everything seemed to be more relaxed. I even started sleeping properly again.

We are back together again and complaints from the neighbours about the cursing of the children began an eviction process. My partner also had a track record of making a racket from her drinking days, so we put in for a transfer to get a house together on the other side of town. We moved in sometime around October 2006, and lived well as a family, apart from when the jailbird made the odd visit. Then fights would break out and things, especially money and medication, would disappear.

Once again Ian and I stepped in to try and make it 'right'. We moved furniture and sorted stuff out and I prepared a meal for the family to eat in their own home on moving day. I set the table and cooked a beef stew, one of Steven's favourites. The little family looked bemused, obviously not used to sitting around a table, let alone eating a cooked meal together. The two boys picked and prodded at the food, asking for identification and then announced, "We only like proper food from the shop" and both left the table, the meal wasted on them. Steven and Eve enjoyed it, obviously hungry.

During these periods I was therefore devoid of stable medication, and subsequently would quickly have attacks of mania. One such episode resulted in me attempting to deck my father. He was an insurmountably large and fully mentally functioning man compared to me. Seeing that I was ill, he used only restraint against my attempt to punch him one. With me screaming like a banshee, I was pinned to a bed by him until the unbelievable and meaningless rage passed. If I'd been him, I would have knocked me out instead. But he was 14 stones plus and I'd withered down from 19 to a miserable 9 through months of not eating. I was lucky he didn't decide to snap me in half. My mother thought I would be better off sectioned, but thought twice about it. I think in retrospect I would have been better off if I had been.

Steven was really going downhill at this stage. Dirty, malnourished, distressed and depressed, he spent time with us when he had the energy. We tried our best to feed him, encourage him to shower and kept an open-door policy. I wished with all my heart that he would leave Eve but she seemed to have some kind of unworldly power over him regardless of how badly the relationship was faring.

I made an appointment to see the local psychiatrist, who turned out to be my old adversary from the first hospital I was in. He basically told me I was a hypochondriac and was wasting his time. I made a formal complaint about him, and later found out unsurprisingly, many other patients had also done the same. He was not to last much longer in the job, at least not in that area. I got a letter of apology from the CEO of the Community Mental Health Team and was asked if I wanted to take it further. I said thanks, but I knew I wouldn't be able to take the stress of any legal goings on.

Shortly after this I became very ill indeed. I felt bleak, blank, dark, and worst of all convinced I was being followed by various people who wanted to hurt me. I would take the longest and least obvious route to wherever I had to go. I was constantly looking over my shoulder and my mind was spinning out of control. I did not feel remotely safe until I had got myself indoors. Then worse still, I began to suffer auditory hallucinations that were so unbelievably real they scared the life out of me.

It began one night when I was sat with my partner at home, and thought she asked me something, I can't remember what. I turned and replied, "Oh, about thirteen". She looked at me strangely and asked why I said that. I said I was only answering her question. She replied that she hadn't asked me anything. I thought she was having me on, but she wasn't.

This became clearer in the coming days, as voices of people that I knew and some I didn't began conspiring to do things to me, to mock me, to hurt me. Then I started sensing people I didn't know walk into the bedroom and discuss me. I thought maybe the kids had come in to sneak a cigarette or something, but these were middle aged people I was hearing as well. These voices put me down, made a joke out of me or made outright threats. After a few days of this I was ready to fall apart. My partner could see that I had gone quite literally mad in the worst possible way and without a word visited my doctor and brought me back a prescription for Olanzapine, an anti-psychotic drug used in mania, schizophrenia and other psychoses. In this case it was a depressive psychosis, or perhaps a mixed episode. Who cares? I'm going to give this a try, I thought.

Once again, I have had difficulty pinning this down to Steven's medical records. Surely you don't just prescribe this at home as a one off without even seeing the patient? If discussed with a GP surely this would be seen as a mental health crisis and appropriate assessment and help should be given? Is this the truth? Did someone give Steven something that perhaps he shouldn't have had?

The first few days it at least helped me get to sleep, deadened down the voices a little, but a side effect of it was that my dreams seemed real and solid and upon waking in the morning I would be convinced the dream was a factual happening from the previous day. Then the voices magnified to a deafening drone. They were telling me to do things, stupid things, like steal my father's car but I just blotted them out, much as it hurt. I gave up the tablets as a bad idea, and within time, the voices stopped. I had some nasty physical withdrawals, mostly muscle spasms in the upper arms that made me look like I was trying to impersonate a kangaroo. Also, the darkness was still with me.

Is this to do with medication, illness or alcoholic polyneuropathy? I was quite ignorant in the beginning of the devastating effects of alcohol but was to learn much more in the years to come.

We had another Christmas (2006) with my parents, and made the long walk back across town in the freezing night. My wife's parents had her down as the black sheep of the family and didn't invite her to meals. Her elder sister thinks she gets abducted by aliens, her younger one believes herself to be a practising witch. Do you see a pattern emerging?

This is the beginning of one of the worst periods of our life. I was desperately worried about Steven. On 13th December Ian takes Steven to see our GP as his mental health is worsening. He is told to stop drinking. I am not sure how helpful that is! On 18th December,

Eve and Steven visit the GP again together to ask for help from the Mental Health Team.

On the 19th the Community Mental Health Team is contacted by the GP as Steven is disturbed and depressed. Steven is given an appointment for 21st at a local health centre to see BL a Community Psychiatric Nurse (CPN). He is still living with Eve at this time, but I am keen that he should attend. He accepts my offer of a lift but insists that I shouldn't stay. With hindsight, that was a disastrous mistake. I suggest that he gives me a call when he is finished and I will pick him up. It is a miserable cold day with sleet blowing in the wind and he looks shrunken and depressed. I arrive at the centre to retrieve him and find that he has gone. I am shocked as he was in a bad way when I dropped him off. I phone him, and he is enraged and upset. "He called me a waste of space mam." Dr M has told Steven his problems are 'just' alcohol related and that he will be referred back to the Substance Misuse Team. So much for caring for those with a dual diagnosis.

I have to go looking in the streets for him and persuade him to get in the car and come home with me. It takes quite a while to settle him down and I too am furious. I phone the mental health team and ask for a meeting re the lack of support or care given to Steven. Apparently, I have to make do until the 3rd January because of the Christmas break. I also write to Steven's GP and ask that he facilitates a second opinion on Steven's mental health and that we do not want any more involvement with Dr M. A referral to a neurological specialist is also requested by me to rule out any brain damage or malfunction. As a family we are becoming desperate.

On 22nd December 2006 we made a Christmas dinner for just Steven and Eve. We could not face having the boys for Christmas day and Steven agreed to the plan.

He was quiet and jumpy and obviously unwell, but they enjoyed the meal and made a brave attempt to be sociable.

The jailbird had been making trouble with his brothers and when he called one night on the phone to intimidate them, I intervened. He said something that flipped my lid and he got a full verbal blasting at the top of my lungs. Despite his threats to come to the house for a fight with me I promised that he wouldn't be a wise puppy to mess with me in this state of mind, or words to that effect. He could also probably hear me punching seven bells on the large amplifier cabinet I was stood next to. Next time I saw him he bowed his head, apologised and offered me a handshake.

2007

My appointment with BL and the local Community Mental Health Team is altered three times at very short notice to 2nd January 2007 at 12.00 noon. I begin to feel that this is a ruse to persuade me to give in. As a result of the changes I have to attend on my own. I am faced by three professionals on the defensive and who really seem to have it in for both Steven and I. It is a very unpleasant interview. The notes to this meeting were never passed to me even though I asked and I was later told they were lost. I am told directly that Steven is 'just an alcoholic' and I feel I should believe Steven's story that Dr M called him a waste of space. The three of them demonstrated very little concern or care for Steven's mental health or personal welfare.

Dr M states emphatically that all of Steven's problems are due to drink even whilst acknowledging that he may have obsessive compulsive disorder or a personality disorder alongside it. No support, treatment or care plan is offered other than the referral to the Substance Misuse Team.

Early in the New Year, when the children had gone to school and my insomniac partner, who wouldn't sleep until daylight, was out for the count, I would wander to the shop and buy a can of cider. Then I would lurk around a nearby graveyard, ruminating over death. I wondered about the stories of the deceased people's lives, and who they had been, what they had felt. I even took morbid shots of the cold, winter frosted graveyard with my mobile phone, then rambled back home and would sleep until after lunch time.

11th January 2007. Deeply depressed, flat broke and it's a miserable January day. I had been into town with my partner, and decided to leave her doing what she enjoyed best i.e. gambling and go to my parents' home where my gear was set up. Knowing no one would be in I wouldn't annoy anyone by turning up the volume a bit. When I got there, I had a can of lager and strummed a few chords out. In the last few days I'd completed my solo album, which I had started in 2005, put on hold for what seemed forever, and recently got onto disc. The title was coincidental to my mood at this time, dark and depressed. I couldn't get in the mood to do anything, nothing constructive anyway. In the fading grey light of a wet winter evening, I sat and read, re-read and re-read again a few old magazines. Then, as the season made clear the necessity of switching on some electric lights, the call came. My partner is in a state, having lost every penny we had in the slot machines. Could I steal from my parents, so she could try and win it back she asked? No way.

I was struggling with the £17.5k debt I'd amassed during my manic periods with bank loans and credit cards. Understandably all now frozen and useless so I had nothing. She was in charge of the money. All the bank accounts and benefits were in her name, cash had a habit of losing its way and disappearing into the belly of a one-armed bandit. There was no way I was going to steal from my parents, but I did have another idea that would end this awful situation, if only for me.

Head down, I walk through the gusting wind. It stings my face and bare neck. Looking up towards the house, I notice an upstairs light is switched on. Surely Steven isn't back? I'm not expecting him. I dropped him off an hour ago in the town centre to meet with Eve.

Sensing trouble, I quicken my step. On entering the house, I call Steven's name and get no response. I throw down my bags in the hall and go upstairs. I am met by a very strange scene. Steven is frantically pasting brown 'goo' onto a wall behind the bookcase on the landing. There are two large ragged holes in the carpet in front of his bedroom door. Inexplicably there is dirt and dust along the bannister rails and over the rest of the furniture. What has happened?

Steven is agitated and incoherent, and he has always been a good dissembler. Garbled tales of looking for a lost CD and moving furniture do not seem to account for the damage. I forcibly take from him the wood filler that he is plastering everywhere, and can still get no sense out of him. He is frantically pacing up and down the landing, and the thought of 'headless chicken' comes unbidden to my mind. I begin to lose my temper with his inability or unwillingness to tell me what has happened, and storm downstairs for the vacuum cleaner and wet cloths. On returning, Steven grabs the cleaner from me and promises to pay for the damage. I am puzzled by the badly chipped wood on the side of the bookcase, and as I examine it, Steven pops up with a paint pot 'to tidy up a bit'. This is apparently for the splintered wood on the staircase that I have only just noticed. How can he have done all this just by pushing furniture about?

I am now very upset and becoming angrier because I know he is lying to me, and I am concerned as to why he would need to do that? I go to make tea so that I have time to think. He follows me and sits down with me as I drink my brew. He looks like a tall, gaunt, agitated vulture and my concern grows. He begins to ramble about 'secret things' that I mustn't tell anyone, and I wonder if he has found the time and the money to drink, or if the threatened manic episode has finally engulfed him.

I can't now remember what happened that made him 'confess' but it seems that Steven has used the keys to his dad's shotgun cabinet and found ammunition there too. That's Ian for the high jump then and a lifetime of guilt. Either by design or mistake the gun has gone off, missing every part of his body, wrecking the landing in the process. He has black powder burns on his hands. I am stunned and upset. I can't remember who I call first – was it a doctor or the Community Mental Health Team? Not the police that came later. I certainly called Ian, who dashed home from work to the ensuing ordeal of yet another wait at the hospital for assessment and admittance. Steven was lucky this time, straight into hospital and admittance to the loony bin yet again, with not much hanging about. I ask the Substance Abuse Manager that if all Steven's problems are to do with alcohol abuse, can she not take this opportunity to instigate a detox whilst they have him? I must have been persuasive because they keep him for a full 7day detox and assessment.

I remember that it was very late when we returned home – about 11.00pm. Emotionally drained and having missed meal times, we then had to face calling the police. Ian reported that a gun had been discharged and shared the surrounding circumstances. No one in the street had reported hearing anything, obviously all too busy watching the TV or eating their tea. (Apparently it is legal to discharge a firearm on your own property.) Ian received retribution by being interviewed and reprimanded at a later date. He was obliged to remove the gun from the house. I gave him grief for being an idiot and keeping ammunition and the gun in the same cabinet. Gun cabinets are by law furnished with two locks and two different keys. These had been safely hidden away by Ian in careful hiding places. This is not a problem for someone who really wants to be able to kill themselves and is prepared to watch and wait and sneak about until they find them. Steven was always deviously organised when it came to having the means to call it a day. So much so that CPNs and psychiatrists never got him to admit too much about his persistent desire to 'turn out the lights.'

The shotgun was lighter than I remembered as I slipped in two shells, but it would do the job; after all I was twelve the first time I'd fired one on the clay shooting range years ago. The sky was turning dark now, not quite as dark as my mood however. I closed the gun, flipped the safety catch off and put the barrel to my throat with my finger on the trigger. I ruminated on what I was about to do, looking down the barrel then putting it back to my head. I must have sat there some time, thinking about the pros and cons of this deed, and finally decided I owed more to my parents than for them to come home to a bloodbath. There would be a cleaner way for me to die, surely? I put down the gun, lengthways on the bed upon which I was sitting. Suddenly there was a massive detonation that half deafened me and made every stringed instrument in the room resonate. I sat there for what seemed like half an hour in shock, but it must have been in reality, only seconds. The shot had fired down and out of the room, just missing my right foot, then out of the open door where it skimmed the landing carpet and blew a hole though the banister. As soon as I could think again, I removed the second cartridge from the gun and locked it away, and feverishly tried to make good the damage. I could fill in the hole, I'd have to make an excuse about the carpet, but as I was making good, my mother arrived home. She almost bought the story that I'd had accident moving furniture, but my dad knew the smell of gunpowder, and also spotted the badly hidden spent shell. Cue the doctor again.

Steven hasn't remembered this quite accurately – Ian was at work and did not arrive home until I summoned him in a panicked telephone call. He found the pellets embedded in the landing floorboards. These were repaired but still have a distinctive squeak 'lest we forget'.

CHAPTER 6: OUR MAN ON THE INSIDE (AGAIN)

2007

The doctor was out very quickly. I can't remember much about who I said what to as I was a sobbing mess with no idea where my life had gone. They maybe stayed 2 hours, maybe only 10 minutes, I wouldn't have known if they had stayed all night. However, I do remember a medical man asking if I would like to spend some time in a psychiatric unit again. I couldn't talk for crying and nodded yes.

Late on that fateful day, ironically my grandfather's birthday, I was taken into an open ward (open as in the ward is locked, but the rooms aren't) and settled in room 9 with a massive dose of sedative Librium to calm my spinning head. I would spend the next fortnight there. My first hospitalisation was in 2001, and I have until now had 4 more stays. This was either the first or second of these probably the second. I can't remember in total how many times I was in this unit, but the future would bring me back here yet not to the same room. I know for a fact I'd been in this room before but when I couldn't say. Manic depression, as I have said, plays havoc with when and where and why. I was there for a fortnight. Drew and his wife came to see me and deliberately didn't mention what had happened. In fact, the sadness in their eyes mirrored mine. My partner came by often, which was a bitter-sweet experience for me. My parents visited, trying to make idle gossip but were pretty much dumbstruck by the situation.

Eve is angry with us, saying that Steven would never do such a thing as attempt to take his own life and we are lying. She cannot cope with the idea of him being in hospital again having attempted suicide. She sees it as a personal affront. I promise to take her in the car to visit in the early afternoon. She is not out of bed when I call about 1.00pm. When she finally answers the door, she is mute and dazed and half-dressed and her lower body naked. She realises she is late and pulls back her long black hair, deftly securing it with a band. She urinates in the hall toilet with the door fully open, whilst continuing to talk at me. She doesn't wash her hands, or her face, and pulls on her jeans without underwear. Straightening the sweatshirt that she has been sleeping in she says, "I'm ready, let's go."

My father brings my partner to see me. She argued persistently that the shotgun incident had been merely an accident, and I would never try to take my life. He protested that there couldn't be another explanation as to why I had a loaded gun to my head. She was nearly ejected from the car for her attitude. Denial is a great coping mechanism. That's what she was trying to do. My dad was right in his anger but for a while, made peace.

The peace in my room was a massive relief, and this unit was modern and had en-suite bathrooms and private bedrooms as opposed to the dormitory ward styling of the hospital I was in back in 2001. I even had my own writing desk with drawers, easy chair, waste bin and wardrobe. Not bad for the NHS! At first I would just stare into space for hours until it got dark. Within a few days, I was reading the few heavy volume books I'd asked to be brought in, and keeping myself to myself. The tranquillizers and sleeping pills were levelling me somewhat. I eventually began drawing little cartoons, like the Birdman Charlie Bronson, then began writing this account about what I didn't yet understand:
"I don't know exactly how I came to be here. A strange unravelling of events that have come together to see me sat alone in a psychiatric unit wondering who the

hell I am on a Friday night. I miss my girl so much it hurts. I miss my life, and boy do I miss my sanity. I know the dark thoughts have been building for some time, slowly, almost imperceptibly; they crept in like silent assassins.

Where did they come from? Theories abound. All I know is they caught up with me with a vengeance all at once. The next thing I know I've fired the gun. No one was hurt, thankfully, but the last bit of faith I had in myself is gone.

I almost have to laugh in a very tongue-in-cheek way, my life has become such a frustrated, confused mess I couldn't even kill myself right.

I heard the shot and felt the black powder spray back, and the incredulity hit me like a bucket of cold water. Why was I holding a gun? I don't know what had put that thought in my head; don't remember loading the shells, in fact I don't remember anything of the last few weeks. It was as if one dreary day just merged into another. Weeks came and went, I didn't notice. And now I'm wide awake and wondering how in hell things could get this bad without me noticing.

Now the reality sinks in. Little flashes of lost time flicker in the soup that is my mind. Yeah, the depression was there but I've always managed before. Oh, and I've just remembered the spiralling debts I've been trying to ignore, and the persecutory voices that have been screaming at me periodically. That's how it's come to this I guess I've just had my head in the sand all this time. Pull the covers over my head and hope for it to go away. Yeah, well…

So why would I want to write all this? It's a bit too late now to undo the damage. It won't fix the hole I blew in the floor or the wall. It won't change the fact I can't be at home with the woman I love when I need her most.

It won't change my well-deserved reputation as a screaming lunatic, won't repair all the damaged trust. I suppose I'm just trying to piece together some explanation from all these fragments of what is left of my mind. I'm ashamed, frightened and partly incredulous. I'm scared of what the doctors may tell me, and equally scared for what they may not be able to.

I hate being alone in this single bed. I hate knowing the torment my girl must be in at home. I wish I was there now. What if this isn't a treatable illness? What if I'm just nuts, plain and simple?

I recognise psychosis when I see it in myself. I thought that would be impossible worrying stuff. Anyway, I digress. If I'm honest this has been coming a long time, but I wish it hadn't manifested in such a shocking and potentially disastrous way. It was fair enough in the past, no one could see the cuts on my wrists and they'd heal. The overdose could be vomited up before it was too late. No harm done, everything forgotten about and back to pretending. But I really blew it this time, literally. I don't want to have to deal with this situation, but I can't ignore it anymore. I feel like I'm locked inside an arena in a red suit and there's a very angry bull in here. How can I ever get my head around this? I've been bottling this up forever and now, literally, bang.

Well, there's not much I can do about anything now except wait and see; I'm not really making anything clearer with any of this. I guess I'll go and continue smoking myself to death and see if the morning brings any answers".

I think I was starting to get some sense of reality back by the end of that fortnight. When I'd used up the few bits of paper I had with me, I asked the nurses if they had any more, so I could write down the songs I had in my head relating to my predicament. I was given some blank clinical report sheets, which I still have today with the lyrics I noted down, though the tunes I imagined have long since escaped me. At release time, I spoke with the doctor and asked for some pharmaceutical help, I suppose to save from this situation happening again. I was prescribed the antidepressant Citalopram, part of the group of SSRI drugs. That is, selective serotonin re-uptake inhibitors, the family of drugs to which my previous runs on Prozac, Seroxat and Lustral belong.

Ironically, the same day that Steven messes with the shotgun, the GP writes a letter for a private referral to Prof C. The implication being that there are no other NHS psychiatrists available to us at that time. We are given an appointment for the 7th February 2007. The system has failed us utterly and we feel that we have little choice. As a family we agree that the money we have spare should be used for private psychiatric assessment once again. I have no recollection of being supported by the GP to get another NHS opinion – we always seem to have to sort it out by ourselves.

18th January 2007 we check with Citizens' Advice – Steven hasn't got enough income to pay his debts and his only choice is bankruptcy. The fate of the TV is all that Eve seems to be bothered about and it is upsetting Steven on many levels. Steven has bought it on 'buy now pay later' and of course the bailiffs may choose to take it back as it is in his name. I call the Rethink Advocacy Service and am frustrated because the numbers on the leaflet are all wrong but P.P. answers the fax number! A wonderful, well-informed woman who inspires hope. We discuss the failings of Dr M, the community psychiatrist and the mental health team and she tells me she is well aware of his track record. "Even his body language says he's not interested." She agrees to support Steven where she can within an advocacy role.

That same day Steven is discharged and is intent on counting out his tablets. "I'm to see someone called BL." I point out to him that this is the same BL who sat with Dr M and called Steven a liar to my face, saying "It did not happen". Steven seems not to care or comprehend. He is reluctant to discuss advocacy or his mountainous debts, although he does sign the papers for the Citizens Advice to go ahead with his bankruptcy and act on his behalf. I am frustrated at his lack of awareness and concerned that he does not seem to be functioning well on any level. I drop him off at Eve's at tea time and give him some cash. What else can I do? I am relieved that he shows a flash of common sense later in the day. He texts his dad to say, "Hello, I'm okay."

Waking up suddenly at 5.00am the next morning I realise that I have no idea what care or treatment has been put into place for Steven. Here we go again.

On investigating that day, I find out that he has been discharged on antidepressants and no care plan in place other than one call from the CPN. I catch up with the CPN outside Steven and Eve's house and he tells me his is just a courtesy call and he won't be calling again as Steven categorically does not have a mental health problem. So yet another mixed message and the brush off. Understandably Steven refused to see him. And of course, antidepressants are not safe or appropriate medication for bipolar on their own.

18th January 2007. It was a bit bewildering to be back in the world, and I felt flat and grey, but no longer black. It takes most antidepressants about a fortnight to take hold properly, and in time I began to rally. I got an enthusiastic welcome home, and waited to see where my life would go from here. As it turned out, to hell in a handcart, but that would be later.

31st January 2007. I am engulfed in sudden gasping choking sobs, as though drowning. The storm passes as quickly as it came. I have just read a description of the love a mother has for her child: "A fierce and overwhelming protectiveness and a desire for the child's survival at all costs." I have acknowledged it for the first time and understand why I keep it under wraps. It is as if I can see into the future.

On the 5th February 2007 I take Steven to County Court and he is officially made bankrupt with debts of over £16,000. He is weak and thin and even in clean clothes looks unkempt and pathetic. After the event it is back home to Eve.

7th February 2007 12.00 noon, we wait quietly, not talking, ready to be disappointed. I am attracted by a pleasant looking man with dark hair and a tidy beard. He's heading for the rest room. He looks directly at us as he passes and smiles gently. When he re-emerges, he heads straight for us and I realise that this is Prof C. He takes Steven away with him, and they are gone for quite a while. Prof C. personally comes to collect me to join the interview. I find myself unable to choose between sobbing and laughing hysterically at his verdict. Tears win, but I restrain myself. I am shocked by his statement that we should consider suing the powers that be – "There is no doubt about the diagnosis." Steven is quiet and calm. "Why are you so surprised mam? I always knew it was bipolar." So Steven has been untreated for 7 years, after being removed from appropriate medication and the original diagnosis of Prof C in 2000. Those 7 years are when the long-term damage to both Steven's liver and his self-esteem really set in, and later we decide to complain officially about the psychiatrist who told us that *"Steven is just an alcoholic."* Even after this verdict things do not go easily. The medication that Prof A wants to give Steven must be written up by his GP, so it takes a further 5 days to get the medication. Shockingly 25 days have elapsed since his discharge from hospital without appropriate medication. By now Steven is climbing the walls and drinking again due to mania and his inability to sleep.

I felt the Citalopram was not cutting the mustard. I got financial help from my family to see a private psychiatric professor who, after an hour or so said he was convinced I had 'advanced' (think he means untreated here) bipolar disorder and that frankly anyone who said otherwise should have their license revoked. He prescribed me Valproate semi-sodium again, along with the anti-psychotic tranquillizer Rivotril. I was to stay on the Citalopram also. I was subjected to several brain scans, the results of which were not divulged to me, but whatever they were, did not alter the professor's mind.

The scans were done later in June 2007 requested by us via our GP at the instigation of myself and Prof C. Steven saw neurologist Dr LF who authorised them. They showed alcoholic brain damage. I did not find this out until after Steven's death and I do not believe the results of the scans were ever discussed with Steven. He believed they were being done to show if he had bipolar or not. I realise that Prof C would not have been informed as Steven was no longer seeing him after July 2007. How did we come to that decision? Was it shortage of cash or Steven now being back in NHS services and thinking he would be okay?

I need to caution readers here. It took me a long time to find out that if one psychiatrist gives a diagnosis and recommends treatment, another can overturn the same if they choose to and that patient has come under their care and jurisdiction. This may be a fundamental flaw in consistent appropriate treatment for psychiatric patients. It certainly did Steven no favours, as his list of 'labels' and medication indicates.

On 18th February 2007 Steven spends the day with us. He is unwashed, hungry and very thin. He admits that he has missed two days of his new medication. I sort him out as best I can, and he spends the day very quietly. I have no idea what Eve is doing and neither do I care.

I agreed to marry my partner, though I didn't see what difference a piece of paper would make. We settled on doing the deed later though, not straight away. For the next couple of months, we went on as always.

However, in the spring, she was popping too many pills. I had started to drink too much to block out the arguing, and one night walked out. I got up and went to a friend's, turning up in a manic state and woke up the next morning in hospital wondering what had happened. Apparently, I'd imbibed a lethal amount of alcohol and by rights should be dead. He'd left me in the living room for a minute with a litre bottle of vodka and when he came back from the toilet I was comatose, having consumed the lot.

On 20th February 2007 Steven walked out on Eve and came to us, and for the first time ever, he was aggressive, argumentative and we could not settle him. It was obvious that he was drunk this time, as well as manic. He was adamant that he was never going to be with Eve again and did not want us to contact her. Ian tried to calm him down, but he was raging and incoherent. Ian's temper snapped when Steven threatened him, and he told him to get out. Steven left quickly and in a dreadful state. I was so frightened for his safety that I insisted Ian went after him. This he did, realising that Steven was at risk. Unable to find him, we called the police and reported him missing and a danger to himself. We rang around all his friends and asked them to contact us if he turned up. I spent the next few dreadful hours with ice in my belly, waiting for whatever was to come. It was later clear that Steven had no recollection of arriving at our home first, before running off.

One friend, having been sworn to secrecy by a manic Steven at first denied that he was with him. Later, he changed his mind when he found Steven out cold on the floor and rang us in a panic. We told him to call an ambulance and the police and tell them that Steven was on his way to hospital. We also rang the police to make sure the information they got was correct. We were so exhausted and upset that we left the medical people to get on with it. I think they called us to confirm a few details, but it was now about 2.00am in the morning. I called the hospital as soon as I got up the next morning and then called Eve to say where he was. I promised to take her by car to see him, but sensing trouble I first went to the hospital alone, intending to pick her up once I had found out the lie of the land.

Just as well. Steven was in the local General Hospital on a drip and very ill. He is also very manic, but the staff were still insisting it was 'only' alcohol and drugs that were screwing up his brain. They were concerned about his heart rate and the amount of Amitriptyline that he had stuffed down his throat the night before. This is not a drug that you take to get high; it is one that can easily put out the lights. I asked for a psychiatrist and as usual was told that one wasn't available. Steven was away with the fairies and talking fast and furious and in a very detached way. He asked me for his clothes. I asked him if he wanted to see Eve and he freaked out, raging and anxious, telling me a definite no, even though he was still confused. I told *him that I was going to fetch her, and left. I have no idea now why I thought that this was the best course of action. On the way out, I again asked for a psychiatrist and warned staff that Steven might discharge himself. They insisted that they couldn't stop him and were uninterested in his mental health state. Where does safeguarding fit in to this scenario? I thought it best to go and get Eve and try and explain to her that he wouldn't see her.*

I was no sooner in the car and on my way to collect her than I got an agitated call from her. She hadn't waited for me, but had got the bus. She had arrived at the hospital just after I had left to find that Steven was already up and gone. Knowing that he only had one place to go, I called Drew and luckily, he answered. I explained the situation. He quickly agreed to come and search the local area. We both knew that if Steven had any brain working he would be heading for Drew's house in a nearby village. I took myself off in the opposite direction to check out our own town.

Against advice, and still manic, I discharged myself and started walking (in completely the wrong direction) to find Drew's place. After several miles, raving like a lunatic, I asked a young lady for a light for my cigarette and directions. I must have appeared utterly crazy, or like some kind of street person. I was pointed back in the other direction. After an hour of walking, I realised the alarm had been raised when I saw Drew scouring the roads to find me. I spent another 3 days with him before going back to my partner.

Steve stayed with Drew for a couple of days and was supported to attend an outpatient appointment with the Mental Health Team. That seems to have come to nothing once more. He capitulated and went back to Eve. I am inclined to write 'like a dog to vomit.'

On the 2nd March 2007 Steven and I composed a letter of complaint to the Chief Executive of the local Mental Health Team at the local hospital in relation to the lack of mental health care given to Steven. These are the words that we agreed upon:

"I wish you to investigate the following complaint regarding the care and treatment I have received from my Community Mental Health Team:

BACKGROUND:

I have had a mental health problem since my early teens and was diagnosed as having bipolar disorder by Prof A in the summer of 2001. I had a dual diagnosis and was hospitalised in autumn 2001 to detox and to be assessed. On leaving hospital I was not treated for bipolar as Dr M did not agree with the diagnosis. I was unwell over the next years with only the support of my GP.

In February 2006 I was again very unwell and was admitted overnight to hospital after an overdose, but was not given appropriate diagnosis or medication. Over the following months I was continually advised that all my problems were due to heavy drinking and not a mental health disorder. In late December 2006 I was again very unwell and was referred back to my local Mental Health Team. At an emergency consultation with Dr M and Ms BL on 21st December 2006 I was again told that all my problems were due to alcohol and was refused any further support or treatment other than from the Substance Abuse Team.

On 11th January 2007 I was again hospitalised as I had tried to commit suicide and was very unwell. I was an inpatient for 2 weeks where I was detoxed without any problems. When discharged from hospital I was given the antidepressant medication Citalopram (inappropriate on its own for bipolar) and again referred to the Substance Abuse Team. The day after my discharge a CPN told my mother that I did not have a mental health illness.

On 7th February 2007 I sought a consultation with Prof C, a private psychiatrist, who assured me that I definitely had a bipolar disorder and prescribed a mood stabiliser alongside the antidepressant. I have been treated by my GP on Prof C's instructions and do not feel that I can expect any help or support from the Community Mental Health Team.

My complaint is as follows:
•   I have not been correctly diagnosed or treated by the Community Mental Health Team over a long period of time (2001-2007) but specifically since February 2006 and in particular at the consultation on 21st December 2006.
•   I have been continually discharged from the care of the Mental Health Team without appropriate treatment for bipolar disorder. This has caused my condition to be unstable and has impacted badly on my life and that of my parents. This caused further distress because when I needed help, my parents had to first contact the emergency doctor and could not always get access to the Mental Health Crisis Team directly.
•   I was discharged from hospital in January 2007 with no care plan in place other than to be referred back to the Substance Abuse Team.

My comments:
•   I would like to be referred to a Mental Health Team outside my own area as I cannot afford to continue private treatment and I have no faith in my local team.
•   I would like an explanation as to the lack of care and appropriate treatment.
•   I would like an apology regarding my treatment at my consultation with Dr M on 21st December 2007 when he was dismissive of my needs.

•   I have decided to complain because I have a severe and enduring mental health condition and have not received the care I needed to stay well and progress. I hope that by complaining others will not have to go through the distress that I am experiencing.
•   There seems to be a lack of communication or cohesion in treating people with a dual diagnosis such as myself. What plans have the trust made for improving the service and care given to patients with a diagnosis of substance misuse and a mental illness?

Please note that I give permission for my parents Ian and Clare to speak to you on my behalf and generally to act on my behalf if needed."

I wish at this point that we had asked for help regarding this as it all went tits up from the beginning, more of this later.

12th March 2007 Steven is with us for the afternoon and is sulky, unwell and irritable. I fuss around him trying to get him to eat and to ascertain if he has taken his medication. It seems that he either can't remember or has not bothered. I retrieve the spare tray of tablets from the cupboard and hand them to him, trying to get him to take responsibility for himself. He is adamant that he doesn't need that 'shit' and becomes more agitated. I ask him once again to take his medication, hoping that it will calm him down. My request has the opposite effect. He snatches the open tray from me and begins stuffing a week's worth of tablets into his mouth. I am initially frozen with shock with part of my brain saying, "Well this would solve it all wouldn't it?" I try once to retrieve the tray but that only makes him shrug me off and chew all the harder. I reach for the phone, dial 999 and ask for an ambulance. When they arrive, Steven is sitting clutching an almost empty medication tray. They talk very gently to him, getting to grips with the situation as Steven is now angry and agitated. I am distraught, thinking that I handed to him the means to kill himself. It is then that the ambulance woman spots that Steven has his hand in his pocket and is trying to open something out of our sight. With great patience and skill, she persuades Steven to show us what he has in his hand. I am shocked to the core to see a bottle of Amitriptyline he willingly hands this over but refuses to go with them to hospital. Having distracted us he heads for the door, and of course they cannot forcibly hold onto him, so they call the police. One of them follows Steven in the ambulance and the other gets on the phone. They catch up with him in a nearby garage block. He is escorted into the ambulance and a police car follows to hospital.

The bottle of tablets has my name on it and a date from 1996. I am careful with medication and realise that Steven has stolen this and hidden it for over 10 years keeping it like a comfort blanket for the day he makes the decision to quit us all. So the desire to 'switch out the lights' was already with him before I handed it to him on a plate.

On 13th March I phone Prof C's secretary. He contacts the hospital, GP and the Community Mental Health Team asking for Steven to be carefully assessed with a view to sectioning due to suicide risk. It is possible that human error caused a miscommunication re fax numbers etc. as I have seen the paperwork with the wrong telephone numbers on it. So, this did not happen, and he was discharged in to the care of Eve the next day. She later admitted to me that the hospital doctor had wanted to section Steven, but she had persuaded the doctor that she could cope with and care for Steven. This is not documented in his notes. This was a lost opportunity to halt the spiral of self-destruction that Steven has fallen in to. The next day Eve sends him back to us saying that she cannot cope with him.

Within a few months the dosage of the Valproate was making me sleepy all day, and I have since cut the dose from 3 doses a day to 1, and as of time of writing, am managing. Before that it was easy to have people make the mistake that I was permanently pissed.

One day I went about my business of recording, after which I fell asleep. I got a phone call enquiring as to my whereabouts with my missus angry on the other end of the phone. We came to a massive, unnecessary verbal argument again and I said that that was that, and with immediate effect began to withdraw from that world again.

Steven came 'home' to us again on 30th March 2007 and I have a note that the police were called on 1st April 2007, an Easter weekend. I believe that Steven is trying very hard to cut down his drinking and has done it too fast. He gets agitated and upset and confesses that he has called the police. "I am worried that I might hurt you and dad." The police are very understanding and supportive. I cannot remember if we end up in hospital or not, these months are dreadful for all of us.

I do remember one similar occasion when the police were called by Steven because he felt so agitated and afraid that he would hurt us. They came and talked to him very reassuringly. Steven took his evening tablets in a bid to calm down but was desperate to go to hospital. He was admitted via Accident and Emergency to be assessed overnight. Unfortunately, the prescribed medication was finally kicking in, with the possibility that Steven had taken a double dose in his distress. As a result, he is now sleeping, zoned out on heavy medication. The nurses don't want to touch him as he is swiping them away, eyes tightly shut, mumbling protests and unable to cooperate as they try to transfer him to another trolley. The emergency doctor who has assessed him in a kind and humane way steps in, and Ian, I and him all manhandle Steven onto the new trolley whilst the others stand by. It is obvious that they have decided that Steven is not worth helping in any way. He is a dead weight and almost unconscious with medication.

Up on the ward we are met by three nurses, two women and a man. It is very clear that the two female nurses don't want to touch Steven and I wonder what they have been told and what they are thinking. They obviously find my son, in his current predicament, distasteful. Steven is not helping the situation. He is absolutely gone on his medication and waves his arms about every time they go to touch him even though he is fast asleep. The three of them finally attempt to get Steven into bed. After watching them struggle the staff nurse comes in and says that she is having none of it and if we can't get him in to bed then we can take him home with us. The male nurse looks Ian and me in the eye and says, "Well let's get on with it."

Between the three of us we slide Steven onto the bed using the sheet on the trolley. I roll him in to a semblance of the recovery position and put his shoes in the locker. It is very obvious to me that some of the nurses are frightened of Steven and do not know how to handle him. Surely, they have dealt with unconscious patients before? I think they have made a number of unpleasant assumptions about my distressed son – alcohol, drugs etc. Of course, he is not looking his best with long, uncombed hair, leather trousers, poor body weight and the look of someone who has just had a 'skinful'. Ironically part of his anxiety has been triggered by him ceasing to drink alcohol. The male nurse takes us to one side and promises to look after Steven.

We go home with a very sour taste in our mouths. A medical ward is obviously not the best place for someone with a mental health illness.

Steven sent this letter to Mrs Tay, manager of the Community Mental Health Team on 17th April 2007.

Dear Mrs Tay,

I refer to my complaint and the reply dated 12th April.

I request a second opinion regarding my mental health from a different consultant psychiatrist, outside of my local area. I am willing to consider any area. I have no faith in the local Community Mental Health Team.

I wish the Trust to note that my alcoholism is a direct result of my mental health condition not being correctly diagnosed and treated. Since receiving appropriate medication and support via a private psychiatrist my condition has slowly improved.

It has enabled me to make important decisions about my personal life and I now have a genuine desire to give up alcohol as I know that I can further improve on my medication, without the need for alcohol. I am awaiting advice on this at an appointment with the substance misuse team on 23 April 2007.

I think the trust has missed the point of my complaint which is that my initial diagnosis from an NHS Psychiatrist was overturned and I did not receive the correct treatment then and over the following years. This resulted in an increase in my alcoholism. I am not satisfied with the response that I have received.

Steven is in hospital again on 24th April 2007 and I have made these notes for the on call CPN at the hospital. This is the information I left for the on call CPN:

Steven Midgley for the attention of the on call CPN

This is Steven's recent history:

7 February 2007 Prof C gave a definite diagnosis of bipolar and prescription was faxed to GP surgery next day. Steven was sober.

12 February 2007 Medication finally issued via GP surgery – PLEASE NOTE 25 DAYS SINCE DISCHARGE have elapsed without appropriate medication and 5 days to get medication via surgery, Steven is drinking again by now due to mania and inability to sleep.

20 February 2007 Extremely intoxicated – had to get police to search for him and they called ambulance. He was taken to the hospital and was extremely ill. Too ill to be psychiatrically assessed. Discharged himself next day whilst still very unwell. I had advised hospital that he needed assessment and of his mental health history. Was found by a friend wandering about the outskirts of the town.

5 March 2007 Second appointment with Prof C. Advised he must stop drinking re effectiveness of medication.

12 March 2007 Steven escorted to hospital after snatching medication tray from me whilst depressed and had been drinking. Escorted to hospital by police as he ran out of house. Prof C had contacted hospital, GP and the Community Mental Health Team asking for Steven to be carefully assessed with a view to sectioning due to suicide risk. This did not happen and was discharged in to care of partner next day.

13 March 2007 Partner could not cope with Steven's behaviour /care.

30 March 2007 Steven left partner with a view to 'staying alive' and giving up alcohol.

8 April 2007 Had cut down alcohol too quickly and became agitated, manic – Steven called the ambulance and police because of obsessive fearful thoughts. Taken to local hospital. Told Crisis Team in hospital that he wanted 'monkey off his back'. They said that they were going to contact you ASAP – perhaps you can check what they said / noted re Steven and alcohol. Steven came home with us early on Easter Monday morning and has tried hard to cut down on drinking. Unfortunately, he is in a vicious circle of his alcohol intake reducing the effectiveness of his medication.

I would like to bring your attention back to the cleft stick in which he is caught:

The local Community Mental Health Team do not accept that he has bipolar or a severe or enduring mental illness therefore will not support him or us as his carers in getting the best / appropriate treatment for him.

Substance abuse services will have to decide if he is a dual diagnosis or **just an alcoholic**. He is losing hope again of ever getting well because no one is co-ordinating care and we are going around in circles. I am aware of the dual diagnosis policy and policy regarding suicide risk. Is anyone going to take this on board and engineer a co-ordinated approach to Steven's care before he does actually manage to drink himself to death in a binge or commit suicide?

He really wants to change, and we have noticed a change in him in these past few weeks since he has had bipolar medication. He has removed himself from a destructive and stressful relationship. He is cutting down his alcohol but struggles to maintain an organised approach to this. He has reduced binge drinking from the level of two months ago. He is looking forward to moving into rented accommodation with a friend but knows that he can't do this until he is stable. Hence, we are all extremely frustrated and exhausted.

Enclosed are two copy letters from Prof C.

Clare Midgely with Steven's knowledge and consent.

24th March 2007 I have an appointment to see Mrs Tay at our Mental Health hospital and I wish I had taken an advocate with me. I became very emotional whilst trying to get my point across. I cannot now remember her official title, but she was the 'boss' I think of the Community Mental Health Team. She was sympathetic and appeared to pay attention to my tale of woe but I shouldn't have been taken in. I really thought that we were going to be listened to. I hadn't realised that the system was concerned with dealing with this 'in house' before it became a fully-fledged complaint. She promised to call in a 'few favours' and even in my confused state I was aware that this didn't seem quite the right solution. She asked me what I wanted – I said a detox for Steven and appropriate medication, support and treatment.

I stayed away, enjoying my new-found freedom, and got a slight rush from this. I had my own money again and went on a minor spending spree. I rescued a two-year old cat that had been sent into the vets for euthanasia simply because her owners did not want her. I did. I thought she might be a nice little sister for my faithful existing rescue cat. When they didn't immediately try to eat each other I knew it would be all right.

Steven seems to be making a real effort and his friend Ron offers to share a house with him. The house belongs to his uncle. They keep in touch, but I suspect that the offer doesn't progress because Ron does not like the idea now of sharing with a drinker. I am excited that it might happen and see it as a new start for Steven. Gradually my hope drains away again.

Eve is constantly at our door and on more than one occasion she is lying on the drive screaming and crying. She comes to the door yet again, sobbing and Steven will not see her, leaving me to sort it out. She asks for help saying that she has been attacked. I turn her away and tell her to go to the police and the doctors. I do not believe a word of it. I am haunted now by the thought that it might have been true and that I did not help her.

My wife and I had a few depressing and berating phone calls between us then nothing. I was single, not interested in anyone else, and just enjoying life as best I could. I became involved as a friend with a married couple. I did not know at the time that they were bisexual swingers with designs on me. I had a lucky escape.

Steven met this woman with bipolar in a recent stay in hospital and got friendly with her and her husband. After discharge they all stayed in touch and they made a real effort to take him out and about. We saw this as something that would increase Steven's confidence and get him back in to the real world. I quite liked them, and they seemed to be doing Steven some good. I do remember the husband sitting with me talking about mental illness and how difficult it was to live with someone with bipolar. He intimated that he couldn't keep up with his wife's sexual demands. I wasn't shocked, but it rang alarm bells with me. I remember looking at him and saying, "As long as you don't have my son selling himself on the streets, I am okay about him being with you." Well they didn't put him out on the streets but groomed him with trips out and free beer and friendship. Steven tells me he has been asked to stay over, what did I think? "If you really must stay, I suppose it is better than getting a taxi late at night. It is okay if you take your medication, watch the booze and come back in a taxi in the morning, or dad will collect you." I wasn't happy about it, but Steven was keen on the idea of some chat and some tunes. He rolls in at about 5.00am angry and dishevelled. "The buggers only wanted me for three in a bed. Even I know when I am being fed booze and being played. I woke up with one of them on each side of me, so I legged it." My suspicions were right. Steven is devastated and let down and they never meet again.

Three months or thereabouts rolled by, but I could not stop thinking about my partner. I can't remember who instigated it but shortly we were back together in a less than ideal location over the road from her ex-partner. When the recriminations died down, we decided to move ASAP to another town and, rather foolishly, marry. We set the end of June as the date. My first experience with marriage had taught me it is a worthless piece of paper and changes nothing, but that's what she wanted to be happy. Like an idiot, I acquiesced.

Eve decides to move again, and they are living in a rented house in a nearby town and Steven, possibly influenced by Eve, does not bother to give us an address. It is a while before we find him living in a hovel. I get the feeling that Eve does not want us to know where they are and certainly doesn't welcome our visit.

This is a scary time for Ian and I as we are aware that we are being pushed out and bad mouthed. We are stuck in the middle again. After a period of time in which Steven had asked us to keep Eve away from him, he has gone back to her yet again. How can I bridge the gap after telling her to fuck off at Steven's instigation? Now I treat her with civility as they are once again 'together'.

Quite quickly they realise that the recent change is not for them and are on the move again. They move to another private rented house on the 14th June 2007. It is no smarter than the one before and is another hovel in a difficult area. It's not even easy for them to get on a bus. As usual we help where we can. At least I know where he is. As usual notifying people of the change of address is not high on the list of priorities and this has ramifications for continuity of care and medical appointments.

Steven continued to see Prof C but is sent for tests and an MRI scan. At this point Steven has not the energy to continue the battle with the NHS. Neither have I. Against my better judgement he decides that if he is back in the NHS system then he doesn't need Prof C any more. He is returned to Prof B as the 'favour' called in by Mrs Tay.

I think Steven was also aware that none of us had the cash for him to continue to see Prof C. Having said that, in hindsight, I would have sold my soul for him to continue to see Prof C.

Ian and I are exhausted and accept the offer of a holiday in Spain from a friend. I try my best to safeguard Steven during the period that we are away and write this letter before we leave.

My letter to the Community Addiction Team in May

Dear Community Addictions Team
<u>Steven Midgley appointment at 10.30am</u>
I have further information for you regarding my son Steven, for whom I am the prime carer. Steven is no longer living with us, having chosen to go back to his ex-partner. I do not know if he will allow me to attend with him tomorrow so please note the following:

I have been asked by Prof B (Community Mental Health Team) and by Mrs Tay, Community Mental Health Team manager, to advise them on the treatment offered by yourselves and on Steven's progress.

If you do not feel it appropriate to advise me as to what action is offered to or agreed with Steven, then will you please advise them in writing of the outcome of the appointment on 30th May 2007 and advise Steven's GP as well.

Steven is still drinking. He has made real attempts to reduce his intake. He would appear to be unable to stop without physical and psychological support. The medication he is using for bipolar disorder is being counteracted to some extent by the alcohol he is drinking. He will under-report his alcohol although I must stress that he has tried very hard to reduce his consumption. His private psychiatrist Prof C has expressed grave concern at the danger of accidental death that Steven is placing himself in when using medication and alcohol together.

As far as I am aware he is not yet accepted into the care of the alternative Mental Health Team as he is still in the process of being assessed and transferred. I have confirmed that there is an open referral on the system for Steven. This means that no one other than his father and I are watching out for his welfare. He has had only two bad episodes whilst with us during the past two months which is a vast improvement on the previous year. I have serious concerns regarding his personal safety and that his drinking will increase and that his mental health will deteriorate further if no one is paying attention to his welfare on a regular basis. Steven can be contacted on his mobile number.

If Steven cancels this appointment would you consider advising me please? I believe you have authority from Steven already on file to share information with me.

After writing this, I realise that no one is concerned about the health, welfare and safety of our son other than us, his parents. At the time I had no awareness of safeguarding issues within services and with hindsight it seems that services were not much interested in Steven. It is on reviewing his records later that I find he is flagged as a vulnerable adult. This did not provide him with the safety net that he needed.

And then Steven drops the bombshell, two days before we are due to leave on holiday. Eve and he are to be married at the local register office on 29th June. We are due to fly back the day before the wedding. Nothing else to do but run away to the sun… We are shocked to our core. Eve and I are still not on easy terms (never really were). I write her this note before we go away:

Steven is still alcoholic and has not stopped drinking. It is essential that he attends the following appointments if you are to have any chance of making a go of it together or his health problems are to be addressed.

Alcohol Services, at XX on Wednesday XX May (TOMORROW)

Nerve conduction tests Tuesday XX June

MRI scan 2.15 pm for 2.30 pm on Monday XX June

Psychiatric appointment: with Prof C in XXX on Tuesday X July 20XX at 12.00 noon.

Steven puts himself at risk every time he drinks particularly if he uses his brown Clonazepam tablets which are only supposed to be taken when he is extremely anxious or manic and not with alcohol.

When he left you, he came back to us by choice. We did not encourage him to do so. Perhaps you need to reflect on why he chose to do that. He weighed only 9st 2lbs and was in a poor condition mentally and physically. You are not responsible for his mental health condition nor his alcoholism, but you are responsible for his deterioration over the past months. You also isolated him from his friends and made him choose between you and his family. Steven needs care and a regular lifestyle even if he cannot accept it himself. If you cannot undertake to help him or make a decent home together because of your own problems, then you both need to get outside help. He has no spare cash; his level of drinking and smoking spends all of his incapacity allowance. Remember, that his illness and his alcoholism in conjunction with your financial difficulties caused his bankruptcy. Remember also, that you could not cope with Steven before. Well, nothing much has changed Eve and by going back to live with you and adopting your lifestyle his chances of ever leading a better life, or of becoming well again and mentally stable, have been jeopardised once again. I would be delighted if you could prove me wrong and hope that Steven and you can both progress.

I now have no idea if I sent this or not! I leave a list of numbers and instructions for my brother William who will 'ride shotgun' if he can whilst we are away. I ask him to do his best to ensure that Steven does not end up with the three in a bed swingers and do his utmost to keep an eye out. Steven knows that he can call on William if he needs to, so we are obliged to leave it at that. I leave a spare tray of medication in case of need and a list of Steven's usual bolt holes if things get out of hand again.

On our return we are relieved that Steven is in one piece, but it becomes apparent that appointments have not been kept. On the morning of the wedding we are delighted that he chooses to come to us and get ready and we have photos of us taken on our patio. It is lovely to see him suited and booted standing with his dad in the sunshine. However, I am ashamed to say that I was embarrassed by the wedding. Steven is gaunt but clean, his scraggy hair freshly washed, and his beard shaved off. He has made an effort and is smiling. Eve (who is only 10 years younger than me) is in an elaborate white wedding dress found in a charity shop. I have no problem with her age or the charity shop, but I think a traditional white wedding dress is pushing it, and she looks overdone. It is a very small affair indeed. Drew and his wife Sindy, my mum, Ian, myself, Eve's two boys and the barman from the local pub who is a long-standing friend. My poor mum who is unwell and recently bereaved of her second husband does not recognise Steven. He goes to hug her as they haven't seen each other for a while, and she is perplexed. He has lost so much weight and has changed totally over the last year.

They have made no plans for after the ceremony and it is a scramble to work out who is going home in which car. We offer to take them all for lunch at the local hotel which is where they are having a one night stay as a treat. It is very near to their current house. This is accepted and of course we end up paying for their lunches. I feel aggrieved because it is assumed that we will sort it out. I only do it for my mum who is completely baffled by it all and keeps asking where the reception will be.

Steven tells me later that on the following day, when they came down late for breakfast, and ended up in the bar, they were asked to leave. I ask him why and he says it was because Eve was dressed like a hooker. I imagine the worst and guess that they were both probably drunk. I wish I could give Steven the benefit of the doubt and blame it on his appearance and his medication. I ask him if he wants to complain and he

*says no. Once again, I am ashamed, and I haven't felt
this so strongly before, what has changed?*

*We do our best as usual and organise a barbecue for
Saturday 30th June, the day after as a bit of a
celebration. The invitation to friends says that this is to
say a big thank you to all of those who have supported
our family through trying times and in the hope that we
can all have some fun!*

*I really can't remember too much about this. We don't
seem to have photos and I don't remember if Steven
and Eve were there or not! I put this down to emotional
exhaustion.*

July: A month later when we were sure the kids would
cope alone, now one at least was over 16 and legally
allowed to take charge, we took a short honeymoon
break. This was pleasurable, if exhausting. I'm talking
about carrying the wife's entire wardrobe in a vastly
overloaded suitcase by the way. And not without
incident, when we were tired from sightseeing and she
had too much to drink. She was very protective over
money, but it didn't keep her off the slot machines.
Even after a couple of wins, a few simple days at the
seaside cost about £1500.

*Where oh where did the money come from? Or is he
exaggerating again?*

On return, things went okay for about two months, but
then went spectacularly wrong. It is August Bank
Holiday weekend and we are at my parents' house
while they are away. We are looking after the cats. My
wife had a cat of her own, and the three didn't mix. It
was just one night, so no problem I thought. But that
morning I woke up manic, internally running at warp
speed, and full of bizarre ideas. My wife immediately
noticed that I was acting oddly. We had sex, which I
am told was rougher than ever before. I began to say

odd things in conversation. Something inside me dared me to streak naked around the garden, so I did.

That evening we decided to go to the local pub for an hour. I suddenly became very paranoid many faces were looking at me. It had been quite a while since I'd spent time in this pub. Apparently, I was having a very odd conversation with the barman, who I knew well, but I wasn't making any sense. Then some yobs started making suggestive remarks about my wife and I felt myself becoming angry. Eventually, before I even finished my first drink, my manic mind went in to overdrive. I tore off my shirt, 'Hulk' style, roared like the lunatic I was, threw over the tables and chased said yobs out of the bar with a cast iron barstool in my hands. They fled. The barman was concerned as he knew I wasn't like this as a rule. He was aware that I wouldn't be likely to cause any further trouble. As soon as my wife went to the toilet, I bolted outside, my head full of voices. I hid under a bush outside the house, talking nonsense to myself. That again was a result of me thinking I no longer needed my medication.

My wife, having spent 20 minutes looking for me, found me under said bush. The following events were further inflamed by the fact that she had consumed a lot more alcohol than I had. We went into my parents' house. I was agitated, and sat with my head in my hands. My totally inebriated wife put in her headphones for her MP3 player and began drunkenly singing at the top of her voice. She obviously hadn't been devoid of refreshment whilst looking for me. She had a reputation for being partial to consecutive quadruple vodkas at record speed.

I went off into the kitchen and decided to open a can. I couldn't take this. I needed something to slow my mind. I tried talking to my wife to quieten her, but she was too far gone in to the land of vodka. She would not remove the earphones and was singing ever louder. I tried to remind her it was late, and we had an elderly lady living next door. She did not comply. I could not take this caterwauling on top of the noise in my head. I removed her headphones and an argument ensued. I was trying, though not all at home myself, to be reasonable.

Steven was generally gentle and reasonable when well and really cared for the elderly lady who lived alone next door.

The argument grew stronger now and I cracked. I pushed her down onto the couch and ran in to the kitchen. I found the sharpest carving knife. It was an evil looking blade with a serrated edge which could probably cut through bone. With the blade pressed into my palm, I ran back into the room. I fell to my knees in front of her. I grasped the lethal blade in my right hand, with the handle pointing upwards. I screamed at her and threatened to squeeze the blade if she wouldn't shut up and listen. She freaked, and asked me not to injure myself. I replied "not a chance." If she wanted to take it off me she would have to pull it out of my hand, and slice through arteries. I said "Go on and do it, it would be the biggest favour you can do for me."

Somehow, she got me to drop the weapon, I don't remember how. She threw it out of the open patio doors into the summer night. It wasn't found until my father was gardening days later. We collapsed sobbing together and took ourselves off to bed.

That night I did sleep, but woke very early, by which time my wife had probably just gone to sleep. In the early morning light, I knew, absolutely, that I was not 'me'. I was definitely someone else. Everything I knew around me was familiar, but I was in a very odd mood that I'd not experienced with this intensity before. I just wasn't ME. I was physically exhausted, but my mind was frantic. I got up and paced around the house. When my wife woke, she was understandably eager to get home. I wasn't, my mind was elsewhere. After a few hours of me rebuffing her requests to go home, she lost her temper. I said that I was staying put in my bedroom for a while, and if she wanted to go, then go. I would follow later. She ran up the stairs and slapped me across the face. This ignited the pile of neurons in my brain that were just waiting to explode.

I regret what I did next; that is to grab her and drag her back into the bedroom and pin her against the window. I snarled that she would regret what she'd just done. I could easily push her out of the window and down on to the paving below. Trying to escape, she beat me, and I restrained her, shouting out loud that I thought she was trying to trick me. Into what, I don't remember. Eventually the confused mess that was my mind let her go. She understandably ran off, I didn't know where.

Next, I had a moment of clarity. I called for an ambulance, saying I may have injured her and that I thought I needed help myself. Of course, nobody was hurt, but I wasn't thinking right, and didn't know what was happening. Ten minutes later I found her hiding in the garden, in shock, but unharmed. I cancelled the ambulance and tried to make sense of the situation, but 10 minutes later a police car arrived to check things out. They clearly suspected something was very wrong but without any obvious crime having been committed, they left. We finally made our way home together.

We arrived home from holiday and met with Steven and Eve at our home a couple of days later. Eve told us what had happened, but in a very manipulative way. Ian later found the knife in the garden border. Steven gives no rational explanation for his bloodstained bed sheets.

From my memory it seems that Steven and Eve spent some time with us to get some relief from the boys fighting. They eventually go back home and by 30th August Steven is on his way to hospital again.

I was under house arrest at home. My wife was understandably uneasy around me. I was under lock and key in the bedroom whilst she slept downstairs. I had crashed from mania to black depression again, especially knowing what had happened. Back on medication, I didn't move from my bed; my wife would come in with food and water, then leave. She was frightened, understandably, and had immediately phoned Prof C. He urged her to get me into the psychiatric ward as soon as possible.

I have no way of ascertaining the truth of this. It is not marked in the records that Prof C passed to me at a later date.

The situation in this country is that it's hard to get a place, but my wife could be very persuasive and after 5 days of badgering the NHS, the key turned in the door, and my wife said, "Come on, pack a few things, we're going." I knew where. We got a bus to my parents' house, so I could get a few books, but first my wife took me to the pub saying she was very worried about me and I should have a stiff drink because this wasn't going to be very pleasant. I had a couple of her trademark quadruple vodkas, which given the situation probably wasn't such a good idea, but with the state my mind was in it didn't make much difference. Then my father drove us to the hospital, where I was checked into room 6 on the same corridor I had been on before.

We didn't find out until later that Eve had been keeping Steven in a locked room with a bucket for a toilet. At what stage can you check on an adult who is married without making a relationship worse than it is? They arrive at our house for a lift and Ian takes them back to Eve's to get some things and then to hospital.

Ian is a long time and I hear nothing. It's 10.00pm and the phone rings again. I snatch it up in my anxiety. Relief floods through me as I hear Ian say "Hello." "Where are you, I was getting worried? It shouldn't have taken that long, they were expecting him."

"Believe it or not I am in the general hospital." I am confused. Steven has just been admitted to the mental health hospital not the general. "What's wrong?" "Eve says she has taken an overdose. She must have done it when we went back to the house to get Steven's gear. She didn't tell me until we were on the way home. I've given her £10 for the fare home and left her to it in Accident and Emergency." "Just come home Ian please." "I'm on my way. Can I have fish fingers – I'm starving!"

Ian has been given strict instructions from Eve not to tell her boys what she has done or where she is. This causes problems for us on all levels. Will they be alright overnight? Will they be worried? We are 'persona non-grata' and they are very aggressive towards us at the best of times. They have previously threatened Eve that if Steven goes back to hospital they will stop her being with him. They do not like the idea that someone else is watching out for her and knows how they treat her.

Early next morning I call Eve, but the phone cuts off. I go shopping; buy flowers for Eve and food for whoever wants it. When I reach the house only the boys are at home, not what I expected. The younger one is sleeping, and the older one is very aggressive and wants to know where his mum is. I have to lie. (Writing this I cannot remember the very good reasoning behind not telling the truth). All he is interested in is demanding that someone should replenish his cigarettes. I go to the shop and buy him some Mayfair and tell him I will be back soon. We exchange mobile numbers.

I phone Ian for advice and he tells me he has had a text message from Eve to say that she is still in hospital. I explode with frustration "Why have you not told me?" He lies and says that he has told me, and he is angry at the whole situation. I return to the shop and buy 'goodies' for the boys and leave them to it. I go home and phone the hospital. Eve is still there. I ask them to tell her that I have checked on the boys and realise that I may have dropped her in it re their welfare. I pass on my phone number and agree a time to pick her up.

First, I go to hospital to see Steven and switch my phone on to silent. The boys are plaguing me with abusive calls. Steven is quiet, almost calm. I have agreed with Ian not to say anything about Eve's latest escapade otherwise Steven might not stay. He is very worried about her, having received a 'strange' call from her. I truthfully tell him that I have visited the house and she wasn't in, and that the boys are okay. We have a long discussion and he shows me some writing he has done. It is thoughtful and insightful. I have hope then that he can be 'saved' from himself, and that his self-awareness is developing further. "I'm proud of you Steven" I say. I tell him truthfully that I am going to check on Eve and dash off to the general hospital. There are no messages or missed calls on my silenced phone.

When I get there, I am told that she has just gone and that she wouldn't wait. I drive to her house and park around the corner. I phone her and still get no answer. I phone the elder son – he is safe at his stepfather's. "Where is my mum?" Then an avalanche of threats and abuse and I have to lie again, as he obviously does not know what has happened yet. I am frustrated at the situation, and tell him that I have been told that she is on her way home. He cross-examines me and I am angry at being put in that position. I get even angrier when he hangs up on me. I am upset and furious. Eve isn't at home and isn't anywhere else that I can see. I decide to post the note that Steven has written to her through the door – what more can I do? Is she missing or a danger to herself? I go home in despair. She is still not answering her phone, so I text her two messages 'as above' and ask her what I can do to help. God will have to look after the rest.

I am no sooner home than the younger son calls me and shouts at me about his mother and hospital and an overdose. I can hear Eve in the background shouting at him to give her the phone - it doesn't happen and he hangs up. I call Eve's phone and it cuts out. It seems that the boys are up to their old tricks and controlling Eve's communications. There is nothing I can do about it.

I saw a lot of old faces, and this being late summer, this time going out for a cigarette wasn't as bad as it had been in January. I would stroll through the internal grounds, central to all wards, useful for visitors and those allowed off the main treatment block. Or I would sit in the small garden allocated to each ward which was primarily used by smokers, or one or two old hands who just liked to stare into space.

There wasn't a great deal of expertise in locating my medical records this time. I was given my sleeping pills, my anti-depressants, and Rivotril, but they said they had no Valproate Semi-Sodium. They gave me liquid Sodium Valproate, which is a different thing altogether, used to treat epilepsy. Valproate Semi-Sodium, brand name Depakote, is the drug used for mood stabilisation. When I went for my dose one night, they had the anti-epilepsy drug ready and said sorry, we still don't have the proper tablets. I spotted a box of them in the medicines cabinet and said, "So what are those?" The embarrassment on their faces when they realised their mistake was hard to hide, not having recognised the brand name. So much for making simple, background checks. This was my third day as a patient without the proper medication. When this was rectified, things became gradually more stable. And soon, I was to meet my new professor of psychiatry.

After a succession of faceless doctors and CPN's who couldn't care less, I was about to be given the chance to speak with a very well-respected NHS professor with a vested interest in mood disorders. The reception staff were locum psychiatrists who wouldn't put their money down on what action to take. This man agreed that yes, I was manic-depressive, or bipolar as they now had to call the condition, and explained the nature of the disease (which I obviously already knew, but I let him do his job). He described psychosis in detail, how mania and psychotic depression differed from schizophrenia, and that he thought I may well have co-morbid (co-existing), obsessive compulsive disorder to some degree, which is apparently common with manic-depressive illness. I'd heard that before too, and agreed with him because I clearly had those traits from early in life. Not in the classic sense of repeated hand washing or counting things, nor fear of dirt or germs. It's just when I get an idea in my head, it bloody well stays there. He stated that the private professor I had seen had been right and that I was to continue the medication then prescribed.

I spent the next fortnight ruminating on my recent breakdown, visited daily by my wife, and every evening by one or both of my parents. My wife's eldest son, who lived with us, (not the jailbird) now nearly 17, came to see me as well. He brought me some DVDs to watch on my laptop. I think he was surprised about how normal and calm things were when we were sat in the grounds. He was expecting something like 'One Flew Over the Cuckoo's Nest' and I think he was marginally disappointed that it wasn't. His curiosity was satisfied, and I was glad he cared enough to drop by, whatever the motive.

Over the time I was there, back on proper levels of medication, my head began to pull around again. It wouldn't be long before I would be discharged. It took a hard toll on my wife, who was making herself ill by insisting on coming through every day to visit. It was a difficult journey. Getting to the town centre was easy, and she had a free pass for that due to her disability. The buses from the town to the outskirts where the hospital was were exempt from the free travel plan and ran at irregular times. They did not always coincide with visiting times. If she could not get a lift with my parents, she would occasionally be stuck at home and that made her very stressed. I don't think I ever sent so many text messages to the same person in one day as I did in this period.

When they started to put my release plan together, I was to meet a CPN who was clearly the most obnoxious woman on the planet. She seemed to thrive on intimidating her professorial superiors. It was to become a personality clash of the 'nth' degree. I found it incredible that these doctors, including my new professor, were so afraid of her temperament. However, she hadn't reckoned on the fire that burned within a manic depressive and his mercurial wife.

It was agreed that the diagnosis of bipolar was clear, probably either rapid cycling or the even more rapid Cyclothymia. I had this explained to me by the doctors and the professor on several occasions. But in steps the CPN from hell. All the big guns cowered before Mein Fuhrer, or as she called herself, Sasha.

CHAPTER 7: INTO THE GREAT WIDE OPEN

2007

10th September 2007. As the release committee gathered, Prof B and the staff nurses, along with some junior doctors assembled to tell me I could go home for the weekend. I should see how it went, and then return to the ward for one or two nights. The length of time would depend on when the specialist could fit me in on his rounds before final discharge. The doctors went into great detail about bipolar disorder once more, but every time it was mentioned, this Sasha would shoot them a dirty look. By the end of the interview, these doctors seemed to be seriously irked by her. I was again beginning to wonder what was what. She voiced strongly that she thought there was nothing wrong with me and the doctors all looked at their feet.

I went home; rather annoyed that this idiotic person would be in charge of my care after release, and gob smacked that these professional psychiatrists would allow their say-so to be vetoed.

Being back home again was yet another thing to get used to, bearing in mind it was only for two days. I took my pills and returned to the unit on the agreed day, but the professor could not fit me in. So, I did end up spending two more nights before discharge. When I saw the professor, he again confirmed bipolar and said he was happy to send me on my way into the 'care' of this Sasha. Enter the dragon, and she again thinks I'm a hypochondriac. Prof B looks at his shoes. I'm sat incredulous thinking, **"grow a pair professor!"** As we file out of the room I garble to my wife what has just happened. The professor slinks away looking flushed even for an Asian gentleman. My wife collars Sasha, asking her what the hell is she playing at. Sasha brushes her off and high-tails it out to an 'important meeting'.

Eve should have been in the meeting but was asleep on the bench outside and couldn't be woken by the staff.

I could not speak from indignation and shock. Basically, I was being called a liar, a fantasist, and the psychiatrists had just allowed this 'want to-be' doctor to urinate all over their diagnosis. When my father came to pick us up in the car, I erupted with indignation. I was to have several sessions with Sasha at a local drop-in clinic. This was as productive as trying to generate electricity to power your lighting circuit with the combustion of methane emissions from the rear end of a gnat.

I believe it is here that Ian, I and Steven ask for a meeting with those involved in Steven's care at the local mental hospital. This is given. We are stunned into shocked silence by the fact that Sasha, the CPN, is allowed so much sway in the meeting and states bluntly that she does not believe Steven has a mental health illness. Prof B says nothing. Yet we have just met with him prior to the meeting (without Steven) where he told us that Steven may have a mood disorder or Cyclothymia and we get the impression that he has placated Steven with this diagnosis – so is he lying to Steven and to us, what is the issue? What purpose is he trying to serve? Writing this I cannot comprehend how we were unable to hold our own or speak out.

I engaged in several such sessions, sometimes just myself and Sasha who would look at me like a poisonous reptile, sometimes Prof B would be there, adamant in his diagnosis until Sasha would shoot him a withering glance. I was doing fine on the pills. I was able to decorate our rented house which had been dilapidated since before we took on the tenancy. Then we decided to move back to my home town as we were fed up with the house and the lousy letting agent who seemed unable to instigate repairs. The place leaked every time it rained, and there were various insects living in dark corners. The agent wouldn't make repairs, even to the lethal gas fire which I got fixed privately. The gas board said it should be condemned, and would petition the landlord. Still nothing.

I help Steven and Eve move to a new house back to our town, and agree to clean up the rented house after they leave. I turn up on the morning to help them pack. I am shocked to find that the boys do not have beds any more, just mattresses. "That's how we like it." They don't seem to have many personal possessions or clothes. I keep my mouth shut and help Steven and Eve pack stuff into bags and boxes. Steven is busy taking their bed to pieces and is having difficulty. He is quiet and distant and seems really ill. I do not know if he is over medicated or hung over. The younger boy decides to solve the bed problem. Steven goes for a screwdriver and meanwhile boy breaks the bed to pieces, truly believing that he has helped. I doubt that it will fix together again. Steven says nothing and continues to pack the broken bits together to be moved. A local small removal firm comes, and we are not ready for them. The downstairs rooms seem to be stuffed with Eve's clothes and broken furniture and bicycles. I am embarrassed by the look on the removal men's faces but keep my mouth shut. It's becoming a habit. It all gets a bit too much for me when on moving the furniture it becomes apparent that the cat has never been house trained. I eventually get left on my own to clean up and it is a bleakly depressing task.

After we left, someone would move in and shortly afterwards be murdered. That was a close call for us then. We started packing, which was a manic operation in the time frame we had, but my mood was fairly stable, if a little distant. During this time, we argued, and I suddenly decided on suicide again. I ate an entire month's worth of Rivotril, and when my wife wasn't looking, stole her Valium and sank a whole bottle. Nothing happened. I awoke the next morning somewhat surprised to be awake at all, and in a surprisingly better mood.

I do not have any awareness of this incident; for once we are not involved. I have got the minutes of a meeting that I attended with Steven in October 2007 where our complaint was further explored with senior managers and Prof B. Needless to say we didn't really make any progress. We asked for an apology from Dr M and asked Prof B to ensure that he continued to give Steven his support. This was promised but none of it happened, it all just faded away. His crisis plan at this time, dated 23 October 2007 does state that he suffers with bipolar disorder and that he should have enhanced care coordination. We are still in touch with the Healthcare Commission regarding the complaint but even they seem disorganised. Emails went unanswered due to us being given an incorrect email address and apologies for not responding to written correspondence were given but with no explanation. By this time, I was exhausted by it all and Steven did not want to continue. He believed that he would be in safe hands with Prof B. How wrong he was.

In the early November of 2007 we had moved into a house on the same estate where we had lived before. I had a couple more sessions with this Sasha, but it was pointless. I stopped seeing her but agreed to stay on the professor's books in case his help would be needed.

Things began to break down now. Psychosis seemed to take over the youngest of my wife's children. The kids all seemed to take after their father, who was a regular nut job, suspected of paranoid schizophrenia. He had spent half his life in jail for armed robbery, GBH, ABH and general domestic abuse. My wife was clingy and needy and was successfully trying to stop me from seeing friends. I can't prove it, but she was probably drugging my water bottles with the opium-based pain killer Tramadol. It left me in bed and zoned out all day. Early in our relationship she told me that she loved me so much that was I to die, she'd ship the kids off to their stepfather and keep my body in the bed and lie next to me forever. This should have set off more alarm bells ringing than it did then, I thought it was a joke, but it wasn't.

The psychotic youngest spent a day arguing with his mother. I could hear this through the haze of my possible drugging as I lay in bed. Evening came, and I began to pull round. The younger boy came into the bedroom and I became aware of having water poured over me by this child. I jumped up immediately. He ran off and returned with a pool cue. He proceeded to attack me, injuring my ribs and my hands as I protected my face. He also attacked his mother as she tried to intervene. I was sore for quite a while. I reported it to the police, but like an idiot I did not prosecute. At our previous house this child had torn a door off its hinges in a rage and smashed it into my head. I had called the police then, and despite the river of blood from my forehead, I had been berated by them for wanting to prosecute a minor. Absolutely ridiculous, I thought.

Christmas 2007 My wife took out an enormous loan and spent most of it on presents for the kids, but I was miserable and on the verge of clinical depression again. About this time Drew and his wife noted that I seemed to be under the influence of something. Without having had any alcohol, I would just pass out for no reason, even mid-sentence. My parents noticed the same. Drew has since said he thinks I was being 'medicated' by something that I was not aware of. Considering my wife had boasted that she had tried to kill her second husband with drugs, I think this is very possible.

Things were so miserable, I was paralysed. I vowed to attempt suicide again. I planned to overdose, drink a bottle of strong spirits, and then take my portable CD player and headphones down to the railway lines. There I would put on some music, put my neck on the tracks, and slowly pass out as I waited for a train to end it for me. But as often happens in deep depression, I didn't have the energy to do anything that involved moving more than from the bed to the lavatory.

Just before Christmas, I was dozing again when I was awoken by my hysterical and ranting wife. I found myself in the middle of another massive argument. She was literally manic herself, although no one had ever diagnosed her as such. She took only sleeping pills, though on occasion still would overdo the booze. This situation escalated out of control. She locked herself in the downstairs lavatory and was screaming that she was going to exit via the window. I tried to work out what was going on, and attempted to talk her down from this fit that she seemed to be having. What cocktail of painkillers and booze had brought this on? She had about six different types of drugs stashed away, including a lot of Valium, and had been known to pilfer my pills also. I tried to force the door to the toilet where she had hidden herself. When I succeeded, she was gone. Luckily for her this was the ground floor, so no splattered corpses to behold. I walked out into the winter night, freezing cold, my breath frosting, but could not find her. That's because she was safely ensconced at a neighbours' home. She had called the police as she had convinced herself, without reason, that I was her violent ex-husband. He had done terrible things to her, and she was terrified. When I couldn't find her, and realised she had left her phone behind, I waited in the house for her. Expressing my great frustration, I attacked the TV with a rubber mallet that inexplicably had been left on the couch. The glass on the TV didn't smash but it never worked again. Then the boys in blue unceremoniously let themselves in, cuffed me, and hauled me off down the station on a charge of attempted murder.

Ironically, when she got back to the house, she had no idea where I was and phoned the police to declare me as a missing person! She quickly realised, with a jog of the memory from the old bill, that I was with them due to her accusations. She did a volte face on this ridiculous delusion. She brought my medications to the station. The police doctor examined me and refused to give them to me until I was released in the morning. I was sent out at 4.00am wearing only a t-shirt and jeans. Released jacketless into a freezing December morning which would have killed a polar bear! Medication in a carrier bag, I shivered my way to my parents' house. I had been released pending a court case and on bail, and advised not to go near my wife until it was over. That suited me; I didn't really want to spend Christmas with someone who'd just had me locked up for no good reason.

18th December 2007. Yet another hysterical midnight call, "Steven has tried to murder me, and the police have taken the bastard away." Reeling with shock, we pull on our clothes and hurry up to her house to find out what is going on. Eve is sitting sobbing in a chair, and the boys are circling her like hyenas and are mouthing off. It takes me a while to realise that they are not just furious with Steven but with Eve as well. Why do they always take it out on her? "He attacked me, and I got away through the downstairs toilet window." Although she is obviously upset and distressed I can see no real damage to her face or the arm that she is proffering for examination. She has a small red mark across one cheek and a red hand mark on her arm. "I ran to a neighbour and then the police came to arrest him. They found him under the bed." I am amazed that Eve 'does' neighbours and even more baffled that Steven would hide under a bed. I am stunned by the story and concerned for both of them.

The boys are joining in like vicious yapping terriers although they were not in the house when it happened. A policeman arrives to take a statement from Eve. He is rude and dismissive, giving the impression, that 'domestics' are a waste of time. As she tells us what has happened, we listen in shock and my heart hardens against my son. Did he really try to kill her? Physically she does not seem much hurt at all. When asked if she is intending to press charges Eve is emphatic in her affirmation. We try to reassure her that we will do what we can to help. With Eve unhurt and Steven arrested we trudge off home. What else is there to do?

We decide not to go to the police station. We sit up drinking tea. Just as well that we don't go to bed because the police phone us about 4.00am and say that they are releasing Steven to be bailed to live at our address. No one asked if it was okay with us! We are not impressed and neither Ian nor I are inclined to go and collect him. "Keep him a bit longer we'll be there in an hour." However, they throw him straight out, and he turns up at our door angry, ashamed, dirty and exhausted. He is minus his belt and leather jacket which he never did get back. It is a winter's night. He is half frozen and has not been allowed to take his medication. Part of me doesn't want to let him in. He has also been interviewed without a solicitor or chaperone present, his choice apparently. Don't the police know anything about mental illness?

We have no bed for him and he is too tired to wash. We throw an old sheet over our bed and he crashes there. Whilst his clothes tumble around in the washing machine we ponder what to do next. This is the beginning of another of the most distressing and challenging periods for us as a family, as parents and carers. It almost breaks us.

Over the next few days, I listen to Steven's denials of violence and both Steven, his dad and I are all very angry – with each other, with the situation and ultimately with Eve. I feel a responsibility towards her, especially if what she says is true.

The next day I go to check on her and I arrive to an upsetting scene of cruel behaviour. The youngest son has thrown her phone and her clothes out of the bedroom window and is laughing at her attempts to get dressed and retrieve them. It is pouring with rain. She is weeping with frustration and he is insulting her every action, using foul language. I tell him in no uncertain terms what I think of him and his behaviour and go and look for the phone in the mud. He is equally insulting about Steven and takes the piss out of his mother because she has been dumped again. Phones and the control of them seem to be a motif that runs through this family. I let rip at him and finally get him to retrieve the phone. This takes some time as he is intent on tormenting Eve. Both boys seem to enjoy seeing their mother in a mess again.

I take charge and get her sorted enough to leave the house. The visit to the GP is humiliating for me. I state briefly what has happened and leave them to it. Eve emerges later with a tear streaked face and nothing else to say. Whatever has happened she is not physically damaged. I arrange to pay some outstanding bills that are troubling her as I feel responsible for my son's actions. I will not give her the cash but take the bills from her and pay them myself. I feel that she is entitled to some support from me, but I find it very difficult. She is hell bent on making things worse than they are. Steven's bail conditions clearly state that he must not communicate with Eve in any way or visit her house. She refuses to accept this on any level and does not understand why Steven will not come home. Steven is furious with her for getting him arrested and telling lies. We do not know where the truth sits.

I try to continue to support Eve over the next few days, but the obnoxious behaviour of the boys and the vitriol aimed at me by Eve become too much. Apparently, it is me who will not let Steven come home. She seems to have forgotten that it was her who called the police. I carefully explain that if he comes back to her, he will break the conditions of his bail and may be arrested and locked up. "I'll withdraw my statement and my complaint", she says. "He didn't hit me anyway." So Steven may well be telling the truth! After that I keep my distance as I have to take sides to survive. Steven is angry now with Ian and I because we believed her story.

At home with Steven we are having real difficulties. Apart from the fact that he has no bed and no personal items other than his music stuff, he is becoming an aggressive and moody monster. Something we have not seen before. I borrow a mattress from my brother and Steven must make do with the floor. I sort out medication and toiletries and he has the basics and a roof over his head. He is bailed not to go near Eve or her home and she makes up for it by continually calling him or visiting. I send her away every time. I am afraid that they will row, he will be arrested and then he really *will be in hot water. She does not seem to understand the concept of his bail.*

Steven insists that he did not hit Eve but held her to restrain her from attacking him. "She's off her head. She thought that I was her previous violent husband." He sticks firmly to this story through the next weeks and during the court case. He will not admit to attacking Eve, so he must go to court. I think he might have got away with a caution otherwise, his word against hers and no apparent harm done.

Steven is a nightmare to live with, blackly depressed and extremely irritable. He channels his resentment into the need for alcohol. Somehow, he finds money for secret drink and we can't seem to catch him at it. He is abusive, aggressive and brings us to a point of despair that we haven't felt before. He is adamant that Eve is lying about what happened and his rage simmers on. He becomes so unpleasant that I tell him that I will not have him in the house – the first time I have ever said it.

Then my mood crashed completely. Waiting for my January 2008 court appearance, I never seemed to get a minute's rest. I slept a lot, but every day seemed to run together. I refused to get out of my bed for days on end. Christmas meant even less than usual to me, my birthday just a reminder of how much happier everyone else was, compared to me.

Steven is very ill and drinking anything he can lay his hands on. He descends into a black angry place which makes it very difficult for us to cherish him. We are at breaking point. Christmas is endured, and we have very poignant photos of Steven trying to eat his dinner, looking sad, bad and hopeless. We have traditional false jollity to fall back on. Ian and Steven are rowing, and I have a screaming fit some time here and threaten to leave them both to it, making a great show of packing my case. This seems to jolt Steven back in to the moment and he begs me not to leave Ian and him. From that moment he tries to curb his drinking with some success, but he is also mentally wrecked. I do not know if we sought medical help. I have a sense of hopelessness and no help to be had. We have been conditioned in to believing that we will not be listened to. I do remember phoning around to see if Steven could be housed somewhere else. I am offered a bail hostel place in an industrial town on the coast. This facility is available purely because he is taking prescribed mental health medication. I talk it over with my brother who is a social worker and he is horrified. "He won't last two minutes – they will eat him alive." So we persevere. My brother gives us a bed for Steven as we are unable to pay out again for another. Steven has previously unintentionally wrecked one bed and one has been moved into Eve's property. It is better than a mattress on the floor.

Simon and a couple of other friends come to visit some time over the Christmas break. Unfortunately, Steven is either drunk, manic or both and the visit is an embarrassing disaster. He is so full of rage at his situation that he doesn't seem to care how that impacts on his friends and is full of self-pity. They can do nothing much to help him and don't stay very long. I have to call Steven to heel for his obnoxious behaviour in front of them and it does no good for any of us. When they depart he is even more depressed and seems bent on self-destruction.

We had problems with Eve who was continually contacting Steven even though the terms of his bail forbade it. We were afraid that this would cause more trouble for him. She somehow gets the terms of bail altered where Steven can visit during the day and must return to us by 10.00pm. Steven tries it, wondering if they can be reconciled. We are afraid for him. All she has to do is construct or provoke an argument and he will be arrested. The boys know this as well and I amazed that they don't take advantage of it. They have obviously found something else to amuse themselves with.

Steven can't hack it and he has decided once again to leave Eve and we endure until the court case in January 2008. Once again, we must find him a bed, cart his stuff away from Eve and redirect his benefits away from Eve's account. She is in pieces and I feel for her, but I am relieved that Steven has made this decision. The boys are gloating and goading her to further distress. I try to reason with them, explaining what has happened, and I ask them not to be so cruel. The smug self-satisfied laughter that this request solicits from the older boy causes me to finally snap. The left-handed crack I deliver to his head is awesome and takes all of us by surprise. He holds his face and tears fill his eyes. "I'll get the police on you!" "You do that. You are a cruel little sod and I'll do it again if you keep baiting your mother like that." I tell Eve that I won't visit again, for all of our sakes. I go back on this just once. I call a few days later to pick up Eve, take her to the bank so that she can pay more bills. With this action, I wash my hands of the whole situation and try to hold my own little family together. We have no support, no CPN, no Social Services nothing so as usual we just get on with it.

It was slow going; I wait for the court date with some trepidation. Though I know they wouldn't do much to me except maybe charge me with disturbing the peace for whatever reason. In reality this was Eve's crime. I think that she had more to worry about, having admitted to making the whole thing up; she was to incur the wrath of the police and lawyers, plus the CPS. However, no charges were brought against her.

CHAPTER 8: FREE FALLIN'

2008

3rd January 2008. Waiting for the court appointment was a nightmare. Eve does everything and anything to get Steven back. "It's all lies, I've dropped the complaint." Well that doesn't wash with the CPS and she is in danger of being done for perjury. Steven is bombarded with notes and phone calls and I have to act as gatekeeper. We drag him off to court. We were there at 9.00am as ordered and I think Steven went in at 2.00pm. He was stressed and probably manic, and the situation was not helped by continual harassment from Eve wanting to speak to him. Steven was raving and frightened and on the verge of absconding. Ian and I did our best to calm him and stop him doing a runner. Eventually we asked security to intervene and we waited with Steven in a separate room.

On the day of my hearing, I was disturbed to find my wife at the courtroom. She sat directly in front of me as I was waiting to be called and I blanked her. She was dressed as if she was going to a funeral, clothed all in black with her long black hair hanging down her back. She had come to hand in reams of handwritten retractions of her accusations. Her lawyer went spare with her, trying to make her insist that I had done wrong. But now more rational, she could see that she had had a 'funny turn' herself. She stood up in court admitting her mistake. I think there is a lot in common with manic depression and her PTSD. I was told my case would be adjourned, come back in a week. That would be nearly a year to the day that I tried to blow off my head. I could see her if I wanted. I was now under a curfew of 10.30pm and was ordered to sleep and live at my parents' house until the case was over. After the initial hearing, my wife wanted to take me to a hotel to talk. Obviously, I was a bit reluctant, but her mind games got me there and one thing led to another. She made sure I was home on time and was eager for me to be at her house as soon as I awoke next day, promising to have me home to meet curfew again by taxi, her shout.

This situation caused us great concern. We were aware that any upset, row or altercation could see Steve imprisoned due to the terms of his bail. We warned him about this and begged him to remove himself at the first sign of a row or trouble from Eve or the boys. I find it hard to understand the hold that she had over him. No matter what, he went back for more.

We went on like this for a while, but it felt like I was punching a clock. I was really down, and much as I loved her, or thought I did, it was getting to feel like I was working the graveyard shift in some dismal storeroom. One day she called to summon me for another miserable day with her, and I refused to go. I said I would not go back. Needless to say, she wasn't there at the final court hearing. Her retractions and no real evidence, plus my innocence, resulted in me being released on a £100 bond to keep the peace for a year. I was free, as I bloody well should be, and as I hadn't, and didn't again break the peace, I never had to cough up the £100.

On 17th January 2008 Steven was bound over for 12 months. His refusal to accept a caution for something that he hadn't done brought him to this point. I also have a note in my diary that he is to see Prof D on 21st January. He works in the alcohol service and is a specialist psychiatrist in relation to addictions and mental health. This appointment was later downgraded to the usual support worker. I also note that he is due to see Prof B on 19th March 2008.

It took me a long time to pull my head together, but that is what I did. I stayed with my ever-dependable parents for a while trying to re-learn who I was. In time I gained confidence, and with money to spend, I went shopping for music and saw friends again. Once more things gradually became 'normal'. I had constant thoughts of my wife. I was perturbed by her persistent phone calls and text messages threatening suicide if I did not return. I had a new-found confidence which gave me a steely reserve against blackmail; I was not responsible for anyone else. Having got back to being 'me', I enjoyed myself. I was trying to make up for the time I felt had been stolen from me. And then I began to destroy myself.

First lesson: Anti-psychotic medication does not mix with too much drink, especially dark rum in my case. Second lesson: Apart from (but including) alcohol, know your limits. Never presume anything. Take your medication properly. Don't forget. Be a good bunny and don't answer unwanted calls and text messages.

The spring of 2008 was glorious, the blossom on the trees reminded me of manias past, yet the manias did not return this spring. I was still a bit stifled. Summer was expansive, and a sea of friends and family poured through the house. My level of poetry output came slowly back up to par again. I normalised what had been my childhood bedroom into my private space once more.

It was a normal life again, but there were echoes of the past every now and again. They usually came to me through phrases in some of my favourite songs. Songs often written before I was born. Soon, I began feeling as if I was living in two different worlds simultaneously. Life on Mars…?

My physical health improved, and my medication was doing its thing. It was keeping me fairly level, but I felt the echoes chipping away at my psyche. Oh no, another downer. In the 10 months I'd been away from my wife, there was nothing eventful to speak of, but depression set in again at the beginning of autumn and by the middle of September 2008, I was sad, frightened and very lonely. By chance, after months of radio silence, she calls me, and I answer. BAD IDEA.

In some moment of madness, I agreed to see her in a hotel nearby. We do the marital thing, and agree to meet up again. There would be plenty of these meetings as she tries to prepare the kids for my possible return. She tells them she's staying with a female friend, and tries to reconcile with me. This would turn out to be insane. Gradually, she persuaded me to move back into our home, and I did but with great misgivings.

Once again, in September 2008, Steven walks away with Eve. We try to stay on good terms with her, but this is difficult after keeping her away at Steven's request. She has a long memory.

We were seriously worried about Steven's safety at this time and had noted how he was like a walking zombie. On one visit to our house with Eve he was talking to me one minute and was asleep the next, mid-sentence and sat bolt upright. I shook him awake and he was as surprised as I was about falling asleep. I helped him to the car to take them both home. He fell asleep immediately. I woke him up and he apologised, saying he didn't know what the problem was, and was grateful for our help and support.

Alarm bells were ringing. Surprisingly, at that time I had no knowledge of how I could have helped by flagging him as a vulnerable adult in need of protection – regrets and hindsight are not helpful, but one can learn from them.

She got me to call off the divorce lawyers. Apparently, I had caused her such a great inconvenience with this process. Again, we tried to reconcile. By and large we muddled though. It seemed to be working and we stumbled through another Christmas together. She takes the boys over to their stepfather then joins me at my parents.

In the New Year 2009 I felt completely dead and lifeless and wondered if I really was being drugged. The new things we had bought for the house were less than a few months old and already broken by the kids fighting; I'd seen it all before. At this point the days began to run into each other again. I was down, my mind was soup, and though I was taking my medicine I think I must have been given something I wasn't aware of on top of this. Very soon I would find this to be evident.

I lay in bed sweating for most of the day, and suffered painful muscle cramps which can be associated with opiate withdrawal. As I wasn't knowingly taking any opiates, I didn't think twice about it. As the first three months of 2009 were drawing to a close, the penny dropped.

On the 27th of March 2009 my wife asked me to accompany her to her parents for a visit the next day and I agreed. The next morning, the day of the visit, I awoke to deafening noise. Venturing downstairs, I could hear her attempting to sing along to the blazingly loud stereo. She was obviously drunk, or on drugs, or both as she was dancing around hysterically and slurring every word. The living room was carnage. We hardly ever played the stereo loud in this terraced house as either the neighbours, or the kids, would complain. She would usually insist the kids keep their TVs turned down in case of complaints, so I knew something was wrong. She demanded I take her to the bus stop immediately to go and visit her parents. The bus stop was barely a minute's walk away. It took me 10 to get her there in the state she was in.

Unsurprisingly, we missed the bus. She was angry, and I took her back home to wait for the next one. Yet again, due to her state, we missed it. All she could manage was a slow stagger around the corner to the stand.

This was apparently my fault and she lashed out at me. I restrained her and tried to calm her down. In her intoxicated state she kicked me down the street, finally knocking me to the ground, and I landed painfully on my knees. She then jumped on me and began to try and tear out my hair and bite off my nose. I managed to roll her off me, made suitable and unprintable remarks slapped her across the face and limped off. I still have knee pain to this day. I kept walking, and she just stood there, zoned out.

This time I did not go back. I went as far as a local shop, my face, especially my nose bleeding profusely, and bought a 4-pack to unwind. I phoned my father to see what I could do now. He said stay put; he was on his way to collect me.

These calm recollections written by Steven belay the terrifying chaotic screaming mess that was his life most of time. The incoherent phone call that Ian received scared us both. It seemed that Steven was on the verge of disappearing and we knew that he was quite capable of doing that. We jumped in to the car and rushed to retrieve him from the off-licence where he had taken refuge. He told us that Eve had beaten him up and bitten his nose. He was certainly bleeding and bedraggled with his elbows, knees and face cut and grazed and a bite mark on his face. He was very distressed and seemed drugged and 'out of it'. And of course, he had turned to the usual panacea of alcohol.

Back at my parents' house, the police were called and saw my blood-encrusted face. They took a statement, asking if I wanted to make criminal charges of assault. I had three days to decide. I chose just to leave that part of my life behind me. Instead the police went around to tell her to just stay the hell away from me.

We cleaned up his injuries and stripped him of his filthy clothes. We call my brother's step son Alan to sit with him. Steven is extremely shocked and angry, and we hope that he will be comforted by Alan's company. We finally got him washed and to bed so once again Steven is home on the 27th March 2009.

Over the next few days we notice a remarkable change in him. He becomes more alert and responsive and tells us that he feels 'different' and 'better' and wonders if he has been previously drugged. This resonated with me. I remember a phone call with Eve who suggests that perhaps Steven is taking something he shouldn't, or someone is spiking his drinks. I know who I think it is, but I have no evidence to prove it.

It is at this point that Ian becomes Steven's main carer and we swap roles. Ian was made redundant at the end of January 2009. It makes sense as I am now working full time with a local charity and Steven needs someone to watch out for him.

He seems stable and is able to go out of the house on a few occasions. The arcade of shops just around the corner from our home has flats above it. In one of these flats lives an unusual and troubled young man who was well known locally. His struggle with his gender identity and his challenging behaviour made him very noticeable. Steven has a soft heart and is easily taken in by a sob story. He agrees to call round and teach him some guitar chords. He comes back home to collect his guitar and tell me where he is going. He is animated and excited and I realise how

*lonely my son is. We agree that he will be back by
8.00pm and will keep his phone switched on. My
instinct for divining trouble is working overtime. By
8.30pm I am becoming worried. I call his mobile and
get the answerphone. I am just putting my coat on to
go and retrieve Steven when he comes clashing
through the front door. "Mam, he locked me in! He
wanted to have sex with me. The guitar lessons were
just a front to get me in to his flat." I am shocked, but
my instincts are vindicated. Steven is not physically
hurt but is distressed by the experience. He was locked
in straight away and offered alcohol and drugs, and it
was made very clear that this man intended to have
sex with Steven. "I was frightened Mam. I just kept
filling his glass up with booze, and distracted him by
playing some tunes on the guitar." I query how Steven
has managed to escape. "I waited until he was drunk
enough to fall asleep and I unlocked the door and ran
back here." Steven refuses point blank to allow me to
call the police and doesn't want anyone to know how
easily he was taken in. Yet another example of his
vulnerability and another let down for a lonely young
man.*

You may have noticed that some of these chapters are
named after Tom Petty songs, which got me through
my mixed-up moods. I really was 'Learning to fly', and
then found I didn't have wings. Then was 'Into the
great wide open', I was the song's character; 'a rebel
without a clue'. And the references to 'Life on Mars' are
also poignant, I woke up in a different world but in the
future. 'It's a God awful small affair…' I was finally free.
And in retrospect, although manic depression has
dogged my life it really is only a small affair in the
grand scheme of things. I was also a character in
Petty's 'Yer so bad'; 'Now he's got nothing, head in the
oven, I don't know which one is worse…' Or so I would
like to believe. I now had to accept that life was life and

the songs were written during my early life or before I was born, though I could find a direct link mentally to all of them.

Steven improves so much that we actually get him into the car for the two hour drive to Scotland to visit his granddad. He might be improving mentally but he looks absolutely dreadful. He is unkempt, thin, with scraggy hair and bad skin. His posture is worse than ever, expressing a complete air of defeat and desperation and he walks with a shuffling unsteady gait. But we still have hope that he will improve further. Sometime over this period Steven does engage with the Community Alcohol Service and is offered medication, Acamprosate, to help him deal with his dependence and wean him away from the booze. Although he agrees with Prof D that he will try it, the reality is different. When I produce the actual medication, he is terrified of taking it and we are back to square one. No wonder they are dismissive of him.

I visited my paternal grandfather in Scotland. We hatched a plan to keep my wife from descending on my parents' home, as she was wont to do if she thought I was there. I decided that any correspondence to her from me would be forwarded via my granddad, making her think I was in Edinburgh. I was dossing on an air bed on the floor of my old bedroom at my parents' home, trying to get back the sense of reality that had been taken from me. I needed time to physically and emotionally heal. The old bloodstains on the carpet were a vigorous reminder of just how ill I had been. I remembered all the girls I had slept with here, even my wife when things were going well in the early days of our dating. I remembered the times of every breakdown I had experienced here. But I had also done wonderful things such as cutting demos and albums and making music. Now the room was practically empty. Since my mother had stopped working in her office room, my musical equipment was moved there, and it is today my studio.

We tried hard to give Steven a new focus in life and encouraged him to set up a recording studio in the smallest bedroom, turning it over to him to do as he pleased.

In the first month of being away from my wife, I began to get the tell-tale 'white-outs' and tingling sensations that I had experienced with Seroxat, this time from the Citalopram. Before any damage could progress, I stopped the drug, and had another fortnight of withdrawal symptoms, though milder than with Seroxat. I gradually stopped having the sensations of head to foot electric shocks and my mood did not take a dive.

Some of the symptoms Steven refers to like tingling and 'white outs' and muscle cramps could well be due to alcohol dependence. None of us seem to have had any awareness of this and I don't know why. This warrants further reflection.

I continued to receive a barrage of insane text messages from my wife, to which I did not respond. I did call her once, caller ID withheld, in response to a completely twisted and false allegation, and to make her see things were final. **Leave me alone.** Then I changed my number but it didn't stop there. She started sending nasty private messages through Facebook, but I soon had her blocked from doing that. I quickly found that I was back in the light, and taking my medication was working, although a lower dose of the mood stabiliser would see me less prone to lethargy. I had my own space again, and practised hard to get back up to par on my instruments, which I had neglected during my 'off' times. I redecorated my room, and began writing again. Endless poems, with little drawings which almost constituted art. My friends were accessible to me again, no more forbidding finger wagging from the black widow, a local name for my wife.

The healing came with time. I spent an expansive 2009 summer with many family members. This culminated in a barbecue attended by nearly all of our immediate family, many of whom I hadn't seen in years. I brought out a guitar when people were suitably relaxed by way of wine and beer, and the late evening became a vast sing-along.

It is a memorable occasion to celebrate my mother's 81st birthday, in July 2009. The sun is bright and warm; the garden is beautifully green and full of family members. Young great nieces and nephews tumble over the lawn, the youngest still needing her Mum's milk. Steven is in his element. He joins in with the children, and then entertains us with guitar and singing. His cousins are suitably impressed. One of them photographs the day and we receive these on a disc much later. One of those photos has pride of place now on the sideboard. Steven is in black leathers, despite the heat, black shirt and shades. He is holding a cigarette and a can, and has one leg crossed over the other. He sits laconically in his seat surveying the scene. He looks totally at ease with the world and his lot. It is not him at his most handsome as life has taken its toll, but it is a picture where he looks most at ease.

That summer I met up again with an ex-girlfriend of Simon's. We'd last made real contact about 10 years ago. She has an excellent blues voice, and she had been part of our rehearsals for the band that we never got up and running. Simon has long since been living away and has a new partner. She had been living away too, but was now home spending time with her parents whilst looking for work. We would go out for drinks and meals, not involved in any kind of intimacy in the biblical sense. We were friends having fun and killing time together.

She had a powerfully intense temperament, much akin to my own; we would spend entire nights awake, just talking endlessly, and drinking beer and wine. We would mess around with songs we liked her singing, me playing guitar. I would laugh to myself as I walked home through the night dead streets, everyone asleep. And then the sunlight at 4 or 5am. I felt that I owned the world as I walked through those empty places.

We would go with our parents to the local folk club. I was likened to Jim Morrison by many. I retorted that if this was so, she had to be Janis Joplin. Not many people got the joke but those who did had a quiet smirk. Having read so many rock star biographies I knew I was right. She obliged by treating the entire club to a classic Joplin song, 'Mercedes Benz', without accompaniment and with enough volume to negate the need of a microphone. Everyone applauded.

I am happy that Steven remembered and took such pleasure in these outings. They didn't happen more than three or four times, but he enjoyed them, and he blossomed under the attention and in the company. He begins to see a way forward. Ian and I take him to the solicitors to finally complete the request for a divorce from Eve. He is still incapable of doing this on his own. He is nervous and physically frail, but he manages the private interview to the satisfaction of his solicitor. So, on the 22nd of September 2009 the wheels are in motion once again. All I can say is Thank God for legal aid because we are all down to our last pennies.

I began to wonder if I was just happy again or could this be one of my 'white' manic episodes. In fact, it was probably both. Even when alone, I began staying up all night, not distressed, but not touching down on the face of the planet. My mind was up in the stars and scrutinising the moon. I would spend these nights writing endless bizarre poetry. I would crash at daybreak. On awakening I would find reams of surprisingly intricate poems that I didn't remember embarking upon. There was often a morning surprise in the form of a half-filled notebook, to be revisited once the fog of medication began to lift. I spent a night writing a short story about a Floridian prison guard who ended up in his own electric chair. It would have been an A-grade essay had I still been at school, and could probably have earned a few pounds as an article in a magazine, but I gave up on it quickly.

I remember Steven first allowing me to read this and I was suitably impressed. He didn't think enough of it to save it digitally, but I have since discovered it amongst his notebooks.

It is probably mania which sparked off this creation. Enthusiasm flares in my mind and many co-existing projects jump in to being. Some are forgotten about, later returned to, but some are totally abandoned and lost. When the black periods come, nothing happens at all for a long time.

It's October 2009 and at the moment my mood feels stable. I'm not too high, I'm not too down. Even with the medication I still fluctuate up or down now and again. When this project is finished, I will most likely crash for a while. The worst I experience now is pure flatness, not sad, not happy just being. I find that somewhat disturbing, feeling like Mr Joe Plastic 9-5. Would I prefer not to have the illness? Well to be honest, no. If having it means being capable of animated thoughts and creativity, new ideas and a real insight into my being, then I will keep it. The depressions are like bleak vacations to recharge the mental batteries before the next big idea hits home. I would have preferred not to have been through the terror and the pain that I have experienced. Without them, would I have the insights I have gleaned from an insane journey through life and lies?

As the year ends, I become increasingly aware of my moods again. I spend much of my time alone, focusing on where my mind will take me next, who with and why. I'm again in the proceedings of getting a divorce from my second wife, begun in September 2009, and this time I will not look back. I made a promise to my step cousin (Alan) that if I were to be tempted back to the black widow, he had the absolute right to forcibly plunge my genitalia into a deep fat fryer. That is how certain I am that it is over. I can't however say the same for my relationship with alternating moods.

CHAPTER 9: ANOTHER KIND OF WORLD

Autumn 2009

There are many kinds of mental disorders. Before my diagnosis I thought I was plain depressed then I began to worry that I might be schizophrenic or just plain eccentric. But with a bit of research I found out exactly what manic depressive illness was, and immediately saw it in myself. But I told myself it could not be true. I thought denial would see me through, and the illness would burn itself out.

Many people have only one severe episode of distorted moods in their lives. Others, like me will have several. The old fashioned methods of treating people as general 'lunatics', simply locking them up forever in institutions and worse were to give way to more modern ideas. For example, the barbaric concept of an ice pick through the temporal lobes to 'let the madness out'. Before the coming of Lithium, most patients were given ice baths and Laudanum.

Thankfully in 1949 the UK began to dispense Lithium Carbonate to manic patients. Discovered by accident in a laboratory test to find a drug to treat depression, it turned out to be a very effective anti-manic drug. Other drugs, now known as tricyclic antidepressants arrived in the 50's. They had been developed to treat schizophrenia, and though they turned out not to help with that condition, they helped those with depression very well.

Nowadays, the preferred choice of drug for depression is one of the SSRI classes, which are also useful in treatment of panic disorders and eating disorders. Lithium, which is useful in both mania and extreme states of depression, is well known to have many side effects, and today is still in use but often substituted by

Depakote. Carbamazepine, an anti-epilepsy drug influences mania in some cases. It is an old drug that causes unpleasant side effects in some, though works very well for others. Treatments for mood stabilisation is very much a 'suck it and see' process.

The third class of anti-depressants are Monoamine Oxidase Inhibitor Antidepressants (MAOI), they are rarely used today due to their often dangerous reaction with certain foods. They react with the tannin present in red wine, tea and suchlike. But they are still an option for a few.

Some patients, and I have been guilty myself, resist the idea of taking medications once they are feeling better, often with catastrophic results. This is a feature of some mental health disorders. Many find the talking therapies useful. Cognitive behavioural therapy and psychotherapy can be helpful, but none did anything for me. Having seen first-hand what ECT can do to a person, I have completely ruled it out of the equation, no matter how ill I become. Yet many swear by it.

Other than the time that we had family therapy when Steven was about 12, I am not aware that he was offered or accepted any of these. The one occasion we got an appointment for psychotherapy was after he was discharged from his first stay in hospital. He was too ill and agoraphobic to go. This was because the appointment was for 5 months after his discharge and he had deteriorated without treatment or support.

Other peoples' reactions to mental illness vary. Some are wary, some will be insulting and call you a freak, and others will assume that due to being 'tapped', you are of an inferior measure of intellect. Some are overly sad for you and some will just accept you as you are. I remember one occasion working in the call centre when I burst out laughing. The lad next to me, a friend, asked what could be so damn funny in this awful place.

I asked him was he blind, could he not see them? Asking what I was seeing, I explained to him that the building was being invaded by flying cats that could morph through glass and were currently making sweeps of our office. He thought for a second in case I was winding him up, then remembering who he was talking to, laughed himself and said, "Sure, Steve." He asked me to describe them in detail, and I think I spent the entire lunch hour rabbiting away about it, with him laughing hysterically, and concluding that I was a complete nut case. I said I knew I was. It didn't affect us being friends; I even got him to cameo on one of the 'Bathmat' recordings sent cross-channel to Drew. The guy who worked on the other side of me also made a cameo appearance on one of these; and while never having sought a diagnosis, he too was prone to alternating depressions, high spirits and visions, and we would regularly exchange bizarre letters and mock-ups of magazines, mostly in Goon show style, in the mail.

In my experience, the worst reaction to mental illness comes from doctors and the police, who will usually presume that you are either drunk or just misbehaving. They don't realise that there is a real problem when you're skipping about laughing with nothing but neurotransmitters intoxicating you. And maybe your depression is a simple bad mood. Many doctors will keep a cynical eye on you for a few days before they treat it as a serious issue. I understand this poses less of a problem in the USA, where patients are required to pay for treatment. Coincidence? Probably not. I have been led to understand that running an in-patient service here in the UK on the NHS costs over £2000 per patient per week (2009).It can also take a long time to get a bed in a mental health unit unless you are sectioned. Fortunately, I never have been, though I should have been on many occasions.

Even being placed in a secure hospital ward is no guarantee that the patient will stay for treatment. Many is the time during my stays that someone has 'gone over the wall', and been returned shortly afterwards raving and incoherent, with the help of the local police. In reality there is nothing to run from except yourself, which is impossible. Hospitals are generally of a much more tolerable and comfortable standard today than when I had my first experience in 2001. Security can be ruled with an iron rod, or if a different rotation of staff is on duty, people may be allowed out out 'for a smoke'. On my second hospitalisation, I went for a walk of about a mile to the nearest shop. I bought some more cigarettes and a beer, then returned unnoticed. Yet most escapees have no intention of coming back, due to their illness telling them they know better than the professionals trying to look after them. I don't want to become that ill again. It is a possibility that I once more may have that experience. The last time I was hospitalised, I had the humiliating experience of being forbidden from closing my door and a security guard sat outside all night lest I try and kill myself. It made it hard to sleep, but I couldn't have slept anyway, not until the medication kicked in a few days later.

Nowadays I sleep soundly in a comfortable double bed, surrounded by music, poetry, books and cats. I enjoy hooking up to the so-called 'idiot box' when my mind draws a blank, talk shows are hilarious. You get to see people even more messed up than yourself without the excuse of mental illness. Why anyone would want to do such a thing in public for no fee evades me. Shows like Jeremy Kyle and Trisha in the UK, along with the various shows from the USA started by the likes of Jerry Springer and so forth make you think 95% of the world must be mad.

If I didn't write poetry, play any instruments or have the small pleasures of TV, music and a drink with friends and family, I couldn't go on. My Valproate levels are much lowered, and I have reduced the amount of tranquilliser I take, and can now just about pass as a 'normal' human being, whatever that is. Gone for now is the florid, psychotic madness to be replaced by occasional, light, white manias. I get lighter non-suicidal depressions that are more like a flatness where all creativity dies for a time. Gone are the days that I was too high-flying or too damn low to look after my appearance and general grooming. I eat these days. During my lowest times I would be too tired to think about getting food and would gladly have stayed in bed and starved. When I was high, I'd be too involved with various hair-brained schemes and plans that I would simply forget all about food. I think I might have packed a lifetime of living into 30 years, there is no longer anything much that would shock me in life. There are things I find repellent, but not shocking.

I don't know for sure where life will take me from now, but hopefully not off my feet, or more importantly, off my head. My energies have gone more towards writing poems and jamming on classic blues, folk and country standards. This is instead of my earlier tendency towards elaborate compositions, where I would use every piece of kit available and multi-track until I'd forgotten what month it was.

I hope this writing will throw light on a very complex and serious condition. Anyone who suspects they may have a mental disturbance should obviously first seek advice from their doctor. If he or she can't explain enough then the internet is a good source of information on your diagnosis and prognosis.

Private healthcare is literally a real life-saver, and whilst expensive gets the job done faster. Friends and family are invaluable; support groups like Mind help a lot for some of those who have no one else to turn to.

The light does come back on even after the blackest night, and whilst the turmoil of these depressions and most serious manias can never be forgotten, things do change. The best way to close I think is a line I wrote whilst seriously psychotic; "time makes ghosts of us all."

Don't become a ghost until you have to.
Steven, Autumn 2009

Steven tried hard to be 'normal' during this time and was desperately ashamed of his bankruptcy, his failed marriage and his illness. In the early part of 2009 I searched for a bank that would open an account for him. I found the Co-operative was willing to take a chance on him. I remember the disbelief and then delight on Steven's face when I presented the details to him. When his debit card arrived in the April he was buoyed up, his self-esteem given a boost and a little self-confidence was restored. However, he was unable to get credit of any kind and Ian had to contract for a mobile phone for Steven rather than a leave him with just a 'pay as you go'.

2010 These days things are stabilising, but as George Harrison sang on 'Any Road' from his last album, 'Brainwashed', "when you don't know where you're going, any road will get you there." On the same track he makes a lot of analogies to extreme highs and lows of mood and circumstance, but I'm not suggesting he was bipolar; it was his black humoured take on his acceptance of his inevitable impending death from cancer. George was a great fan of Monty Python and apparently would laugh at nearly anything weird. If he could laugh at cancer, I can laugh at my condition.

My moods are more stable but now I'm just like everyone else. Some mornings I feel bloody awful and don't feel like moving, but it isn't anywhere near as bad as the frosty, bleak dark night of clinical depression. Some days I get a bit hypo-manic, but being deprived of a credit rating, I cannot go overspending on these occasions, but still do mildly foolish things. Nothing on the scale of what would happen in my full blown manic episodes though. Basically, I'm 'normal', but still very eccentric and beholden to medication for the foreseeable future, possibly for my entire life.

Many patients will not stick to this and repeatedly, sometimes tragically relapse. For me, a downer day sees nothing being done. A high day sees me writing and making music until morning. But as night follows day, the occasional soaring high uses energy, and results in an exhausted crash. Happens to everyone, I'm sure, just with me the fluctuations are a bit more intense. I dread to think how intense without my medication.

I would hope anyone who believes they may have this condition will seek medical help. Should you, as I have frequently thought, think the medication or care you receive unacceptable, speak to the highest order you can reach in the profession. I personally fought a psychiatrist who thought he was above and beyond medical protocol and was offered the chance to sue him, but was too ill to be bothered.

However, medication is only one of the many ways to get well, doctors do make mistakes. You may have to wait and see what your solution is. There are a range of mood stabilising medications. It is trial and error, and therefore not surprising many patients end up self-medicating with drink and drugs. Sometimes it works… but not ideal so you must try and avoid it.

I like a drink and a packet of smokes as much as your average Joe, but with me, the cancer sticks pull me out of the sedatives I'm prescribed, the drinks put me back there again. I must say it's not wise to drink on certain prescribed drugs, but I do this only sporadically, it may not be safe for all, but I know my limits.

I have found in my area that some of the local CPNs are useless, some even on harder drugs than me (and illegal too). I have had little or no help except from the doctor, and even then, often only because of massive protests when I was lucid enough or when a family member stepped in when I was not. I don't need a CPN; I know what to watch for, as do my kin. But many have no one. Some areas have much better services than there are in mine, the NHS post code lottery. So, I'm not here to 'brainwash' anybody, you can do that very easily to yourself. I am here to give a personal account of my roller-coaster ride thus far.

They do say what doesn't kill you makes you stronger. Well, maybe sometimes. If I hadn't had to hang on in there through my own personal torture, I probably would have gone to bits every time my second wife used emotional blackmail against me. The overdoses, the bulimia, the time that she cut into her arms sitting on my parents' kitchen floor knowing her son (who was annoying her) and I were watching. The stress I felt when I had to peel the brothers apart during numerous fights. Most people would have wanted to lamp them one instead. I just had to watch in mute horror the aftermath of the knife fights, the punching, the destruction and be damn quick and calm with my finger on the 'call' button of my phone, 999 was already tapped in as soon as I got wind of any trouble. Maybe my ex had characteristics of bipolar, but apparently that had been ruled out by top psychiatrists. Who knows? I only know **I don't have to care anymore**.

Maybe two schizophrenics and one bipolar of the 3 kids she acknowledged. Same answer.

Hell, I lived there, survived, but my parents damn near cracked up with the stress and they were only getting it as a second hand account from myself. With experience, it's not just her and her kin that I've been better able to tolerate. I tend to find I'm nervous in ordinary situations, but when all hell breaks out my brain kicks in. When everyone else panics, I seem to be calmer and know what to do.

I feel like I've been through the mill. Without experiencing my problems, I would have never been able to survive anyone else's. I have played much down to save space by the way; otherwise the book would have just been one enormous bitch. If I hadn't broken free I would not have survived. I do quite all right alone as a manic-depressive, thanks, and it's steeled me for almost anything. Almost.

Take good care of your sanity in this world. It's the most precious thing you have, and I'm just getting mine back. Therefore, I bid you farewell (not in the terminal sense though) and wish the best to most, if not all, of you.

But that's just for now, because I'm not telling you the entire truth.

CHAPTER 10: THIS IS THE END...?

2010 has wrecked my mind again. In the late months of last year, 2009, after swearing I wouldn't, I tried pot again. No problem. I enjoyed a drink. No problem. All was well. Suddenly, I developed an infection in my left lung and was told it had affected my digestive system. I recovered.

This is a very brief statement from Steven about a challenging and worrying time. He seems to have not remembered the facts here, which is probably because of how ill he became, or he is glossing over the truth, because it is too painful. We had to support him both physically and emotionally to see a Solicitor to continue with his divorce proceedings. Each trip out was a trial for all of us, but he was determined this time to go through with it and proceedings were reinstated in January 2010. Mentally and physically his health was deteriorating, and I was afraid for the future. The GP is called on Thursday 25th March as Steven is so weak and unwell. Blood tests follow. I am committed to teaching a Bach training course in the house during the weekend of 27th and 28th March even though my son is fading away upstairs. I put a brave face on it as usual. Ian's stepmother dies that weekend and we just grit our teeth and ride it out. The doctor is called out again on Monday for Steven and again, on Tuesday. Fortuitously, I am technically on compassionate leave from work.

Steven is admitted to hospital on Tuesday 30th March 2010 after much haranguing by me, his dad and our GP. It has taken about 3 weeks for us to secure his agreement. He is weak, in pain and his belly is swollen with ascites. He hasn't eaten properly for weeks and is not getting up except to make it to the toilet. His bed is soiled and he fights me when I try to change it. He seems to want to lie there and die. It takes me a lot of nagging to get across to Ian that there is something very wrong and that Steven may be becoming seriously ill. After a nervous wait of about two hours, I accompany Steven in the ambulance and his belly is too swollen for him to lie down comfortably. He has got himself washed and dressed with a bit of help and is putting on a brave face. I settle him in to the ward and book in his details. I must confess that I am relieved when I walk away and leave him.

Ian visits on his own, on the Wednesday, as I am away on a training course. On Thursday we can't attend as we are with Ian's dad, Ed, in Scotland at the funeral of Ida, his wife and Ian's stepmother. It is ironic that the fact that Steven is in hospital allows us both to attend and support Ed.

On Good Friday we find that Steven has been moved to a side room because he is disturbing the other patients and won't 'behave'. He likes the private room better, but he is distressed and angry. He is not eating and tells us that he has not been given his proper medication. He has a drip in his arm and is being given fluids (and what else?). I come away from the hospital wondering how he will get better, if at all. Once again there is no one available to discuss his treatment.

The insistent ring of the bedroom phone disturbs us at 6.25am on Easter Saturday 2010. We know from past experience that this can only mean trouble. I scramble to answer it, already on high alert. It is the hospital. "Can you come and calm Steven down please? Can you come straight away? We have had to call the police."

Shocked and upset, we throw on clothes; grab cash and phones and make our way to the hospital as fast as we dare. Panic seethes just below the surface, and we must deal with the situation unwashed and without breakfast or a cup of tea.

It is cool and showery as we park the car. I shrug down into my old fleece, aware of my constricted throat and churning stomach. Ian and I head up to the ward to find a consultant waiting for us in the doorway. He appears upset and rather breathless.

"Steven tried to leave the hospital. I have had to pretend that I was getting a taxi for him to get him to come back inside. If he leaves the premises I have to call the police. He has a cannula in his arm and he is only partly dressed. He is so ill that he could die, and I can't force him to stay." Where does safeguarding fit in here? On reflection it would have been better here if Steven had managed to abscond. Without doubt he would have been sectioned at that time and it might have saved him from himself.

We try to take in the situation and the sight that awaits us. Two uniformed policemen are in Steven's side room. They are standing against the wall looking bored and uncomfortable. Steven is half sat up in bed. He is wearing a stained t-shirt and underpants and his skinny bruised feet are dirty and bare. A large multi-tubed cannula is fixed in to the back of his right hand and he is picking at it. This is quite difficult for him as he is handcuffed to the bed rails.

Steven recognises us, but he is totally psychotic. "This thing in my hand is eating me. Is it a squid? Take it out mam." He struggles to pull it out and I hold his hand gently and explain that it is important that it stays where it is. Ian stands the other side of the bed and reassures Steven that he is safe. "No, I'm not. Those guys over there are aliens and they are going to take me away. They take their skin off with their uniforms and you'll see what they really are."

The policemen shuffle their feet and one replies, "No, we are policemen Steven. We are trying to keep you safe." Steven gets more upset and struggles against the cuffs. "I want to go. The nurses are in false skins and they are going to kill me. I want to go home."

I explain carefully to Steven the current situation. "You are very ill Steven. You need to stay in hospital or you will be even more poorly. The squid thing is a cannula to give you medication. You need to lay quiet pet. We will stay with you." He protests and tries to get out of bed. He is uncoordinated and confused and the cuffs are obviously hurting him. Red weals are evident at his wrists.

"Selfish, selfish...." mutters one of the policemen.

I turn on him. "He's not selfish, he is ill, and he can't help the way his brain is working. When are you going to take these cuffs off?" The policeman leaves the room. He comes back with the consultant who wants a private word with us.

"If we take the cuffs off he might leave, and he will die. I don't want to be responsible for that. Will you stay with him?"

The three of us discuss what to do. We ask that a psychiatrist is called to assess Steven's capacity and state of mind. We are told that one is not available. We ask if he has been given his bipolar medication and I can't now remember the answer. We discuss the apparent psychosis and the guy says that is due to alcohol and his damaged liver, which it may well be, but Steve has been in hospital 5 days now, without alcohol, so we don't think that is the whole truth. The specialist wants to sedate Steven to keep him in bed and to further medicate him. His intention of keeping Steven alive resonates with us and we are in a state of distress and shock. We agree to this as we are told the other option is to put him 'out' with anaesthesia and this will further risk his liver function. I can't remember if we are asked to sign something or not. (There is nothing signed by us in his records). We ask again for a psychiatrist and are fobbed off with the promise that the hospital CPN will assess Steven "as soon as possible." this does not happen until the next day, Sunday. We do not know what to do for the best as there is no one to advise or support us impartially. We sit with Steven as his handcuffs are removed and the police leave. We stay for about 5 hours and gradually Steven settles down. He is upset and frightened but is aware of who we are - "I know you don't I?"

We note that he seems dirty and unkempt and apparently is not eating his food. I go to check with a nurse. This is difficult. The few nurses on the ward are rushing about and I can find no one in authority. I go back to the room to check Steven's charts. It seems he is not eating and then I notice the little plastic bottle of fortified food sitting at the back of his locker. It is half empty. I am pleased that they are trying to feed him, and I pick it up to check the ingredients. Cow's milk features at the top of the list. In my fragile state this infuriates me. Steven is extremely sensitive to any cows' milk protein and it seems to have contributed to psychosis in the past. If this is all that he has been having, then it will have exacerbated any psychotic state or brain toxicity. Clutching the bottle, I go off to find someone. Eventually I find a staff nurse who does not want to talk to me. "It's not my fault" she says. So much for professional responsibility! I know that she is not personally responsible, but she is after all in charge of the ward at this moment.

"When I booked Steven in I gave the information that he must not be given any cows' milk products. Why is this information not available to the staff on the ward? You've been giving him something that will contribute

to his mental health illness. No wonder you are having problems with him."

She is angry and resentful and makes a great show of writing out a notice which says 'No dairy products' and tapes it to the room door. Her whole attitude makes it clear to me that she doesn't like Steven and wishes that he wasn't on her ward. On a roll, I ask why Steven is wearing dirty clothes and seems unwashed. I have made allowances for his bare foot foray in to the outside world. She states that if he doesn't want to be washed or doesn't want to eat then she can't do anything about it. So much for nursing care! In his current medicated state how is he supposed to feed himself and change his clothes?

At staff change over in the afternoon a senior staff nurse comes to talk to us all. She is literally an 'angel' and puts herself out to build a relationship with Steven. With her support and input we feel able to go home about 3.00pm and leave Steven in her care. She manages to persuade Steven that he should stay and that she will keep a good eye on him.

However, during my hospital stay (regular hospital, not psychiatric), I was removed from my usual 'head meds' and became convinced certain medical staff were CIA agents packing guns and tried to run for the hills, thought the police who handcuffed me to a gurney were impostors and I hallucinated black dark slave pits on the wards from which I must run until the day of my release. Mental hospitals, though horrible, are generally kinder on the psyche. I was being loaded with Librium and couldn't even walk to the toilet on my own, for God's sake. That shit makes you shake like a jelly and your legs don't work. You go down like a sack of spuds.

On returning the next day, (Easter Sunday) we find out that Steven has already been highly medicated with some sedative drug and can't even make it to the toilet on his own, a cause of great embarrassment and distress to him. No psychiatrist, no CPN and not many staff visible. We are in turmoil and Steven lies in a not too clean bed and hasn't been able to eat. He seems more mentally 'with it' but very sullen and upset. Ian helps him to the toilet, gets his face and hands washed and helps him change his pants. It is hard for him to keep him upright. Steven complains that no one comes when he needs to go, and it does seem that the sheets have suffered because of this. Due to the danger of brain toxicity from liver failure, he is being given very high doses of Lactulose, a laxative. He is extremely embarrassed and distressed by his predicament. I note that a couple of nurses come and change the sheets whilst we are there. Are they afraid of Steven when he is on his own?

On the Easter Monday when we visit, the hospital CPN catches us on the ward. He has assessed Steven and believes that he has mental capacity at this moment in time. He does not have the power to do anything else for Steven it seems, and there is still no psychiatrist available until later in the week. This is in spite of the fact that Steven is unable or unwilling to eat or get washed, or engage with staff. Over the next couple of days, we become increasingly worried that he will 'do a runner' again. We negotiate Steven's care with the 'angel'. She seems to be the only one who acknowledges that Steven is a human being and our son.

Eventually we get a discharge for him on the Thursday, after 10 days in hospital. He must attend the outpatients' clinic with the specialist for liver disease. It is agreed that he is not doing very well in hospital and would be better off at home. We are given no instructions or advice on what his needs might be. Common sense tells us that he must take the raft of *medications and supplements that he has been given and we become aware of the importance of him having regular bowel movements so that toxins do not build up in his body.*

I lecture Ian on the importance of putting good quality food in front of Steven and ensuring that he is helped to stay clean. I must try to continue with getting up and going to work. Fortunately, I have been given two days compassionate leave for Ida's death and this is tacked on to the Easter break. I return to work on Thursday 8th April 2010 the day that Steven is discharged.

We muddle on through the next few days trying to stay calm, feed a reluctant Steven and ensure that he takes his medication. We are also making sure my mother can attend her numerous hospital appointments and I am packing up her flat as she prepares to move into a bungalow. We have to ask my younger brother for help with this. He does a little and then backs off. Apparently, he does not agree that mum should be moving. I'm guessing that he would prefer her to be in care so that he could absolve himself from any responsibility at all.

Not surprisingly I can no longer ignore my increasing chest pain and must see a doctor again just 4 days after Steven comes home. I have previously been given an inhaler which has not helped. The GP is concerned about clots etc. in my lungs as I have recently started HRT. I have to have an urgent blood test the next morning. I am contacted at work late on Wednesday afternoon the 14th April and told to get myself to hospital immediately. I am already stressed, and the shock makes me shake. A colleague drives me to hospital where I am checked over and given a preventative and protective injection re thrombosis. I must come back tomorrow as all the scanners etc. have shut down for the day. Ian comes to collect me.

He arranges for my brother to take him to my office and drop him off so that my car can be retrieved. I need it the next day to attend for tests.

I spend all the next day in hospital, where they look after me very well. I have x-rays, blood tests and scans and am sent home at 5.00pm with a clean bill of health. This is a great relief, but I still have chest pain. After mulling it over and using my knowledge of physiology I realise the shortness of breath and lung pain could be a sign of profound stress. This was a feature of a holiday in Derbyshire where I continually had pain and shortness of breath. I now recognise the beginnings of this pain as a warning sign that I need to deal with stuff and chill out. My lung function is checked out later in the year and the results are again inconclusive.

Over the next weeks we concentrate on keeping afloat. Steven needs constant supervision and is very weak and frail. He gradually puts on some weight and by June 2010 he is remarkably improved.

On fear of becoming ill again I ditched alcohol, cigarettes and went back to avoiding consumption of anything mentally upsetting.

He has been able to stay dry for a couple of months but by July he is feeling so well that he decides that he can drink 'socially'. We are not able to do anything about this, or his final refusal to attend for specialist appointments in relation to his liver, after attending just twice. Ian took him for these appointments and Steven refused to allow him in to the interviews with the specialist. Ian is a bit put out by this and feels that all he can do is ask Steven how it has gone. He is of course non-committal and brushes off enquiries and now refuses all interventions. We have no way of knowing what was said or what else was offered to support his well-being. With hindsight it is easy for me to criticise Ian for not being more assertive and asking for information. However, the outcome would probably have been the same. Steven is an adult apparently of sound mind and does not wish to share personal information. Where does this leave parent /carers? How do we give Steven the appropriate care at home if we do not know his physical state and what is required to support him to improve? On checking his hospital outpatients' appointments for his liver condition I find that Ian has had to cancel a scheduled appointment with a note that a new appointment will be sent out. I had left this responsibility to him and it seems that the appointment never came, and Steven has refused all further appointments, so he drops off the radar again re his physical condition.

We move my mum in to her bungalow and immediately afterwards celebrate her birthday with a family barbecue in our garden. We also manage a holiday with my sister and my mum in Derbyshire. We are very worried about leaving Steven but arrange for two of his friends to take turns at staying with him. Bad mistake. They are friends, not parents, carers or medical people. Whilst enjoying a 'garden party' with these friends Steven manages to burn his hand whilst destroying a guitar with fire and the aid of lighter fuel.

I set fire to a broken guitar for a 'laugh', egged on by friends, and the explosion of the flammable gas I had filled it with nearly blew off my left hand. I couldn't play for about 3 weeks because of second-degree burns.

Ian has to return home within two nights, leaving me to get on with it. He will come back at the end of the week to pick us up. I have been left with my sister, mum, a wheelchair and no car. I soon tire of the isolation and become stressed and worried. Whilst we are struggling in Derbyshire, Ian organises the GP for Steven yet again. After one visit we end up dressing the hand ourselves as Steven then declares that he has enough of GPs and refuses further intervention from them. We use Manuka honey every day with a clean dressing and gradually the burn granulates and heals.

I got myself sorted again then the world sowed its rotten seed of horrible darkness within my head once more. Everything scared me rigid and once more I lost all hope. My moods swing back and forth many times in the day. I drink like a fish and am not scared of that. I ignored the doctor who told me to increase my medication, thinking I knew better. I became so scared of my thoughts and manic 'noise' in my mind that I called the police on myself in case I did something stupid. I saw other people's blood everywhere. They were very understanding and, since I hadn't done anything, they simply 'talked me down'. The next day I committed myself to the psychiatric hospital again. This time, it was hell.

At the beginning of July 2010 Steven has yet another admittance to hospital for psychiatric care. After our GP calls in the Crisis Team Steven is admitted to hospital again on the evening of 8th July 2010. I think he was only in a few days, and Ian has noted in his diary that a new male CPN is coming out to assess Steven on 16th July. I don't believe that this assessment took place as Steven is still not in the system at the end of August when we need help again.

I note that Steven has had the August appointment with the psychiatrist Prof B cancelled and no follow up yet arranged, also the CPN misses a regular monthly appointment to visit Steven. In amongst this chaos of Steven's illness, my health scares and moving my mum in to her new bungalow there is a bright moment. Steven comes out of the house with us to have Sunday lunch at a local pub – a rare foray in to the outside world.

Steven improves a little and concentrates on his music. This letter written in August 2010, to Ally Gourlay, the producer of internet radio station K107FM, demonstrates the existence of hope. I don't know if the music was appreciated or played. Ally died in February 2016, so I can't now have that conversation.

Dear Ally,

Hope there's something useful on these discs for you. My first album is pretty much grunge. Track 1, 'I really don't want to dance' is a good one. The second album is a mix of stuff I did over 2 years and pretty much sums up a nervous breakdown. The third is 50/50 covers recorded in a very weird state of mind; some remastered from years ago, some new.

Our group existed for one album only, then Simon the lead guitarist moved to Germany. After that I was on my own, with a bit of help here and there from Drew Wood. Some of the remastered recordings feature Simon, and the odd thing I pulled out of the vault.

The first album is probably the best musically if you like that style. The second is a right mix-up, 'Lullaby' and 'Oxymoron' are maybe the best tracks.' Silly Girl' and 'She Lied' are good original tracks done in pure 60s style but the former has a very long, weird intro. Fusion is a project I've run for over 11 years live with various musicians, on the disc it's mostly me but with Simon and Drew popping up now and again from archive. 'Sweet Talkin' woman' is a good take, as is 'Flirting with time', 'Alabama song' (done the Doors way) and 'Out of the blue' (one of mine).

I'll leave it up to you to decide if any are play-worthy. I'm not easily offended and like I said before, if you hate them you have 3 new coasters!

Let me know what you think. Be honest. I know some of it is crap.

Best wishes to you, keep on with that show!
Yours faithfully
Steven

Late in August 2010 Steven deteriorates further and has been unwell mentally for over a week. We have asked the GP to call and he agrees that there is trouble brewing. Steven is very distressed and wants to be hospitalised so that everybody will be okay.

Our GP asks for the Community Mental Health Team to assess Steven, but as he is not currently listed with them they decline. Our GP then asks for the Crisis Prevention Team to call as a matter of urgency. 4 days later we are still waiting, and Steven is climbing the walls! We decide not to take him to hospital because a) he refuses to go to Accident and Emergency and b) it will do no good and delay things even further.

The team eventually arrive – two capable looking ladies who initially deal sympathetically with Steven's plight. It is 6.00pm on a Thursday evening 26th August and we have had to call the GP again to put a bit of pressure on.

They talk to Steven and to us and suggest that he can stay at home and be given an urgent appointment with the community psychiatrist. "When will that be? Will it be tomorrow?" I ask. "We can't guarantee it will be tomorrow, but it will be very soon." "We've waited over a week for you to respond and you are telling me it won't be tomorrow?" I am angry, but in the controlled clipped way that channels my energy and gets the job done. When Steven asks when he will see someone who can help him, he is told it will be after the weekend. Unfortunately, it is a bank holiday weekend so that means Steven must stay with us for another 4 full days (Thursday pm to Tuesday am) with no guarantee of seeing someone on the Tuesday. The team ask if that is okay with us. Well no, it's not and they are surprised when we tell them that as carers we can no longer cope with Steven and his illness, and that he needs to be hospitalised. Steven is distraught and begins to pace and talk incessantly. He is terrified of being left with us in case he does us harm. The team then get a bit uppity and say that there are no beds available, but they will check. "What about a bed in Newborough – you might be able to have a place there?" This is said in a manner as to put us off. Newborough is a minimum of two hours' drive from us and impossible by public transport. Visiting would be difficult even with a car and a real challenge without and horrendously expensive. We look to Steven for a reply "I need to go. Please, I'll go anywhere, just take me away."

Miraculously a bed materialises locally, in our new and modern psychiatric hospital which is 15 minutes' drive away. The team disappear to organise the admission and we pack Steven's bag for him and drive him to hospital.

On reflection I realise that this incident really does show the gaps in the system. The only means of help when you are mentally ill and not in the system is via your GP or Accident and Emergency. Both avenues will call for a psychiatric assessment which is not always available or prompt.

We find out that there is no connection between acute mental health services and the Community Mental Health Team. The team are there to keep you out of hospital and I expect they get a black mark if someone needs to be admitted. The Crisis Resolution Team can only come and resolve your crisis if you are already receiving services, and yes, they can get you the help you need. If you do not have a CPN then you cannot access the Crisis Team out of hours without going to

Accident and Emergency and waiting in the queue. Our perennial problem was that there was no help whenever we needed it.

As usual Steven had been bumped from the system and had no CPN to watch out for downward spirals. A profound lack of resources and an inability to look at a problem holistically blight the Mental Health Services in our area. This really pisses me off.

After a 4 day stay in hospital I was ready to eat my own head. I was on the right dosage of mood stabiliser and my head pulled round very quickly, so I discharged myself out of absolute boredom and lack of sleep. It felt like prison rather than the haven it had been in the past.

Message to all mental health patients:
Do not stop taking your medication just because you feel better. The condition can and will recur.

Discuss any side affects you may experience with your doctor. Don't keep quiet. If a certain medication doesn't suit you, speak up and get it changed. But bear in mind some conditions, bipolar included, means **LIFE** on medication, even during the 'normal' periods. But what is normal? You make up your own minds, because I'm damned if I know.

All I know is that my head is beginning to settle again. I'm still manic enough to be spending modest amounts of money on things I don't need on the strength of a whim, but since I have money now instead of credit, who cares? Before long I'll be suitably level and boring again. I love these gentle come-downs. But I bet when I'm level again I'll wonder where to put all this stuff I bought. I moved all my amplifiers into the studio today. There's no room to move, but it's functional, if somewhat red-hot already. That's before several thousand watts of electrical equipment gets running. And it can only get worse, knowing me.

Ian and I have a Carers Assessment on 16th September 2010 but I had to ask for it rather than be offered by the powers that be. The woman who does it is compassionate and professional. It becomes apparent that what we need to be able to carry on is for appropriate and regular care for Steven and some hope for a better future for him. Unfortunately, this is outside of the remit of what carers can hope to ask for in terms of support.

We have a new boiler fitted at the end of the month and Steven struggles with the disruption, becoming more anxious and moody.

Steven's divorce finally comes through on 22nd September 2010, but he does not consider it our business so keeps the information to himself.

December 2010

I now have a very approachable CPN (the like of which I have never met before) and am starting to level out. I sleep soundly in my own bed and my pills are doing their job.

The CPN visits on 17th December but things do get worse, and by Christmas Steven is looking frail again. We all enjoy a visit on Christmas Eve from the young family next door. We have supper and chat and enjoy some music. Steven is persuaded to play for us. Our neighbour is so pleased that he videos the occasion. As I watch I note the difficulty Steven is having now in singing and playing guitar. The choice of song is prophetic 'I won't back down…' and his last words on the video "I can't do it any more" are prophetic.

We enjoy our Christmas and our dinner and Steven seems in good spirits - we have photos to prove it. As the New Year begins, Steven seems to be failing in health and is obviously depressed. His CPN seems to work well with Steven, but no long term solutions are offered. Nothing much changes.

2011

Steven has bought a ticket to see the tribute band 'Doors Alive' for 25th January but is too unwell to go even though they are appearing very close to home.

On the evening of 27th January 2011, Steven falls on the landing, unsteady with either drink or medication or both. He crashes to earth against a tall storage cabinet and his weight splinters it completely. I have to climb over debris and the cabinet contents to reach him. A crescent shaped wound is seeping blood where a wooden shard has entered his arm. It is deep and ragged and obviously needs stitches. We eventually persuade him to go to hospital with his dad in the car. Our bargaining tool is the concert that he wants to attend with Rob the following evening. "If you get the wound sorted out you can go, otherwise you stay home." Ian and Steven are away ages and return home about 4.30am. Ian comments "It's like a war zone in there. I'm glad we are out of it."

The next evening Steven goes with Rob to a concert 'Mr Nice' in a local town and he seems to enjoy the outing. We are surprised that he has managed it.

We plod on with nothing much changing except Steven seems to be fading away. He is thin and weak with a poor appetite. He is having difficulty climbing in and out of the bath and we all agree that we need a walk-in shower to maintain his independence. He rarely allows his dad to help him wash and he is managing with an old-fashioned strip wash. It is clear to Ian and I that the ascites is returning.

The GP visits, takes blood and medication is prescribed. Steven refuses to have a transfusion of platelets or any other treatment. He has developed a strong and positive relationship with this older GP, Dr Mac, a genuinely caring doctor of the old school and known to Steven all of his 31 years. Even he can't persuade Steven to have the transfusion.

Although his health is deteriorating Steven has not yet given up. In the middle of April 2011, he takes delivery of a wide screen TV, a Blu Ray player and a stand to put them on, all paid for by him. This suggests that he has hope for life and a future. It is also the point at which he discovered that you can order cases of wine from Tesco on line, for a timed home delivery. These come through the door when our backs are turned.

Monday 6th June 2011. Prof B comes to see Steven with his CPN and Ian is included in the consultation. There is a full discussion on the medication that Steven is using, and blood tests are taken with a view to changing it to Lithium. "We may now need to treat Steven as a case of Bi Polar disorder." Prof B and the CPN will visit or telephone to discuss this at a later date.

Wednesday 8th June 2011. We receive a phone call in the evening asking for Steven, who is fast asleep. It is a doctor from Haematology and he is desperate for Steven to go into hospital now and have a transfusion. His platelet count is dangerously low at just 13 with a haemoglobin count of 8. The normal platelet count for adults is 150 - 400. We readily agree that we will insist he calls the hospital as soon as we can get him to wake up. Steven does call, and he refuses all intervention. "What do we do if he bleeds?" we ask the doctor "You call an ambulance." he bluntly replies.

July 2011

Steven perks up when Kay visits and she manages to get him to leave the house – success – but he is very unwell and looks it. She tells him to get himself sorted out. He tells her he is afraid of pain and afraid of dying. They spend a few weeks together before she has to return to her own responsibilities. Steven is bereft and lonely. His frustration is compounded when his computer fails, but this may have been a blessing.

I find out that he is being harassed by a female 'troll' who is causing problems amongst his Facebook friends. I offer advice, but he will not allow me to sort it out or do anything about it. This person is evil and is continually sending him pornographic mail both electronically and in the post. He shows me a padded envelope stuffed with vile photos and a porn DVD and a letter that is frankly threatening and repulsive. He is near to tears but won't allow me to help.

I believe, with the gift of hindsight, that this is when he starts to drink heavily again. Something has finally snapped within him as he realises the finality of his situation. He believed that he could not heal, and his existence became untenable for him. This may have been the culmination of other difficulties he was experiencing at the time.

Steven's belly was swelling again, and he agreed to allow a home visit from one of our GP's. Whatever was said during the consultation, Steven was left with the expected diuretic medication and nothing else as far as we know. Maybe the GP, who was not familiar with Steven and wouldn't discuss his visit with us, laid it on the line and Steven just gave up.

Towards the end of July, I organise my mum's birthday tea in the garden with family and friends. Steven won't or can't come down. He is unwell and has an abscess behind his ear which he doesn't want people to see. He does occasionally look out of the window at the noisy group below. He won't join in; he is too ill and too ashamed. My mum comes up to have a word with him and this is the last time she gets to see him.

I am furious when I find out about his ear. I don't understand why the GP hasn't spotted it during the recent home visit and why Ian hasn't mentioned it either. I feel that I am the only one who can deal with matters promptly and I am stuck at work when I should be at home. I treat his ear with Magnesium Sulphate paste and this is surprisingly successful.

Two days later Ian and I have a long talk with the CPN. This time Steven refuses to see him. I like his ordinary chunky strength and kindness, but that is not going to help the problem. The CPN spotted this downward spiral with our prompting, but it was not actively dealt with. "We'll see what Prof B has to say about him." Well the Prof had other calls on his time and the appointment within an under-resourced Mental Health Service never materialised over the following 8 weeks.

Steven is still waiting for the discussion on changing to Lithium. The CPN cancelled his own visit the week before Steven died and rearranged it for later. What if those two visits had taken place? What if.............

Steven sleeps a lot now and his appetite is non-existent. It is difficult to persuade him to eat and we are pleased when he manages something as small as some soup and garlic bread. Kay calls and manages to get him out to the shop. This is a victory as he has slept until 3.00pm and had only two bites of pizza for sustenance.

Steven's computer is returned to him, but a lot of his personal music has been lost. He is upset and grumpy. More so because his phone is now on the blink and he has no way of keeping in touch with friends, having knocked Facebook on the head for the present.

He is hoping for a visit from Simon who is back in the UK and Kay has promised that she will spend some time with him too. He is frustrated because he is out of touch with his friends and no one can call him because of the broken phone.

Looking back at this I don't understand why he didn't just call Simon or Kay from our land line? Maybe he didn't have the numbers stored anywhere else. He is angry and upset when Simon doesn't get in touch and Kay doesn't come at bank holiday as promised. He sinks further into depression and self-pity.

25th August 2011

My niece Louise is staying with us with her mum, my sister, in preparation for a trip to Scotland. The task is to take my brother in law's ashes to be interred on a family plot. Steven will not come out of his room, but he does allow and seemingly enjoys a chat to Louise who is brave and generous enough to go and talk to him.

We go to Scotland with my sister, Louise and her dad's ashes and leave Steven in bed. He is resentful and ill and I am glad we will only be away 1 day as there is no one to look in on him. The journey is rather exciting with flash flooding on country roads and spectacular thunderstorms. But my mind is on Steven.

1st September 2011

As soon as bank holiday is over Ian and I go to visit the GP and ask for help for Steven. As usual, nothing is immediately available. The expected visit from the CPN is overdue and the appointment with the psychiatrist has not yet materialised.

4th September 2011

Steven is a little more forthcoming today after a long period of not wanting to talk. He enjoys his evening dinner of roast pork and eats it all, a change for the better.

I go up to say goodnight. Steven is a little more talkative than for many days. We discuss Kia the cat's arthritis and how she has improved on her daily doses of Metacam. Ian comes in to say 'Good Night' as well and the three of us have a short but pleasant conversation.

I cuddle Steven good night and kiss his brow, feeling his dry smooth hair on my face. He winces as I release my hold. "You don't need to be in pain pet. We can sort it for you. Good night sweetie."

My last words to my son.

Part 2: The Aftermath

Monday 5th September 2011 6.35 am

Another Monday morning and I heave myself out of bed. Heavy with sleep and utterly exhausted I head for the bathroom. As usual, the bathroom light is still on. What is not usual is the sight of my son lying on his left side on the floor. The blood, piss and shit that are pooled around him do not initially register with me. His absolute stillness matches my frozen shock. I have seen him look deader than this many times before, but I realise that this time is probably for real. Kneeling on the floor, I struggle to turn him into the recovery position, whilst shouting for Ian to dial 999. Steven is jammed in between sanitary ware and the door frame, and I can't manage to move him. Ian comes to help with the phone in one hand, taking instructions from the operator. I attempt to open Steven's airway and am initially baffled by the solid sticky content of his mouth. It is not until later that I realise this is his tongue. We are both checking for a pulse and I imagine I have found one. It seems impossible for us to get him onto his back to do CPR. As we struggle, the doorbell announces the speedy arrival of the paramedics. Ian runs down to let them in. We are unceremoniously bundled out of the way and must go downstairs to wait.

We don't have to wait long. After the initial urgency of the paramedics' response, we both register the slower footfalls coming down the stairs. The guy looks more stricken than he should, but he carefully tells us what we already know. Steven has been dead for quite a while, and that further attempts at resuscitation are pointless. The post mortem staining of his skin has shown them that he has been dead on the floor for hours. We are told to stay put until the police arrive, not allowed to go upstairs or anywhere near 'the body'. The police arrive quickly. Gently and apologetically we are questioned about what we know or don't know.

They commandeer the medication from Steven's room and have a quiet poke around. Without thinking I have already automatically picked up and disposed of the two empty wine bottles from the floor. After liaising with the paramedics, the police remain and the ambulance leaves – empty. We must now wait for the undertakers to arrive and remove his body to the morgue for a post mortem. The police wait in their car outside. This allows us to be with Steven, in painful silent shock.

I sit on the floor in the bathroom doorway. I lean up against the jamb for support as I stroke Steven's hair. It is very soft and cool. My nose is running with snot, and the tears drip off my face and down my neck and chest. Ian stands behind me for a while. He goes down to make tea and I take a break.

Kia cat is wandering about, so I pick her up and take her to Steven. She hates being carried but this time she doesn't struggle. Putting her down close to his head, I sit back down on the floor. She takes a casual look, a sniff at his face and wanders off again. It's old news to her.

The undertakers arrive; the two policemen politely introduce them and then leave. Again, we are ushered in to the living room as Steven's body is expertly bagged up and carried away. We are told 'what happens next', provided with phone numbers, and left alone without our son.

Without our son, forever.

Struggling with our emotions, the only logical thing to do is to clean up the floor and make more tea. All that first day we are analysing what has happened, what could we have done to prevent this? We reflect on the events of the evening before. I sat on Steven's bed and chatted to him about Kia's new medication and the fact that she seemed more cheerful. I talked to him about his own health and reminded him that he did not have to be in pain. He didn't say too much, but he did talk to me – a vast improvement on the previous few weeks. I hugged Steven 'Good Night' and kissed his cheek, noting that he winced in pain and held me off, even as he accepted my kiss. Ian also paid his evening visit before going to bed. Neither of us were unduly perturbed or noticed anything different.

During the past weeks he had been quiet, depressed, with poor mobility and unable and unwilling to leave the house, spending much of his time in bed. Even his CPN was concerned about him and had agreed to bring the psychiatrist for a home visit. The appointment had been arranged for the week before Steven died, and they cancelled because of another commitment.

I had woken during that last night. I heard Steven mumbling in his sleep and then call out incoherently. Usually I would get up and check on him, and he would resent the intrusion if he was awake. This time, I was so exhausted and drained that I waited, listening for further disturbance. I heard a strange guttural noise but I have heard Steven make that noise before. He seemed to settle, and I drifted off to sleep. I do wonder now what I might have found if I had got up or what I could have done………

The next week passes in a blur, and I do not have much recollection of what happened or how we spent our days. We inform friends and relatives, organise a funeral and accept calmly the fact that there will be a post mortem.

Tuesday 6th September

Ian and I are awake early, as usual. For a moment I do not remember the events of yesterday. We have not slept much, and conversation is at a standstill. I am just drinking my first cup of tea at 8.00am when the phone rings. I snatch at it, still stressed and tuned in. It is the call centre for Call Connect, my mother's alarm service. "Mrs Farrow has activated her alarm and we can't raise her. Are you available to check on her straight away?"

I slam the phone down and share the message with Ian. He is grabbing car keys as I fumble with shoes. We are silent on the short journey to mum's. I find out later that we both are thinking that it might be a double funeral. I unlock mum's door and call out. She is sat with her back to me on her bed. Struggling with her underwear she turns around to see who has come in. When she recognises me, she asks if I have brought her pension. I bite my tongue and ask her if she is all right. All this time her call alarm is sounding and I can hear the operator shouting down the line "Are you there Mrs Farrow?" Ian sorts the alarm out whilst I try to explain to mum what has happened. "Of course I haven't set the alarm off! That woman has been gabbling on for the past half hour and I don't know why. What does she want Clare?" I explain that she must have set it off by accident and that 'the woman' wants to know that she is all right. This is accepted with bad grace and I am beginning to lose my temper. Her actions seem initially selfish when we are facing up to the death of our only child. I realise that mum is as upset and stressed as we are. I brusquely take my leave, agreeing that the next time I come through the door I will have her pension with me. Ian drops me at the Post Office and it is just 9.15am. I am ready to go back to bed and hide.

On returning home, Ian says "You have a visitor." I am surprised to find my GP sat on the sofa. My mood has not sweetened. "What are you doing here?" "I've come to see how you are. We are so shocked at the surgery to hear about Steven." "We didn't expect him to die." I am taken aback by the statement. "What do you mean you didn't expect him to die?"

Ian and I expected him to die, but we too were surprised that it was 'now'. That's what death is like – you don't usually get to choose. I realise that I am being rude in a trying situation. I apologise for my shortness of temper and we make conversation. She gets up to leave and warmly clasps both of my hands. I am glad that she is my GP. I later send a box of biscuits and a thank you card to her and the surgery staff. My anger was justified but not my rudeness. Is it possible that we are the only ones who realised Steven was deteriorating? A doctor had visited about 6 weeks before and the CPN also knew the state of affairs.

Wednesday 7th September

Drew and Sindy visit and are as gutted as we are. Sindy brings apple pie which is gratefully received. We talk about all the 'what ifs' and then get down to some planning. Drew says that he would like to 'do the flowers' for Steven. We have agreed that we will have only one floral tribute with any donations going to Steven's beloved Cats Protection. Drew says he has an idea for the flowers and would we trust him? We trust him. We give him cash so that he can work on his idea. They trail off home, maybe as sad as we are.

We are relieved when the phone call comes telling us Steven's body is to be released. We can begin to organise the funeral using the Coroner's certificate of statement of death. We are cautioned that cause of death will not be known or debated for some time. We always knew that he wouldn't make 'old bones' but we did not expect death to arrive so soon. Had he decided to end his life? We agree that we can drink as much whiskey as needed until we know the outcome of the post mortem. Three months plus later as I am writing this, I do not think that pact was such a good idea.

The undertakers and the Coroner's officer are unfailingly supportive and professional. They have done this before, but we haven't. As Ian commented "it's really hard to get your head around." After caring for Steven in ill health for over 16 years, the whole dynamic of our marriage and lifestyle is thrown out of kilter and it mixes in with the loss of our hopes for Steven's recovery and independence. A raw and unsettling way to be.

Thursday 8th September

I go into work and am gently welcomed by my colleagues. A hug, a quiet word, all appreciated. I sort out my emails and outstanding work, preparing notes for my colleague. I am due a week's leave next Monday (thank you God) and want to leave everything in order. By 1.00pm I have had enough. I tell my manager that I am going home 'sick' – we only get 3 days compassionate leave and I have had it.

We also have a lot of emotional support from the undertakers who visit in a pair. The woman is humorous and gentle and knows just how to talk to us. The other guy is learning his trade but has been mentored very well. We discuss my orchids and swap growing tips. He goes upstairs with Ian and on being shown the recording studio, talks knowledgeably about guitars and music. He spots Steven's Titanic memorabilia and we are surprised to find that he can chat with authority about this as well. God seems to send just who you need in difficult times.

A word of advice regarding funerals - they are horrendously expensive. This one, at a cost of £3000 plus was paid for on a credit card and that embarrasses me deeply. It is easy to say, 'be prepared' but how do you prepare for the unexpected?

Friday 9th September

On the Friday Martin, the Humanist Celebrant, the guy who will lead the funeral service for Steven arrives by appointment. I like him immediately. The idea is to share our thoughts about our son and the way he lived his life, so that Martin can get a real sense of who he is, to share with the congregation. Three of Steven's friends arrive to contribute to the process. Martin stays over two hours, longer than he had arranged. He looks at Steven's room and his books, music and checks out the recording studio. We all seem to find it therapeutic and enjoyable, with laughter, tears and the dawning realisation that Steven is definitely not coming back.

Martin's job is to create a sense of Steven's character, achievements and history to share. He does this with skill and sensitivity. We also need to choose music for the service. This is easier than it sounds. We resist the urge to suggest 'Fire' by the Crazy World of Arthur Brown. Steven would have appreciated the joke, but Ian's dad and my mum would not understand. We settle for Mr Blue Sky by ELO. It is an uplifting track with an upbeat tune and words and seems fitting to leave the chapel with. It has great significance to Ian and to Steven and is perhaps where Steven began his musical adventures. I think it is significant that I found a CD compiled by Steven with his favourite tracks on it. This helped us choose the rest.

We have not yet found Steven's Will. He always said to put him in a black bag and throw him out with the rubbish. For propriety we decide a cremation will be appropriate and then become embroiled in the practicalities of the choice of coffin. We initially agree that the cheapest one will do because it will be burnt, and Steven hated to waste money and we have none. We know that he did not want any real show or religious ceremony, but it is difficult to lay your son to rest in the cheapest box. It doesn't seem respectful or loving. And that was when we spotted the custom-built coffins in the catalogue. Yes, even undertakers have catalogues! Created from cardboard, the coffins were illustrated in a myriad of beautiful designs. After much discussion we agree on a showy creation shaped like a guitar flight case and coloured a beautiful shade of dark red. Steven would have abhorred the cost but loved the joke. We decide that he should have his one last grand moment, sent off into the wild blue yonder in appropriate musical style.

The cremation and all arrangements are settled for the following Tuesday. We do not place a notice in the local paper. The last thing we feel we can cope with is the second ex-wife with rabble in tow. This is a big issue for us, and we agree that if she does attend we will keep our distance and our dignity.

Having notified most of Steven's friends via Facebook (it has its good points), I type and copy an appropriate notice and push it through neighbours' doors. Many of them do not realise that Steven has died and it creates a huge response of sympathy, cards and letters. A neighbour calls, and is in tears as soon as he gets through the door. He is moved by our loss. His own son was killed in a motorbike accident some years previously. I think it was kind and brave of him to visit, but we are faced with someone else's grief when we are trying to come to terms with our own.

A note to family and friends of other bereaved people who want to offer help and show support. Cards are appreciated, personal notes and letters more so, and handing them over in person instead of slipping it through the letter box shows guts and empathy. Visits are also appreciated but do not stay too long, don't ask questions to satisfy your own curiosity, and please bring food that can be reheated without any preparation.

Ian and I hardly had the time or the energy to prepare food and eat that week as we were inundated with visitors. We were moved by how many other people were grieving for Steven, but found it draining to be obliged to comfort others and put on a brave face. The show of support from Steven's friends and family was overwhelming and appreciated.

We welcome the visitors the best we can, but are a bit taken back by the neighbour who asks us "When are you moving to a new house?" I query her line of enquiry; "I couldn't bear to live in a house where someone has died." Ian and I look at each other in amazement she is talking about our son as a 'someone'. Ian comments that her house is as old as ours and quite a few people will have died there over the past 60 years. She changes the subject.

I am informed by the undertakers that Steven is now in the chapel of rest nearby and that he can receive visitors for 'viewing'. Ian refuses point blank, but I am desperate to see Steven one last time. Only Alan, Steven's step cousin was brave enough to visit. I think he had to be sure that we were telling him the truth when we said Steven was dead. He handled it bravely for such a young man, and he and I made the first visit together. I am touched by his sensitivity and his tears. Steven is dressed in the clothes that we have provided, leather trousers and waistcoat, his trademark dark glasses, white shirt and his black Stetson hat to sit beside him. He lies in state looking as if he will wake up and be ready to go out with his mates. I realise that it is such a long time since he has done that, and begin to cry quietly.

Saturday 10th September

Friends rescue us from our stupor and insist on giving us supper and drinks on the Saturday evening. They get it just right, allowing us to talk about what has happened but also to be 'normal' and discuss other things. We enjoy the music, the food and a couple of drinks. On walking home under a sky studded with stars and scudding puffs of cloud, back lit by the moon, I realise my emotional state is demanding release. Unfortunately, my inner being decides that the bowel is the most efficient way of doing this. I don't make it to the door. I sob in shame as I strip off white trousers and casual shoes in the darkened street. Ian has gone ahead and unlocked the door, and I rush past him in a storm of tears. He is also shocked and distressed. When I have cleaned myself up and come back downstairs, I find my trousers neatly bagged in the outside bin and my shoes clean. He helps me find my IBS medication. I realise how fragile we both are emotionally, although we do not want to share this with anyone else.

Sunday 11th September

The day is passed in exhausted dumbness. I make us a 'proper' dinner as we have not eaten well this week. I find myself beginning to serve up three portions and stop to gather myself. This time last week Steven was happily eating roast pork and stuffing and I was pleased to see him eating well. I am not eating well. I find it so very difficult to swallow my food.

Phone calls are fielded, and television is stared at. We make up Steven's bed for my sister and her eldest daughter. We try to arrange the room in a way that will not be too evocative of 'dead man's shoes'. I realise the room is very much alive and still Steven, but Steven's Spirit is insensible to me and I am relieved. He has gone, and I am telling myself that he is safe from harm and pain, wherever he is now. Looking towards the next week, our supposed holiday, I search the internet and find a pub in the borders, which I book for the end of the week. Time to run away.

Monday 12th September

We spend the day checking the arrangements for the funeral tomorrow. Friends call to check details and offer support. I shop and cook, ready for my sister and her oldest daughter who arrive that evening. We eat and drink and comfort each other - then to bed, with a sense of exam nerves and apprehension.

Tuesday 13th September

My sister asks if she can see Steven so we three women, big niece included walk down to the chapel of rest. It is a bright day and windy. I know what to expect as I have visited before. Ian again refuses the offer.

Steven lies in state in his usual leather trousers. The black Stetson sits on his chest, and sunglasses hide his closed, dead eyes. His best white shirt is a bit worn, but his leather waistcoat shows its quality. Under the half cover, as usual, he is not wearing any shoes. His beard has been trimmed, just enough to make it respectable and his hair is clean and combed, just the way he liked it. He does not look dead, just fast asleep, and I stroke his hair. It is soft and dry and airy. I lean over to kiss his brow, but I can't reach. His splendid red coffin is set just that bit too high on the bier. I make do with stroking his cool face. The lid to the coffin is set against the wall and it is beautiful. It gives us something distracting to quietly talk about as we all stand around. As far as I know, no one else chose to 'view the body'.

As we leave I let the receptionist know that she can now have Steven prepared for cremation. In other words, they will remove his finery and fasten down the lid, in readiness for his last journey on earth. I hold myself together very well.

The house is all hustle and bustle. Breakfast is made and forced down. Shoes are cleaned, blouses ironed, dishes washed, anything to keep busy. We all agree that we must eat before the ceremony which is 1.00pm. Traditionally the ham sandwich comes into its own. One of my younger nieces arrives, having travelled on her own from Gloucester and I appreciate the commitment. She had visited us with her mother just 3 weeks before and had talked to Steven for the first time in years. His death has shocked her as much as the rest of us. It is even more poignant that the previous occasion was to take her dad's ashes up to Scotland. Steven was left alone in the house that day, unable and unwilling to come with us.

Ian goes to collect Rob, one of Steven's closest friends and suddenly the house is full of people. Cars, and Drew and Sindy's motor bike are parked along the length of the street. Ian's dad Ed is here, having travelled alone all the way from Scotland at the age of 82. Bobby his dog is kennelled in the back of the car. Ed is so upset that he is unable to eat and leaves to go ahead to the crematorium, refusing help or offers of a lift. He cannot face following his grandson's coffin. My friend Meg arrives, she is a Spiritualist Medium, and quietly informs me that she won't be at the crematorium but will meet me later. I understand perfectly. My younger brother arrives with my mum who needs careful handling. And suddenly the cortège has arrived, and the moment has come to swallow hard and get on with it. I am choking back tears as I write this 6 months later.

I realise that I have no desire to be crammed in the back of a hearse with others so Ian and I elect to drive ourselves. This elicits a moment panic from Rob and one of Sindy's sons, who are obliged to travel with my sister, nieces and mother who they do not know. They 'man up' and get on with it.

Steven is walked the 200 yards down the crescent and then we are off, with the cortège motoring along sedately and Drew and Sindy trying to keep the Harley under control. It must be difficult to ride it in a dignified manner – it's just not made for it. I am grateful that we are by ourselves. I do not think I could have kept my control in company. I need the space, and the comfort of my husband.

We arrive at the crematorium and I am instantly overwhelmed by the number of people milling about. I am not quite sure what my role is, and I go in to 'hostess' mode. I meet and greet as many people as I can as we make our way to the entrance. The funeral directors have seen this all before, and have given us time to do this.

I am amazed and moved to see three members of the older peoples group, which I support through my work role. My manager and my work colleague are also in attendance. For some reason I did not expect this. At some unspoken sign, the cortège forms up and we file into the chapel. We have chosen 'The Last DJ' to walk in to. I recognise neighbours, friends, Steven's mates, Ian's acquaintances. The chapel is packed as is the overflow gallery. The sight of the glossy red flight case coffin causes a murmur of conversation and a few wry smiles.

And then I focus on the flowers as created by Drew and Sindy. They are amazing, inventive and very fitting. A red and white 6 stringed Stratocaster guitar created from silk flowers stands beside a small black amplifier. This acts as a vase for a fountain of gladioli and fresh carnations – an explosion of colour representing joyful music and noise. My throat constricts with emotion and I choke down my sobs.

Martin, the Humanist Celebrant takes the lectern and begins to speak. He tells Steven's story as he knows it, with humour, sensitivity and authority. I find myself listening intently, as if Steven is a stranger to me and I need to know as much as I can about this man, before he disappears completely into the fiery furnace. There is a gasp of consternation from the congregation when Martin speaks: "Steven said that he must have had a very bad mother........." I know what is coming and it makes me smile. The congregation relax as he tells how we allowed Steven to tinker with quite dangerous items and perform risky experiments. The music chosen for the contemplation is 'Rising Sun' and we walk out to 'Mr Blue Sky' all of them Steven's old favourites.

As we stand outside in the bright sunshine, I notice a lone spray of flowers on the concrete slabs. This is nearly missed by both of us as we have requested no flowers and everyone else has complied. These have been sent by my friend who lives in Canada,expressing her support and love. I pick them up and take them home with me. I can't remember too much about afterwards but we make our way to our local Sports Club where a buffet has been prepared. My poor old mum helps in the only way she can by paying for the funeral feast.

Steven's friends chat quietly to each other and a couple of them choose to sit apart, seemingly shocked and withdrawn. I try to talk to everyone who has come, and it seems like we are having an afternoon tea party. I am necessarily devoid of strong emotion and again play the hostess.

My friend Pat and her husband have set up some sound equipment and a CD player and Steven's music is playing quietly in the background. I wonder how many people realise that it is him singing at his own wake? A little later, when people have begun to drift away, Simon sits with his guitar and quietly plays in tribute to Steven.

Amid hugs and kisses friends begin to leave, and I invite close family back to our home. My sister and oldest niece are staying with me; younger niece has left for her train. An evening of drinking, tears, family talk, music and reminiscing ensues, and I think Steven has had a decent send off.

Our family leave the next day, including Ian's dad who has spent the night with his dog in a hotel, by choice and necessity. His stepdaughters have done good service and kept an eye on him.

We spend the rest of the day tidying up and preparing to go away for a couple of days. Drew and Sindy will watch the cats, and nothing else matters much. I visit the dentist in the afternoon and pretend that all is well, desperately trying to be 'normal' when all I want to do is weep.

In Mourning
15 September 2011

We are loading up the car on the Thursday morning, our 38th wedding anniversary, when Dr Mac, another one of our GPs calls in. He offers his condolences and tells us that he did not expect Steven to die. I hold my tongue and chat to him as if he is any visitor calling in for coffee. He offers his support for the future inquest and Coroner's report and we accept gracefully. Seven months on I have not yet taken him up on this, but I will if I need to.

It seems easy to drive up the road on our own. Steven has not been away with us for years, and we managed a few short breaks in that time. We head for the borders and spend a couple of days pulling ourselves together. On settling into the hotel I reach for my phone and begin to key in Steven's number. I stop myself as tears wet my face. We always would let him know when we had arrived, but I expect he knows now anyway. Again, Ian's regular check on him morning and evening by phone is hard to resist. The same thing happens as we drive home on the Saturday. Steven, ever obliging, would check on milk and bread for us and we would call to tell him we were on our way. It is very difficult to walk into an empty house, but the enthusiastic greeting from the cats does help.

Sunday is spent in mundane tasks like laundry and dusting, much neglected over the past days. I prepare to go back to work. Ian will be responsible for the supervision of the fitting of the new bathroom which also begins the following day. Steven will now not be disturbed by the upheaval or benefit from the changes. During the last few months we had decided to improve our bathroom so that Steven could cope more easily. It was something he was looking forward to and needed. We are later much distressed by the fact that fitting equipment and boxes of tiles are crammed into the edges of Steven's room. We decide that we must just put up with it. We realise that Steven would never have coped with the disruption, noise and lack of privacy and of course, now he doesn't have to.

On telling the fitter that we have had a recent bereavement (to explain our odd behaviour!) he asks why we didn't put him off. "What difference would it make now?" asks Ian.

On Monday I set off for work in good time and wonder what sort of reception I will get. I am not sure how I should act or react. I am greeted quietly with hugs and smiles and they get it just right. I work with lovely people. It is however very hard to concentrate with a continuing tinnitus of grief echoing in my thoughts. To cope with work, I try and shut my emotions down. I really want to go away and have a good cry, but there is not an emotional space for this to happen. This desire will continue for many months.

Steven always wore jewellery around his neck, a jet birthstone that we bought him, silver chains, and a leather neck thong, again bought by us as a gift. In the last couple of years, he treated himself to a variety of silver pentagrams. An age-old sign for protection and safety, maybe it helped calm him. The undertaker asked me to sign for the silver chain and pentagram that had been powerless to protect him from death. It was removed before the closing of his coffin and cremation, as was his leather waistcoat and Stetson hat. The clothes are returned to me in an upmarket yet sombre purple bag and the pendant is in a classy little jewellery box of the same shade. I am intrigued that undertaker's colour coordinate their accessories.
I wear the pentagram every day for more than 4 months. The five points are fine and sharp and not enclosed in the silver rim. A scourge for my grief, they

prick me to remembrance between my breasts and close to my heart, during every dark night. Ian wears its brother around his neck. It was not obsession that caused Steven to have two the same. The original was swallowed up by his sheets and quilt one night and he refused to let me strip the bed to search for it. He just bought another on-line. Of course, the original turned up one laundry day, falling from inside a quilt cover, and he was pleased to then have a matching pair.

We gain some comfort by getting in touch with the local Cats Protection to donate the money given at Steven's funeral. We have topped it up to £250 and encourage them to gain some publicity from it. I write the editorial and photos are taken of me hugging kittens. The article appears in the local free paper and in the larger regional one. It is not a popular charity for bequests, but it is exactly what Steven would have wanted. Kia cat gave him love and emotional support for 12 years and she was rescued by this charity. I am delighted when her photo is recognised as 'Susie who had her kittens under the stairs'. Kia continues to give Ian and I lots of love and cuddles when not being molested by her little sister Nellie.

The bathroom is finished, and we are relieved. It has been a difficult time for us and the upheaval has been more than we expected. The workmen have gone, and the gear is tidied away, and Steven's room is free from building mess. The finished item is beautiful, and Steven would have loved it. I cry because he will never use it. I still have flashbacks of Steven on the bathroom floor and maybe the new look will help me get over them. Ian later admits that he has them too. I sleep fitfully that night as usual.

I am startled into wakefulness by the sound of the bathroom door clicking open and the light being switched on. It is on a pull cord and makes a distinctive sound. Ian is beside me in bed and I am frozen with shock as I realise that the light is indeed shining across the landing. "Well Steven, if you have come to visit I had better get up and see what you want." I cautiously move across the landing and peep around the door. I am confronted by a wide eyed and frightened Nellie cat who is crouched down in the new giant sized hand basin. It seems that she has pushed the door to investigate, climbed into the basin and has had a swipe at the pull cord for good measure. She is as shocked as I am at the brightness of the wonderful new down-lighters. I remove her, switch off the lights and shut the door firmly.

I am sat watching the TV with no real interest. I am exhausted as usual and thinking about going to bed. "Mam.... mam.... I couldn't help it mam" the voice speaks inside my head. Steven's voice, I am a bit surprised. I wasn't thinking of Steven and there he is. I wasn't trying to hear him or communicate with him, so maybe it is him and not my imagination? What is it he couldn't help? Was it dying, being ill, drinking himself to death – what? At this moment in time, I do not know. I tell him I love him and that he must go back to where he is supposed to be, to rest and be healed.

I have begun to sort out Steven's affairs and the sadness of it chokes me. I rummage through his papers. I find a heart-breaking mixture of old birthday cards, photos and poems. I sort out the legal stuff first and am relieved that I find his decree absolute, dated as late as 22nd September 2010. We currently do not need probate because of the lack of value of his estate and neither of his wills that I find are valid. I do open the letter that he left to go with his will. I am once again destroyed by tears and the lost potential of a beautiful soul, my son.

If you are reading this, it is because I am dead. Please do not see this as a negative thing I'm no longer in pain.

I don't know how death occurred at the point of writing this. I may have died of natural causes, I may have had an accident, I may have drunk myself to death, or I may have committed suicide.

Whatever the cause, don't upset yourselves because I don't (did not) value life in the slightest. If I was murdered, they have done me a favour, unless I suffered a painful death or was tortured in which case screw the bugger(s) to the wall if you so please.

I wanted to make sure that after my passing my thoughts on existence and my life would be known. I have spoken these words whilst alive, but I don't think anyone ever really listened because they either did not believe me or did not want to.

Since I was 9, I started realising that this planet isn't a very nice place to be, to put it mildly. By my early teens my experiences of humanity only confirmed that I was right to be ashamed to be part of it. It's no one specific person's fault (though there are many who were, and almost certainly still are, particularly unpleasant).

Bearing in mind that death is inevitable for all of us; it doesn't really matter when it occurs, more how it occurs. I'm scared of pain (life), but I'm not scared of death in the least.

Anyway, I know the coroner and consultant psychiatrist will be having a fucking field day with this by now, the toe tag will have some insane legend penned upon it assigning me with some mythical new illness (whichever vaguely accepted mental condition is in vogue just now, you know, whatever 'label' is drawing in the bucks at the moment).

Because death's so very serious and bad and nasty, isn't it? The inevitable scares the living shit out of some of you doesn't it? Why?

Let me make it clear; Life = pain. Death= freedom.

You work to live, and you live to work. Is it just me or does that sound just a bit like a waste of time?!

The only way I can think of explaining this: if you don't like life, the mental health 'authorities' will have you sectioned as a suicide risk because they don't understand that someone who doesn't want to live can be sane.

That's like having someone put away against their will because they don't like eating bananas despite the rest of you loving them!

I just don't fucking get it guys… surely, it's up to me to make the decision as to whether I choose to continue with this farce or otherwise?

I've felt like an old man for a lot of years. I was world-weary at 11. I'm totally fucking shattered now.

I apologise to my close friends if I've been a prick or seemed distant in the last few months/years… whatever… it wasn't your fault and I was probably far from ideal company, but I'd had enough of life and couldn't carry on with it. I love all my friends. And I appreciate everything you ever did for me. Your company was always appreciated.

There are individuals I particularly want to thank for their friendship and involvement in my life. But as there are so many I refuse to list them in case I forget to mention somebody. You know who you are in any case. I love you all…

Don't hate me for dying. It wasn't a dig at anyone. It wasn't for histrionic purposes (what good would that do me?) I don't even know how it has occurred at this point anyway. I might have been hit by a bus. If it was suicide, however, there was nothing 'selfish' about it. It is more 'selfish in my opinion, for a person to expect someone they care about to live through hell because that person can't cope with the idea of someone they know dying. WE'RE ALL GOING TO DIE, PEOPLE! Accept it. NOW! And we'll all be at peace when the gift of death takes away the pain.

There's no such thing as right or wrong.

It has become increasingly clear to me over the last few years that everything is relative. If it seems right to you it probably is. But others won't necessarily see it that way. Quite the philosopher at times, am I not? (ha fucking ha)?

I know few people will get what I'm saying. If you actually be YOURSELF, it all becomes clear. Falsities like 'society' and 'morals' and ingrained concepts are all guilty for making worse this bad deal we have known as 'life'. Did you ask to be born? I fucking didn't. It's the worst thing that could have happened to me. And if anyone is stupid enough to want to live, take my life. You're welcome to it. I don't want it and I don't need it. But then, if you're reading this I don't have it anyway…

I sincerely hope the rest of you recognise that the worst thing you can do is bring children into this world.

It's not fair to inflict this world on someone who hasn't asked for this painful farce known as life and it's not fair to inflict another human being on the world.

This is not an attack on my parents in any way. They weren't to know what I would think of this planet. But I do hope they know how much I loved them.

I can't stress enough: There's no right or wrong. There is no 'God'; there is no point or reason to life. It just happens.

I am glad to be deceased and whilst there is no heaven or eternal reward, there is no hell either. End of story.

If there was a 'God', he/she/it would be the cruellest and most despicable entity that had ever existed. Or just very, very stupid.

Anyway, it's too late to care now. I'm where I want to be. All there is left to do is to clarify my wishes regarding my remains.

I'm not an organ donor. Don't even think about it. Chances are there's nothing worth harvesting anyway. But if there is, tough fuck, you're not getting it.

I don't even want an autopsy if it can be avoided.

I'd like to be laid out somewhere for the maximum possible time before burial (doctors often make mistakes, believe me) and then I wish to be buried without ceremony and without a headstone, MOST IMPORTANTLY OF ALL in Un-consecrated ground.

There is to be NO RELIGIOUS BULLSHIT WHATSOEVER involved in my burial, and no funeral of the traditional kind. If I did have a headstone, the epitaph I would choose would likely be 'At last' or 'Thank fuck for that' or something else along those lines but I seem to feel that it would be frowned upon by the masses. The wake is up to you; just make sure that if you must have one, everyone gets suitably pickled.

Anyway, I've gone on long enough now and I can't think of anything else that needs saying without repeating myself and I think I've made most of the points I intended to make.

Just remember that I'm glad to be out of the rat race.

In closing I must reiterate my thanks to the many, many people who have loved me and been my friends throughout this awful thing known as life and who even, on occasions, actually made it seem vaguely tolerable for a short while.

I leave you with these words:

The only thing better than thinking outside the box Is ending up inside one without delay

May you all find true peace

Unless I didn't like you, in which case I'm only sorry there's no such place as hell... oh wait, there is, and it's called 'Earth' and I'll leave you to it.

Over and out

Steve

Well, there isn't much more to say about that is there? The letter is not dated but I do remember Steven handing it to me and asking me to keep it safe. And once again I sit and weep for what might have been.

My birthday is spent sharing a meal cooked by Ian with four friends. It is at this point that we give Kay and Rob the pick of Steven's remaining guitars. It just seems the right thing to do. Drew and Sindy have already chosen. We choose not to part with the infamous 'beer guitar'. This was Steven's first guitar, customised later with beer labels and it became the envy of many of his acquaintances.

I plod on with work and attend an awards ceremony with some of the students I have taught. Their group has also won an award and I am there to chaperone and enjoy the moment. Someone asks me how my son is, and I bluntly reply, "He died." She bursts into tears and I have empathy for her shock, but I am pissed off with the world. I don't have the resources today to comfort others.

November and December 2011

Mum says to me one evening "People are asking me how you are. I tell them you are bearing up." I mentally explore this connection. I gave birth to a son and 'bore down' to deliver him. Now I survive his death and 'bear up' to cope. I always did like words.

Just before Christmas 2011 I attend an event at work with one of my volunteers. She has become a friend, an older and wiser lady than me, who has also suffered bereavements. (Who hasn't?) She hands me an envelope and asks me not to open it until I get home. When I do open it, I am touched to find that she has written an eloquent poem about love and death and I cry again.

Work plods on and I am asked to help another worker with a Christmas event. Ian and I agree to help serve a Christmas dinner for about 40 people. I enjoy the hustle and bustle and we manage not to drop anything even though the plates are scorching our fingers. As we take a break the caterers discuss the choir they are in and begin to sing, we both join in, and snatches of various carols follow. I am delighted that my voice is passable in a group. We decide to serenade the oldies who have finished their lunches. They cheer us on and have a whip round! We plan for a better future as I take the number for the choir and promise to get in touch. Seven months on it is still a pipe dream. The event totally uplifts our spirits.

8th December

Too knackered to go to work today, cystitis or something nasty is brewing. I make my doctor's appointment before I make the breakfast. I reach for Steven's dairy free margarine from the fridge, as we have no butter. I am disappointed to find that it is almost empty. Something more of everyday Steven is melting away. I notice that the best before date on the tub is his December birthday, one that he will not be celebrating. These are the everyday things that twist my guts painfully.

I bury my face in Steven's grey woollen coat. He wore it on the days he was able to pop around to the shops. Surprisingly it smells only of clean wool and I am disappointed. Only the feel of the fabric is familiar. No other sense of him remains. I place it in the charity bag where it sits for a long time.

Steven's room does still hold a memorable fragrance. Sitting snugly in a brightly coloured tin decorated with yellow and black flowers and birds, is his favourite candle, given to him by his grandmother, my mum. I light it regularly. In the week before Christmas it burns away to emptiness and the fragrance begins to fade. I feel sad as I lose something more of how things used to be.

I write a personal letter to Prof C and ask for access to Steven's medical records. I state that I need the information purely to put a time line and a framework to Steven's book, assist my recall and give some background to Steven's illness. I have obtained permission to examine Steven's other medical records. My GP facilitates this at our surgery and I am allowed to take notes and pull out papers for photocopying. My initial aim is to put a structure around Steven's book, filling in dates and hospital visits and admissions. I reflect further. I need to understand how our family came to this place of fractured potential and bitter loss. I am treated with quiet sensitivity and given coffee and cake. I sit for over 4 hours and am overwhelmed by the story only partly told in Steven's notes. I am heavy with sadness when I leave. What a mess! What a waste! I take a couple of visits to wade through all the folded papers and I am treated with quiet respect.

I am overwhelmed by catastrophes, missed opportunities and some misinformation that doesn't help Steven's cause. He has certainly refused to accept some services and help, but many opportunities to help him have been missed by the powers that be. I need someone to explain to me why information from the neurological specialist Dr LF was not passed on to Steven. Could it be that it initially went to the wrong surgery as Steve had moved to a new address at the time and when it was forwarded it was just filed? I believe that if the information had been shared with Steven and us, he might have been able to realise the dire situation he was in due to alcohol. I am also curious about a letter received from the Mental Health Team about a 'contentious' meeting that we attended. It has been written on by hand and then had that writing blacked out.

Unknown date

I wake suddenly, and irritably turn over in bed to ease my discomfort. I am further irritated by Ian lurking in the shadow of my wardrobe in the far corner of the room. "What are you doing over there? For God's sake get sorted out and let me get back to sleep." I am puzzled as to why Ian is standing so still and silent in the corner – what on earth is he doing? I turn away as I try to make sense of his actions, or lack of them and bring my sleep filled senses into focus. I hear the splash and dabble of a shaving brush in the bathroom basin, he's having a wash. I turn over again to stare at the figure in the corner. It is tall, gaunt, shoulders bowed, but now unmistakeably Steven. Unlooked for, unbidden, and standing silently in the corner looking straight at me. He has not appeared to me well, or happy or healthy or like an Angel, but as he was in the last weeks of his life. I am perturbed at this lack of wellness. I talk to him. "Why are you here pet? You should be away being looked after, being healed. There's no need to hang around Steven we'll be alright. Off you go now Sweetie. Thank you for trying. Go and have the rest you need. We love you."

The shadow melts quickly away.

Christmas is fast approaching along with all the emotional baggage which that entails. As I write out my Christmas cards I enclose a note about Steven. I realise that it will dampen some peoples' sense of holiday, but I don't know how else to do it that is manageable for me. This elicits several enquiring phone calls from distant friends and relations which I cope with quite well.

One of Steven's special friends Neil calls and he reminisces with us about school days and Steven's eccentricities. He reminds us of the time that Steven took home his teacher's clock and fixed it aged just 6. Later that week we have a visit from Simon and his dad and once again the talk is about Steven. It is a challenging time as Christmas day is Ian's birthday and Steven would have been 32 two days later.

We spend Christmas Eve with the youngsters next door. After admiring the beautifully set table, ready for Christmas dinner tomorrow, I drink most of their gin. We are shown a video clip on the young man's mobile. We are both overwhelmed and pleased to see Steven showing off his studio and playing guitar and keyboard. This was filmed last Christmas (2010) and I am surprised that it has been kept on a phone for so long. "I show it to all my friends. Steve's amazing!" The pictures and sound move me to tears. We are promised a copy as soon as he can work out how to move it from his mobile.

We spend Christmas day alone after checking on my mum and on Ian's dad by phone. We can't face other people's emotional baggage and the day is subdued but peaceful. Ian's dad visits on Boxing Day and we share a meal. Nothing much is said about anything.

We have invited friends and visitors for Steven's birthday and a few call in but it is never going to be the same as the noisy house parties of the past. All is changed. I become quite tearful as people drift away. The celebratory firework for the time of Steven's birth at 3 minutes past 9 in the evening makes a poor show and I cry even more.

The next day I am completely knackered and give in. The rest does me good and on the 29th I begin clearing books and CDs as I look for the rest of his music. It really pains me to put more than 60 VHS videos recorded from the TV in to sacks. There is comedy and films and lots more. I put them on Freecycle as reusable. Because they are 'pirated' I can't sell or give them away or take them to the charity shop. The young man next door decides that he would like them and they find a good home.

I find Steven's mini-discs, surprisingly few, and worry because I can't locate his own CDs which I have put away somewhere safe. It is important that I gather all of his compositions together and keep them safe.

I lie awake in the early hours and my loss is upon me. I try to remember if I have any personal notes from Steven. I am one of those sad people who don't easily hold on to cards and letters. I keep them for a while and then they are purged. I am so very sad that I no longer have a particularly loving Mother's Day card sent to me by Steven. I had kept it for more than 3 years, but then it was ousted. I wish I had it now, just to see his writing, and the words written especially for me.

I am also responsible for throwing out cards written to Ian and I am full of regret.

In the afternoon I speak to our GP about joining the Mental Health Working Group. Will I be of any use? The information seems complicated and over my head. I tell him that I don't want to be dead wood, and that there is a danger that I will bring my baggage with me. He reassures me that my input will be welcomed and that I will bring experience as a Carer. We shall see!

New Year's Eve 2011

We spend the evening next door with the youngsters and their families. I take food and booze and feel awkward even though we are made welcome. I am pleased when I am introduced to some people I know, and I have a good gossip, politely skirting around the subject of Steven's demise. We return home, all of 10 yards, about 12.30 am. I have set out the 'mouse man' table with a Christmas cloth and a bottle of good Jamieson's whiskey. The glasses are Steven's, given to him from his granddad Ed. They are very heavy cut glass. A candle is lit beside his photo. It all looks a bit cheesy and it makes me tearful. We give an emotional toast in his memory and it is all a bit flat and sad. I do not enjoy the whiskey. Steven is not here with us to welcome the coming of a new year and the finality of his death is etching ever more deeply into my heart.

January 2012

New Year's Day is spent quietly. I feel ill and out of sorts and all I manage to achieve is to cook dinner. Ian and I take a plate to my mum at tea time. The day fades into nothingness. The following day we go shopping, just for the sake of getting out of the house. I buy nuts and seeds and health food supplements, hoping for a disciplined start to the New Year. Discipline will be needed as I discover that I have bloomed in weight and need bigger clothes. Ian is experienced in sourcing the right shaped tops and the correct length trousers for me and I come away with a new collection of clothes which fit. He would make a very good personal shopper.

I attend the Mental Health Task Group meeting on 4th January. I meet a couple of people that I know, and I can contribute to the discussion. It centres on the plan to involve mentally ill people with 'social prescribing'. This is about involving people in local activities, classes and hobbies so that they increase in confidence, are not so isolated and get involved within the local community. A health link worker will have the job of supporting people by linking them into activities within the community. Whilst I support the plan I wonder how this will benefit people who have a long term severe illness, lack the skills and confidence to engage with others and they need more than information and signposting. Steven would certainly have benefited from a 'buddy' system to get him out of the house. He needed someone he could build a long term and trusting relationship with, who would support him in social activities and stave off the profound loneliness and isolation that we knew he experienced. This type of service was never offered to Steven and we were unable to find a service provider who could help us. A regular visit from a CPN does not get you out of the house or necessarily help prevent loneliness. And when the visits stop because you are deemed not to need them anymore, nothing else is put in place. I hope to be able to continue in this group, but will have to see how open-minded my employers will be. It will mean unpaid time off work and I don't know if I can afford this.

The next day I have a very welcome physio session. My therapist queries the state of my lower spine. I can feel no discomfort whatsoever until she touches me. Survival demands that you numb out the most severe pain and keep on going. Now that I am no longer afraid for my son, the pigeons are coming home to roost and I am becoming physically aware of the tension and damage in my back. The focus of my awareness is my neck and cervical spine. The pain and lack of mobility is constant, and I realise that this increased soon after Steven's death. I reckon it was always like that and now I must deal with it.

We have company that evening, and I enjoy a couple of drinks, three chocolates and lots of conversation. In the night I am troubled with stomach cramps and only just make it to the toilet. My bowel is once again protesting about something and I sit in the cold for nearly an hour. I return to bed, reflecting on the confirmation that long term stress wrecks the digestive system as well as the immune system. Maybe it was the physio session, or maybe the chocolate, but it's just another pointer to remind me that I must pay real attention to my health and habits. Ian and I have agreed that we will make up for lost time and opportunities in relation to our marriage and I want to be well enough to get the best out of these.

Saturday 7th

I call on mum late in the afternoon. As usual I find something for her tea, see to her medication, switch the TV socket on, and undo the milk bottle and her squash bottle. I empty the dryer, fold clothes and chat to her while she eats. After washing up and seeing she is settled I realise I do not need to rush home. Ian has gone to the pub and I am a free agent! Not used to that at all.

I decide to visit a long term friend. We have wine and a coffee and enjoy the chat. I ask her husband, an experienced musician about getting Steven's albums reproduced. He reminds me that they will need remastering and the sound sorting out. I take secret pride in telling him that it is not needed because Steven had already done it himself. I realise that not many people know of Steven's skill with a sound desk and mixer. I decide now is a good time to leave.

The sodium street lights cause my pupils to 'pop' and the cold wind numbs my face and thinking. My booted footfalls match my heart rhythm, beating into my skull, echoing my persistent feeling of loss. Steven will not be at home to greet me. Kia cat acknowledges my arrival and demands a touch, pinning my knee with her claws. Just me and the cats then until Ian returns from the pub.

Monday 9th

Four months since Steven died. Back to work today after my break. Although I would rather lie and doze, I am up before 6.00am. Sleep is always sporadic. The time I get out of bed is unimportant, only the number of hours that I manage to keep my eyes closed matters. I rarely achieve more than 2 hours at a time. This is the result of a mother listening out for a son, a carer for their charge, plus the hormonal chaos of long term stress and the menopause. All have taken their toll on normality and circadian rhythms.

Work is undemanding, nothing urgent, but by the end of the day I am weary. On the journey home, in the frosty dark, I am held up by an accident. Blue lights flash on both sides of the road as two vehicles await recovery. I wait patiently, without upset, until I pass between the flashing lights, waved on by yellow coated police. A sudden surge of adrenalin flashes anxious thoughts of Steven through my brain. For that split second, I forget that he is dead. In almost the same instant I recall the bitter fact. Anxiety tightens my belly and throat. The association of pulsing blue lights, ambulances and yellow reflective jackets has triggered a stress response in my brain; Steven is ill and in trouble once again. As I calm down and settle, I acknowledge that my son will now never be 'at risk', and my anxiety drains away, leaving a void where it usually sits.

Saturday 14th

I have arranged for Bob to visit and service the Hammond and the Leslie. I set off to pick him up at the bus station and I play a tape of Steven's in the car. The lyrics really begin to mean something – reflecting Steven's struggle with life, black and gloomy but meaningful. How come I didn't notice it before? I am late picking in Bob up as the traffic is horrible as usual.

At home after coffee and biscuits Bob sets to work. Ian helps him move and open the Hammond and he gets to work. The woodwork is full of cobwebs, dust and mouse droppings. I remember that the cats spent a recent summer bringing us live mice. After much chasing about and rescuing chewed up objects, we installed humane traps. It took us 2 months to remove the mouse family who had set up home under the stairs. The memory makes me smile as I recall Steven chasing around the house with two wine glasses and successfully capturing and removing little furry creatures.

As Bob works, I busy myself cooking curried lamb with apricots and onions, a favourite of mine. It is strange hearing the notes of the organ again. The sound is so rich, strong and vibrant – I realise how much I have missed it and how much I miss Steven. Bob chats away as he works, telling me anecdotes about organs and his life. I learn why Hammonds must be lubricated with light oil. Ordinary lubricating oil contains lanolin which will dry out and gum up the delicate works and wreck the instrument. On Bob's instruction Ian had gone in search of clock oil the previous day. Apparently the £5 bottle is enough to last a clock repairer many months. I also learn that Mr Hammond originally made clocks. Bob moves on to the wooden Leslie speaker and tells me that the rubber seal from a Federation Ales beer barrel perfectly fits and replaces the seal on the slow speed wheel of the speaker. What a great fact for a pub quiz!

I sit with Bob and have a cup of tea. We chat about music and loss and his varied career – a chemist, a sound engineer, a musician, an IT specialist and lots more. Unfortunately, that means the curry is well and truly burned and we are forced to have Co-op chicken pie and chips. I take Bob back to the bus station and then visit mum to settle her for the evening.

After talking it over with Ian I put the Hammond and Leslie on to eBay. I am grateful and moved when I find the right photos on Steven's computer. He has kept a good record of his beloved instruments. The organ was purchased on 13th April 1996 for the huge sum of £565. The listing provokes a lot of interest and questions and I am kept busy for the next 10 days answering queries. Over the next months I get an adrenalin rush by listing the rest of his vintage musical equipment on eBay. Steven would have enjoyed the fuss.

Friday 21st

I have a really busy day at work and have to catch up on the work that my colleague was unable to complete and I work flat out. This makes me feel resentful and hard done by – not nice! I moan to another colleague about the situation and then immediately regret it. Should have kept my mouth shut. I'm too knackered to call at mums. Go to bed early but IBS kicks in and I vomit as well. That will teach me to try and unwind with a glass of wine! I take an Amitriptyline tablet in desperation. I am restless until about 3.00am and then sleep until 9.00am. Brilliant! Unfortunately, it buggers me up for the rest of the day although I have less pain. I don't make it to mum's and arrange with her that I will have a proper visit on Sunday afternoon.

In the evening I note that there are 96 'watchers' interested in the instrument and the price at auction is rising nicely. As I check my eBay I am idly amending my mobile phone saved numbers. I delete the ones for the mental health Crisis Team, Rethink advocacy, and the ward where Steven spent quite a bit of time. I cannot yet delete Steven's mobile from the list. Maybe I am expecting him to call from beyond, who knows?

Drew and Sindy call for a visit, parking their little camper van 'Gomez' outside the house. Drew and Ian go upstairs to catalogue Steven's musical equipment against the list of gear I have located from Steven's laptop. Sindy and I go to the Co-op. I am too tired to do a big shop and we have nothing much in. We buy cream cakes to have with a coffee – very extravagant.

I am bombarded for the next couple of days by queries from Hammond fanatics, desperate to own Steven's set. I am really fed up with being asked questions that I can't answer. I have to do a lot of research to earn the selling fee. I discover that pre-1960's models had felt under the keys and after that foam. The felt hardens and cracks, spoiling the instrument. I am relieved that ours seems to have foam. Apparently, a plus point when selling. A battle ensues between Holland and Italy and Italy wins. Luckily the buyer seems to have his own British carrier, and after receiving payment Ian contacts the carrier to discuss collection. "Make sure you get paid, I've 13 of his organs sat in my warehouse." An obsessional collector it seems.

Saturday 28th

I sleep late after medication, great not to remember tossing and turning all night. Stagger downstairs for toast, tea and a cuddle from Ian. I spend the day trying to put sensible prices on Steven's music stuff. I have to call Drew to find out what a MuTron Phasor actually does. He tells me not to worry – that anyone who deserves it will not need to know that. I search the web for information and make a stab at a reasonable price. It is draining, depressing and somehow addictive. I ask Ian why he doesn't help with this. He says it is because he doesn't know how to. I don't really believe him. By 6.00 pm I have had enough. My feet are freezing, and my mouth is dry, and I am troubled with my guts again. Time for a cup of tea or maybe even a whiskey?

The money from the Hammond will go towards the funeral costs, rather ironic but fitting. It is somehow shaming to have paid on a credit card because you have no other means.

I investigate accessing Steven's mental health records and am amazed to find that I need letters of administration or probate. Legally we do not need these as his estate was of low value. So, we have to jump through some more hoops just to get access. Apparently if we had been named in a valid will we would have been given access straight away. This irritates me tremendously. I need the records to put a structure onto his story and find out where he missed opportunities to progress. We complete the paperwork at the end of January. I have to look for Steven's decree absolute to go with the application. I am so glad that he was no longer married to Eve. I wonder if she even knows he's dead? What does it matter? She wished it on him many a time. A financial statement and the Coroner's notification of death are included and then we must wait.

February 2012

I observe myself in the mirror dispassionately. Around my neck is the pentagram that Steven valued so highly. Behind me the archway into the dining room is illuminated, and the brightness seems to fix on Steven's picture, lighting it up. The dark green leaves of our ancient peace lily drape themselves protectively around the top of it. Steven looks at me, and I look at him. We know each other. I hold my whiskey glass. He sees it. He knows that I know. He took delivery of 8 cases of wine between the 22nd July and 2nd September 2011. Believing that there was no way forward except to linger a bit longer and then die of liver disease, painfully and without hope of recovery, he made a decision. The drink was killing him even when he was dry, the damage too far gone. No way forwards, no redemption, no going back. Two bottles a day, hidden because of guilt and shame. Deceiving us, so we didn't get upset and give him more grief. I imagine that he was drowning in guilt and grief and despair. "What the fuck, if the drink is killing me then let's get on with it." I wonder if the Coroner will work that one out, or if he will literally let it lie.

I raise my glass towards Steven's knowing gaze. And we forgive each other and ourselves. Ian cannot, he blames himself.

Thursday 16th

I have my breasts scanned today. I am off work for 2 days and I am exhausted. What was happening 2 years ago when I last had this done? Steven was ill in bed and needed hospitalisation but wouldn't entertain the idea. Am I more stressed or less? It is grief that fills that space now.

I am having flashbacks of Steven lying on the bathroom floor. They do not panic me, but it makes me so sad. I am sure I heard him call out and that I heard him die. Why didn't I get up? Would it have helped to save his life? I feel distanced from Ian and this worries me. I am fat, complaining and ill. Why would he still want to be with me?

Tuesday 21st

The journey from work is non eventful, but as I make the turn towards my garage, I can see the upstairs windows of our house at the bottom of the road, caught in my headlights. The lights bounce off the front porch and illuminate for a moment the landing window. I expect to see Steven's silhouette against the interior waiting for me. Of course, he is no longer there. Saddened with remembrance, tears painfully prick my eyes.

The inquest takes place in 2 days' time and the undercurrent of tension between Ian and I is palpable and uncomfortable. I make no comment at the bottle of whiskey brought in by Ian with the weekly shop. He is tense and irritable and spoiling for a fight. I ask him to help me find a power adapter that belongs to some musical equipment that I have sold to a work colleague. "I'll get it for you later." And later – "Did you find it?" "It can wait I'll bring it in on Friday." "Why should it wait? I'll get it." I place the item in my work bag and Ian explodes with irritation. "You just couldn't leave it could you? I said I would bring it on Friday. He doesn't need it anyway!" "How can you say that Ian you don't know that!" He sulks and fumes for quite a while. A pointless exchange of words but he is obviously wound up about Steven and the inquest.

Last week he asked me to order him a new waistcoat. He intends to wear it with his suit at the inquest. 'Why do you need a waistcoat?' I ask. "I just do" he replies.

The suit had its last airing at Steven's funeral. The occasion of the inquest feels worse to me. The process is unfamiliar and threatening.

I wake after a particularly vivid dream. Just out of my line of vision, Steven is walking quickly ahead of me. I can see myself struggling to keep up, my head down. '"Slow down Steven." As I bring my head up I observe that we are on a path through a graveyard. "Slow down Steven, I can't catch up, you are going too fast." "Hurry up mam. I've got to be somewhere" and he walks briskly away, fading into my right peripheral vision. "Steven!" I call, "I'm losing you!" Well, you don't need a therapist, a dream manual or a qualification in Bereavement Care to work that one out, do you?

As usual I have woken up knackered. My sleep was fitful, restless, hot and not refreshing so nothing new there then. My guts are living on a different planet to my current time line. I sit in my dressing gown on the toilet knowing that I am already late for work. To hell with it, why am I struggling on? I phone in sick and go back to bed. I sleep for 4 hours. The next day follows the same pattern except I stir myself to check on my mum. "I think the fridge needs a tidy up Clare." I throw out mouldy cheese, a plastic box of cooked beetroot with thick grey mould rampaging inside, and deliver three disintegrating tomatoes to the dustbin. There isn't much edible left, but I salvage something for her tea, knowing that her shopping will be done tomorrow.

The following day is a bright crisp morning with the sun glaring through my windscreen as I set off for work. This irritates me, and I become even more annoyed as Steven pops in to my head. "I can't think about you all the time Steven! You chose to drink and wanted to die. Well, you got what you wanted and I'm still here to get on with it." A tiny ripple of relief registers before I push it down and hunt for my sunglasses. They are not mine, they are Steven's favourites. They are the ones we chose for him to wear when he when he was laid out, and no, I haven't felt the need to wash them. They give me comfort. The plastic frames have absorbed the gentle familiar fragrance of his bedroom. He kept them in the same drawer as his oils and incense. I focus on the aroma, searching for it and remember Steven in his bright sunny room. Sunglasses are good – no one can see you cry.

A work colleague sneaks me a small chocolate bar to brighten up a tedious day. I open my hand slowly to reveal a miniature bar of Cadbury's Fudge in its bright orange wrapper. Instantly my brain is singing the jingle 'a finger of fudge is just enough.......' and I giggle. Steven and I created a very rude alternative and now it is uppermost in my mind. I can see him rolling about with laughter, the wicked glee of being 'naughty' all that is needed in that moment. And the thought of 'that moment' fills me with a painful joy at being able to remember and still feel the loss of him.

Wednesday 22nd

I have not had any antidepressants for 4 days now, and last night I slept for 6 hours - a record this year. I am up at 6.00am and sit in my dressing gown scribbling words as I drink my tea. Kia cat exchanges cuddles with me and then goes back to sleep beside me. Her feet and tail are all tucked up tight and secure, awaiting the sunshine to warm her delicate bones. Chilled, I reach for my fresh mug of tea.

Thursday 23rd

The day of the inquest finally arrives. I have a consultation event for work in the morning, but I am glad to leave it in the hands of a colleague and rush off home. I strip off and prepare myself. An inquest demands appropriate attire. If Ian thinks he needs to wear a waistcoat with his suit, then I can at least find a skirt and stockings to fit the bill. After much rifling through clothes I settle on an outfit and we gather ourselves together. I use my Rescue Remedy drops but Ian rejects them. I feel dizzy on the short journey to the Coroner's Court and am relieved when we arrive a little early. We are escorted in and taken through security by an androgynous and pleasant person in a simple uniform. We are lead to a small waiting area with very tired chairs. They serve their purpose.

We flick through the magazines and try not to watch the clock. I am grateful to find a current edition of Gardeners' World which distracts me for a while. At 2.25pm, and 15 minutes late, we are escorted into an empty courtroom. The policewoman who attended at our home is present, having been kept separate from us, and is unrecognisable in her civvies. The room is large and well ventilated, with a pleasant temperature and unobtrusive air conditioning. It is typically late 50's early 60's and has glorious red leather seats set out like a cinema. They are the most comfortable seats that I have ever sat in. The aroma of wood and lavender polish, akin to a country house, is very pleasant. I feel safe and calm and would like to sit here in peace all day.

The three of us stand on the instruction of the clerk of the court as the Coroner enters. He instructs us to sit and I appreciate immediately his calm yet detached manner. The policewoman is called first and says not a lot, other than that foul play was not apparent or looked for. Ian is called. I find it hard not to join in and twice I ask for permission to interject. Permission given, I add my piece in support of his answers. I am really annoyed when the Coroner mentions a previous diagnosis of Asperger's (given when Steven was about 15). I am somewhat mollified when he also mentions a current diagnosis of bipolar. Evidence has been gathered from Prof B and our GP, the police woman and Ian and I feel left out.

The Coroner is calm, authoritative and measured in his enquiries. I call him 'Sir' when I ask permission to speak – Ian has turned towards me for clarification of a point. We have no dispute in accepting the verdict that alcoholic poisoning is what killed Steven on the day. Ian does not have an issue with the verdict of 'Misadventure' - what else can it be without other proof? But my intuition is telling me otherwise and I am at odds with him in my theory that Steven may well have taken his own life. He knew that if he increased his drinking he would die. I believe that he did this when he became aware of the degree of damage to his liver – no cure and no going back. But there is no proof, so misadventure it is. Why do I feel angry at the verdict?

Over the next few days I am unwell. I sleep badly, have IBS and vomit, pick fights, drink alcohol, reject love making, buy clothes and wander the shops in search of an electric tin opener for my mother. We also visit the records office to research my family tree. Not much point though when you are never going to have any grandchildren and probably just as well when I read the newspaper transcripts of the trial of my great grandmother for the murder of my paternal great grandfather. She is declared criminally insane and spends the rest of her long life in mental hospitals. I remind myself that genetics are thought to play a part in some mental health conditions.

Ian takes Steven's brand new Blackberry phone in to a shop to sell it. I wait outside in a strop. We are having real difficulty talking to each other and I am in a foul mood. He comes out of the shop with a decent price and I look him in the eye. I put my arms around him, and he says, "Shall we start again?" The truce is sealed with a cup of hot chocolate in a nearby café.

The weekend is a little better – I try to do nothing but it doesn't work. Monday is busy at work and I also have to sort out the doctor and dentist for mum. She has finally realised that she is getting the run-around from the NHS and has agreed to let me do something about it. She has been receiving treatment and appointments from a myriad of specialists over a period of 2 years. She can't chew or swallow without pain and she is very breathless as soon as she moves. This is from a thyroid goitre which is slowly enlarging its stranglehold on my mother's neck. After a few phone calls to the Patient Experience team I am in touch with a specialist who is prepared to try and help improve my mother's quality of life. Within two weeks of the first phone call mum is called in to discuss radioactive Iodine treatment. Four weeks later she receives her pill. She was first offered this a year ago and then it was withdrawn as an option. When I query this, I am told it is because they had to ensure that mum did not have any other heart or lung problems. There is silence when I ask if this would normally take twelve months.

The Hammond Organ and Leslie speaker are finally collected on Monday night 27th February and it feels like another bereavement. Realistically, it is losing Steven all over again. The Hammond epitomised his skills. Rescued from the back room of a working men's club in 1996, Steven had restored it to fine working condition. We had fallen in love with it and it is part of the family. It had returned to fill our hall when Steven's first marriage ended in 2001 and he had left it with us for safety's sake during his other relationships, not wishing any harm to come to it.

The carrier is 'Mr. Phil,' a pleasant man wearing a proper blue trades' apron. Ian chats with him as they decide the best way to move the beast. "This will end up sitting with the others until he pays me for the carriage." Apparently the purchaser is an Italian dealer and he has approximately 13 Hammonds waiting to be shipped from Mr. Phil's warehouse. The organ is lifted and skilfully eased through the door frames with the help of a thick magazine lodged between it and each of the two frames. It is carefully worked through the tight gap with this aid. What a trick – no damage to its beautiful dark oak or to our tatty chipped frames. Evidence there from when it came in, that we did not have that knowledge.

The hall is huge and empty and echoing, like in an empty house and I begin to cry. Ian hugs me and we begin to clean up. I gather up the resident spider and tell her she is moving home – either that or certain death inside the vacuum cleaner. After putting her in the porch, we sweep up the dust and cobwebs and then stand hand in hand, gazing at the space. This is our house as we haven't seen it in about 12 years. I cry again for all that has gone. The space here is as unfamiliar as our life together now. Time to wash the dust away. We make love that night for the first time in weeks.

I have attended our local Mental Health Task Group again in the hope that as a lay person I will do some good. I find the discussions a bit complicated as I am still not clear what the group does. The local Primary Care Trust has allocated funding to produce a set of very good booklets about common mental health conditions. These have previously been used by me in my therapy work. I support the move to spend money to republish them with updated information.

There is a discussion around the table about what extra information could be usefully added. One practising GP suggests that the contact phone number of the Mental Health Crisis Team should be used. I am shocked! He obviously has no understanding of how the team works or how they are accessed. I wait for someone from the eminent gathering to comment. Nothing happens so I say my piece. I explain that this number is absolutely no use to someone with a mental health illness unless they are 'in the system' and have a CPN. You can only access this emergency service via your GP or in your personal care plan if indicated.

I am further shocked when my comments get a response from the guy who manages the Crisis Team. It seems that there are only two professionals in the team for the whole Mental Health area. No wonder they don't have the capacity to turn up when needed! Everyone around the table is paying careful attention and I am dismayed when I realise that I probably know how it works better than most of them.

I meet with a professional colleague later and we discuss the Mental Health Working Group meeting that we have both attended. I share my shock and disappointment with her that at least one of the GPs still did not understand what the Crisis Team do. If GPs don't know how the system works, what hope is there for the rest of us?

March 2012

Spring is coming. I gaze out of the landing window at the newly leafed greenness showing on the trees. A young boy strides proudly past on the pavement below with his two dogs – a wire haired pointer and a tiny dark, rough coated terrier. The boy looks about 9 or 10 yet he is handling the dogs with confidence and skill. I wonder who taught him about dogs? Maybe his dad goes shooting? I am moved to tears by his bright happiness and obvious pride in his dogs. I have lost so much.

Thinking so much of Steven this morning and the sadness is paralysing. I go back to the moment when I reminded him that he didn't have to be in pain. Is that when he decided to numb it all out with Tesco's special offer deliver to the door wine? How numb did he want to be? Did he drink it down in the full knowledge that the booze would end his life, or was he seeking oblivion for one night only?

Tuesday 6th

The Coroners' letter has arrived (in triplicate) stating that Steven had a lethal amount of alcohol in his blood. I am saddened further by the information – the primary cause of death is alcohol poisoning, secondary is end stage alcoholic liver disease and the verdict is misadventure. Although forewarned, we are devastated and ashamed for him, but not of him. The words of his GP sound in my head: "We didn't expect him to die."

Steven's bipolar illness was heart breaking, but honest. His alcoholism is more difficult to accept. It was shaming and insidious. When will society accept that alcoholism is an illness and not a moral failing? He realised his mistake early in the process, but by then his liver was already damaged, and he believed it was beyond redemption.

He took a way out that we wouldn't necessarily spot; the heavy consistent consumption of good quality wine. Only the best for Steven. He was well aware that his system would collapse. I don't believe that it was misadventure, it was suicidal despair.

Ian is gutted that no one medical professional had the courage or decency to tell us that Steven had end stage alcoholic liver disease. We both knew that his liver was affected but not that he was dying. We had no specific support or information given to us in relation to his care, or advice on how to alleviate the pain that he must have been feeling. Has Steven been given this information in plain language at any time? He never mentioned this to us if he knew. The emphasis from the medical professionals who talked to us was always on Steven's blood counts and the risk of bleeding or stroke. Ian and I knew that Steven's condition was serious and life threatening, but that is because we are intelligent people. No one advised us how to specifically help our son. Did they assume that we knew what to do because we had previously made a good job of rescuing him from tight corners? Or did they leave us to get on with it because they had given up and it was the easiest thing to do. A hopeless case and a mad bad patient.

Thursday 8th

I get up early, my sleep again disturbed by pain, soaking sweats and persistent thoughts of Steven. Yesterday, I received a thoughtful and measured letter from Prof C, Steven's private psychiatrist. He has agreed to allow me to meet with him to discuss this book. I am moved by the sensitivity of his letter, he has pitched it exactly right. It is the first and only letter of condolence that I have had from any of the professionals dealing with Steven's mental health. He cautions me against taking on too much. I have already acknowledged to myself that 'campaigning' is a part of the grieving process and must be handled carefully, rather like leashing and muzzling a fierce dog.

Tuesday 27th

The day of our appointment with the probate office arrives. I have missed breakfast because I can't eat. Work is okay, but my manager is late for our meeting and I know that I will not get my lunch before I need to leave. Serves me right for not giving her my updated diary! Missed and rushed meals are a 'no-no' for stress and IBS. The meeting is productive, but I have 10 minutes before Ian is due to collect me. I try to eat rice cakes and some soup but choke on my irritation. Ian arrives, and we leave in bright brittle sunshine. It is a spring day full of rare warmth and of hope – a day to run away into the wild blue yonder and start a new life, leaving old cares and worries behind. We find our way and the parking angels give us the one spot we need, taking the anxiety out of the situation. The court building is modern, and we are checked through by two jolly older men who do not seem to fit the job description of security guards.

We approach a window labelled Probate and hope that we have arrived in time. The paperwork has warned us in legal terminology that we will be severely penalised if we are late and will be turned away. The guy at the window does not give us eye contact or ask our names. I introduce myself and volunteer the information and he swiftly and efficiently checks identification. He does not say our names or even good morning. Is he legally allowed to assume that because we have provided the paperwork that we are the people it refers to? He has Steven's file to hand and we wait to be directed to a seat to finish the process.

I pause for thought – Steven's legal entity as a person has been reduced to a file of paperwork. Nothing else of him exists. He is becoming deader and more distant with each process we go through. The guy in the window asks for the new death certificate that gives cause of death. Dismay sets in as we realise we have forgotten it. "You can post it." "Do we need a reference?" "No, it's got his name on it hasn't it?" Well let's hope there is still just the one Steven then.

We wait for something more to happen and realise we are not going to be offered a chair, meet with anyone else or be interviewed as advised in the paperwork. We stand at the window and just watch as he shuffles the paperwork and completes his tick list. I can't even remember how the process ended now, but we are both shocked at the efficient and soulless way the process is completed. All in less than three minutes – this guy is really good at his job when it comes to time and motion.

We feel numb as we leave, and both agree that we expected more ceremony and respect to be embedded into the process. It seems that despite the dire legal warnings on the paperwork, that this is a dry civil process. It seems disrespectful to Steven in its cold efficiency. Maybe it's because he has no estate as such, no tax liability, no real legal need for letters of administration, that his paperwork has been dealt with in such a cavalier fashion. He is not important to anyone else but us, even as a dead person.

A few days later I apply for Steven's mental health records now held at a local hospital. I must send the recently acquired probate and evidence of his divorce.

It is the 31st March 2012 as I write these words from notes in my battered note book. I see a reference written at the same time as the notes 'The convergence of the twain' by Thomas Hardy. Steven has shared a poem with me about the sinking of the Titanic, and it is very nearly 100 years to the day. I have also been cleaning Steven's room today, and have removed a large number of books about the Titanic, ready for eBay. I wonder if the coincidence has any significance to this process I am going through.

At what point did Steven give up hope? There are several items in the studio still in their retail packaging. Items bought new with a purpose – to make music and record it. This is testament not to manic overspending but to creative purpose and intent. What was it that sapped his self-esteem and his energy? I can't agree with Dot from EastEnders who quoted: "Suffering produces endurance, endurance produces character, character produces hope."

I am cleaning in Steven's room again. Well, cleaning is probably not the correct word. I am sitting on the floor going through his remarkable music collection from ELO, the Doors, Tom Petty, Wilburys, George Harrison and so much more. The shelves and boxes are dressed with dust and cat hair and I carefully remove it. How long will it be before every physical part of Steven is gone?

We are watching John Bishop and his tremendous achievements for Sport Relief. He comes across as a caring family man and the shots of him with his sons are heart-warming. He says how much he loves his sons. Ian's face sags and crumples, "I miss my lad so much. Everyone says it but there are so many things I wish I had said to him." My eyes are streaming as I write this up. I suggest that he finds another way to say what he needs to say to Steven. He squeezes back his tears and mine trickle unbidden and unchecked. We both sit quietly staring at the TV. I get up to blow my nose as I can no longer breathe properly. Ian is sitting with his hand across his face. I reach for my pad and begin to write. "What are you writing?" "Thoughts" I reply.

I see a wonderful sunset on the drive home from work and I think of Steven and how much he would have appreciated it. "Good photo opportunity mam." When I get home, I realise that Ian is not well but he will not share it.

Thursday at work, a quote from a colleague that makes me smile - "Blessed are those who are cracked, for they are the ones who let in the light." Again Steven's struggle is to the forefront of my mind. I hear that his friend Rob is going to Agricultural College and I am thrilled to bits for him and feel very emotional. He has survived and will progress.
Hard luck Steven.

April 2012

I am late again, after another habitually restless night. I dash off to do a presentation about my work project and am amazed to be confronted by an audience of 84 people. I have to count them for monitoring purposes! They look at me expectantly, waiting to be entertained and informed. A true trouper, I take the microphone and on with the show.

I hurry back to the office to take part in our ISO audit which is very important to the organisation. Fortunately, all goes well, and as soon as I can, I leave work to meet mum at the doctors. Her blood sugar is sky high and she has been summoned to be sorted out. "Don't you come in with me" she orders. "Stay where you are!" She struggles, walking slowly with her stick into the consulting room and the door closes. Eventually she re-emerges desperate for a drink of water and to use the toilet. In her hand she clutches a prescription for insulin which will be administered by a daily visit from the District Nurse. Cream cakes and steroids have finally worked their wicked magic. I collect the prescription, settle her in and head home. I am pleasantly surprised that IBS medication is still effective when downed with a whiskey and lemonade.

I am in overload. Since taking the books from Steven's bedroom, the past two weeks have been crammed with news and documentaries about the 100th anniversary of the loss of the Titanic. Steam ships, particularly the Titanic, were one of Steven's passions. His knowledge of these was encyclopaedic and he collected and absorbed books, films and memorabilia. These were shared over many years with a particular friend. I have written to him and asked him to take the books, beautiful hard-backed reference books packed with pictures and stories. He has not responded in the past,

I hope he does now. I would hate the books to end up in the charity shop. That said, it is painful to be constantly bombarded with information which would have had Steven glued to the TV, arguing the toss over the veracity of any report. I miss his quick wit and his ability to absorb information, shuffling it quickly about to create measured and incisive comment. He was always a joy to converse with and our bickering would get on Ian's nerves. He is not a fan of noisy conversation.

Later that day the Songs of Praise programme of remembrance, marking the anniversary of the sinking, comes from a church in Belfast. The music is wonderful and I enjoy it all. Thoughts of Steven take up all my remaining head space. I empathise with all those people who were bereaved by the disaster and cry again.

Just like the Titanic, I am sinking. I have no emotional energy left and am physically going downhill fast. I have visited my GP. Crying in front of her has left me ashamed and desperate. I am weary of the 'brave face' and of 'bearing up well', I am not depressed, I am grieving. I have had over 18 years of juggling work, family, caring, trouble shooting, firefighting, battling for the survival of my marriage and my son. You cannot make the transition to a different world on three days compassionate leave. Every break or holiday since Steven's death has been taken up with the needs of other family members and Easter was the straw that broke the camel's back. I am tired, bone tired with no reserves to draw upon.

For the Bach people reading this I am using Oak, Olive, Star, Crab Apple, Walnut and Agrimony. I could have been signed off three days ago, but of course I have work that needs to be done. No one is indispensable, so I have agreed with my GP to see her next Monday morning and let her sign me off. Now I am worrying about what will happen if I am not available to facilitate the training course at work due in 10 days' time. I decide that I will take a week off and hope for the best, but it will not be enough. I have to do this to avoid collapsing with exhaustion. I hope my remedy will help me through. I have warned my manager that I am not well but I cannot bear to talk to her face to face. I am determined not to cry.

I end up taking nearly three weeks off. My GP and I decide what will go on my sick note. Even now, with all of my knowledge and experience I will not allow her to put 'stress'. I am ashamed that I can't carry on. We settle for IBS that well-known, stress-related condition that has incapacitated me frequently over these past months. My time is spent sleeping and sitting in the garden. When I feel well enough I frantically throw stuff out or shuffle it from room to room.

I don't tell my mum that I'm off work ill as I can't be doing with the fuss or the attention. She is also unwell and I do not think it will help the situation. During the time I am off I have to reorganise her care. Her social worker has increased her care hours and mum and I do our best to communicate with the manager of the Care Provider Company. She comes to visit, and I am dismayed at how unprepared she is. I have provided details of the care mum needs and worked out a weekly routine. She seems to have brought no information at all with her and we waste time going over old ground. I am hopeful that it will all sort itself out.

May 2012

The sound of the doorbell jolts me from sleep. Lurching upright with shock, I see that it is just after 3.30am. Ian stirs beside me and swears. Is it the police? Has something happened to my mum? I get up, grab my dressing gown and open the landing window. Laura, our elderly neighbour is standing at the door. Hunched is a better word – she walks with two sticks and has severe osteoporosis.

"What's the matter Laura?" "I've knocked my chair over and I can't get to sleep." I try to make sense of the statement as I go downstairs to unlock the door. She is unable to step over my threshold because of her disability and the fact that she is terrified of cats. "Where's your cat?" I ignore the enquiry. "Laura, what's the matter?" I am starting to get irritated. "I need someone to put my chair right, so I can go to sleep. It's tipped over." I still don't understand the connection, but I put my coat on and follow her along the street. I carefully lock Ian in before I leave.

Laura walks very slowly and with some difficulty, so I bypass her and enter the house. In the living room, her large easy chair is on its back. The contraption that raises its height, so she can get in and out of it, is dragged to one side. She tells me that she has caught hold of the back of the chair and it has tipped. I am at a loss as to how this could happen. On further interrogation she tells me that she has fallen and perhaps caught the back of the chair for support. After checking that she is not injured, I proceed to tell her off. "Why aren't you wearing your personal alarm? Why haven't you pressed your buzzer for help, instead of coming out in to the street in your night clothes? What if you couldn't get up or you were injured?"

Laura sleeps in her chair most nights. She can just about get into bed but she has such pain and difficulty getting out that she doesn't bother much. After struggling with the concertina contraption that raises her chair, I quickly realise that I can't reset it by myself so I press her alarm buzzer and ask for assistance. The woman that arrives efficiently stamps mud into the cream carpet, and looks as baffled as I am. Between us we struggle to lift the chair and manage to reseat the chair castors in to the raisers, but it still wobbles. We check that it cannot tip, instruct Laura that it will have to do, until the Occupational Therapist team can sort it out. My 'assistant' leaves.

I quiz Laura about her pain relief. "Oh, yes, it's due now." I have seen a bottle of Oramorph in the kitchen. After much faffing about Laura takes her medicine and I begin to settle her in her chair. I talk to her about getting some further help. It seems that she has been assessed for mobility but has no other help at all. No one has seemed to have mentioned social care or help towards living a more fulfilled life. Laura often wanders at night, not because she is senile, but because she has severe anxiety and cannot settle. She agrees to allow me to contact Social Services on her behalf for another assessment, and to ask the Occupational Therapist to come out and sort her chair. "Laura, you will have to lock the door after me." It is no good me putting the keys through the letter box as she can't bend to pick them up. She struggles back up from the chair with her sticks and sees me out. She is very apologetic about coming to my door.

I come back into my home and put the kettle on, all hope of sleep disappearing. I am wide awake and sweating profusely. I realise with dismay that this is the first night I have slept through until 3.30am in months, maybe years. Well, the doorbell and Laura's visit will have just told my brain that Clare doesn't do sleep, and will wake up in the night. I am really pissed off but I don't see how one can leave a neighbour in need on the doorstep. It is then that I remember that Laura was the neighbour who took Steven to hospital when he broke his fingers as a teenager.

We have a significant appointment later that day, 2nd May. Steven's private psychiatrist, Prof C, has agreed to meet with us locally. He has waived his charge other than the room rental. We take an unedited copy of Steven's book and ask if he will be involved with the story. I would like him to check out technical details etc. He cautions us about names and the NHS and litigation.

Saturday 5th

We are off to my sister's 60th birthday. It is uplifting to be able to go away for the weekend. Drew and Sindy are checking on the cats and my brother is on 'mother' duty. It is a sobering thought that this is only possible because Steven is not here anymore. Wherever he is, he is physically not in danger from callous people and he cannot be hurt any more. Emotionally he cannot be afraid or distressed. He does not exist on a human plane and the concerns of our existence will not trouble him. He is not. I am, and I must deal with the baggage I am left with. Maybe it is easier to clear his room than it is to 'sort my stuff'.

The visit is pleasant and we meet up with family. The best bit is walking with Ian along the Gloucester docks on Sunday morning. We are out for hours in bright sunshine and take the occasional break in a coffee bar or on a waterside seat. We discuss our future, wondering if we will have a house boat or a smart riverside apartment. We begin to realise that we can choose now to do anything we want. On that thought I venture into an Antiques shop and I'm immediately attracted by a ceramic cat. Steven is in my mind still. I often would bring him a cat object as a gift if we had left him for a day. This puss is a funny and stylish Italian lady from the 1960's. She reminds me of Kia cat when she is inviting me to play. I chance asking the price and it is 'cheap as chips.' She comes home with me and I am sad that Steven will not be there to admire her.

We return to my sister's via the Cathedral. The building is busy but respectfully hushed. We walk around the familiar aisles and think of things past. When the organ sounds in the loft we are both moved. We stand and listen closely for a few minutes. I can read Ian's face so easily. He is holding back tears. He tells me later that he was thinking how much Steven would have loved the noise and the music. We move in unison to light a candle. I hold it and Ian guides my hand towards the flame until it flares. Settling it in the sand we stand and stare. I think the flames must be hurting our eyes because now we both have to turn away. Love and remembrance of Steven is burning in our souls.

Sunday 13th

Steven's photo is posted to my Facebook wall to celebrate Mother's Day, but not by me. He is a happy smiling toddler and the sight of it breaks my heart. I thank the person who has done it for their lovely words. I then ask them to remove it all. Mum has given me a Mothers' Day gift of a tiny soft pink bear holding a flowering plant. I understand immediately what she is trying to say. She isn't good with words or emotions, so a pink bear is how she expresses her solidarity, her love for me and her acknowledgement of my loss. I accept the gift with grace, but hate it on sight. Needless to say, I don't want it in the house. It reminds me I will never again have the standard Mother's Day greeting from Steven. "Well do you want chocolates, booze or flowers Mother, or just a nice cheap hug?" I take it to work and give the little plant to a volunteer. The pink bear sits on my desk and is handy for a quick stress relieving squeeze. Now his 'Mother's Day' tag has been removed he is quite lovable.

Thursday 17th

Poor mum has to see the gynaecology specialist today. Ian is mini-bus driving and I am at work, so we have arranged for her to be accompanied by one of her friends from church. Mum is brave and tells the specialist that she is not prepared to have a biopsy done again without an anaesthetic. That took lots of coaching from me. He compromises with an ultra-sound scan which is not uncomfortable. Mum is tickled that she can see her insides on a screen. She must have a biopsy and it is agreed that she will be recalled after the doctors have had a case conference about her treatment. The C word is not mentioned but of course it is hanging in the air. Mum has been having treatment for this particular case of abnormal cells for about four years. I try to reassure her that she is the same person she always was. I look at her thin straggly hair and her stooped body and I am close to tears again. She has spent most of the past two years going backwards and forwards to hospital and it would be good for her to have a bit of peace and quiet now.

Saturday 19th

Saturday nights are my favourite. I will have done my duty and visited mum. Ian usually has a drink with his friends and watches sport down the pub, and I have a couple of hours for quiet reflection. He comes home mid evening and we have supper together followed by some constructive TV viewing. Both of us enjoy a drama, and we have developed a liking for Swedish and Danish thrillers with sub-titles.

'The Bridge' is a particularly complicated yet satisfying story about the usual human failings; adultery, betrayal, jealousy, revenge and lots more. It is uplifting in its portrayal of positive emotional development in the characters. The climax of the story is the sadistic murder of the main character's son. This is an act of calculated revenge in response to a betrayal of trust. The portrayals of grief and regret expressed at this death have intruded into the private place in Ian's mind. The place where he keeps his pain walled up. The father – son relationship and its heart-breaking ending have moved him, and I sense the shift in his energy. I realise that this is a good time to get him to open up. I quiz him gently. "I could have done more for my son. I still feel guilty. At least you kept him alive when you were looking after him. Maybe I shouldn't have given him a drink at Christmas?" I try to comfort him. "Nothing we could do would have stopped Steven drinking or dying. The damage was done in the very beginning when he did not get the treatment and support that he needed. You did all that you could and that's it."

We develop the discussion to encompass the plight of humanity (a huge topic for a chill-out Saturday night). We agree that you should always do what is right if you have the resources to do it. This quote, supposedly from Edmund Burke, comes to mind "All that is necessary for the triumph of evil is that good men do nothing." Ian has recently given information by choice to the police about a theft in the local Co-op. The point he makes once he knows that his information has helped convict the thief is pertinent to the discussion. "If he doesn't get caught and punished this time, what might happen next time if one of the assistants tries to stop him? Someone will get injured."

We agree that you have to be brave enough to stand up for what you believe is right, even if you are proved wrong later. We are both tearful by the time we have finished discussing the journey of the human Spirit. Each lifetime it is born into ignorance and must gather something better during its time on earth so that it develops and grows. It is sorrow and loss that tempers the mettle of the Spirit.

Our TV viewing is quite selective in general. I do like DIY SOS now that it seems to help real people with real disaster stories. I am moved by the plight of a middle-aged father suffering with Motor Neurone disease. His friends and family have rallied around to call in the team to adapt and renovate his house. He will have a better quality of life spending his remaining months with his wife and three daughters.

I reflect on the public perception of who is in need. Would the public have voted to help someone struggling with schizophrenia or bipolar? Probably not. Mental illness is not glamorous and does not create a good public interest story. It frightens the ignorant and fuels scary stories in the media. People really need to begin to recognise the effort and strength of will that it can take just for someone with a mental illness to get out of bed. I believe that those who keep trying under such difficult circumstances eventually develop a purity of Spirit. Suffering burns self-obsession from their souls.

The run up to the Olympics also provokes some thought. Tom Daley is a lovely shining example of British youth, a credit to his parents and the country. His Olympic fame has generated an interview on TV where he talks about his career and his new book. I am so sad. No one has chosen my son for anything – no award, no honours, no recognition of the effort he made to battle the odds against him. I cried then and I am crying now. It makes me more determined for people to read his words and hear his music.

Sunday 20th

I have had a lovely morning with Ian and felt well enough to make mum her Sunday dinner. I am in her house when she returns from Church and dinner is served. Whilst she eats I check the fridge. The bottom chiller is stuffed with vegetables, fruit, salad and bottles of juice. I remove it and sort it out. I spend the next half hour throwing out rotten food and salvaging what has been bought this week. I show her a cucumber, still sealed in its wrapper that has turned in to a green slimy soup. She does not seem much bothered. I accept that the care workers may think it is an imposition to go through the fridge with her, but I do wish they wouldn't just pile new stuff on top of what is going rotten. Mum has great difficulty standing at the fridge to look through it, so it is up to me.

I return home, have a late lunch and try to chill. That evening Ian and I settle to watch a drama and he fetches me a whiskey. I take my first sip and am disturbed by the telephone. The Care Alarm services are on the line. "Mrs Farrow has fallen and our staff are on their way." Ian quietly gets up, puts his drink on the table and heads to the garage to start the car. I scramble to put some clothes on, trotting out of the house bra-less and in very dodgy looking leggings. We arrive just after the care worker, who is getting her lifting gear out of the van. "I couldn't get in", she says breathlessly. "The key safe number we have on file is wrong." I say nothing as I know the details I gave previously are still correct. They have had to access mum's bungalow previously for the same reason and have accessed the key before.

My mum is sat awkwardly on the corner of the hearth, which must hurt a lot. She is bleeding from inside her nose and from a cut on the bridge, where her spectacles have made contact. The large bump on her temple is showing angry red and shiny. She is desperate to get up but we cannot lift her until the second care worker arrives. Mum is furious about this and complaining bitterly. I wash the blood off her hands and give her some Rescue Remedy. She is shaking with shock and demanding a drink of water. I ask Ian to bring some pillows so that we can make her more comfortable. The paramedics arrive before she can be picked up, and after a very quick but efficient examination, they hoist her up by her armpits before we can stop them. The care worker and I exchange a look but say nothing. Mum refuses to go to hospital and although her blood sugar is high, her blood pressure is good. I send Ian home and help mum to bed. After I have her settled, I walk home in the cool dusk, it's relaxing after the upset and I sleep well that night. I do wonder how long I can go on with all this disruption to our lives. I want to look after my mum as well as I can, but I now know that this ability is time-limited. I choose not to think about the 'what-ifs'.

Monday 28th

A knock on the front door disturbs my pottering. I lean out of the landing window to check who is calling. A man and a woman look up at me expectantly. After a moment I recognise the man as Len, Ian's best friend at school and the best man at our wedding, surprising really as I haven't seen him for 39 years. "Can you wait while I put some clothes on?" I hurriedly dress and let them in. They offer greetings and condolences and tell me of Len's mother's death. They are in the area clearing her house and ask "Do you want a stair lift?" The meeting is cordial and yet surreal, and they go on their way with a promise to stay in touch which we all know will not be kept.

June 2012

Work is okay and I am bored. I realise that this is quite a good place to be when you are overtired, stressed and grieving. I do feel adrift, not knowing how my future will develop. Who does? After talking with Ian, I decide to pick up my Bach Practitioner work again. I leave my details with a new clinic in the town and I also begin to promote a Level 1 training. It is a positive step, and I do believe I am emotionally stable enough to work with clients again.

I speak to my friend, a fellow Bach trainer in Scotland, about it at the weekend. I realise she has something on her mind and eventually she spits it out. "I have been asked to take part in the Level 3 Train the Trainer", she says. I feel gutted. Why haven't I been asked? I truthfully tell her how pleased I am for her and we discuss the situation. "It must be because of the number of courses I have taught and the work I have done to promote Bach recently." Of course she is correct.

I suppose by those standards I am a poor relation. Over the past two years I have managed just four training events. I think that is quite an achievement when your son is upstairs dying, but only Ian and I know what that entails. I put the phone down and I am really irritated and close to tears. I could do with a dose of the Bach Remedies Impatiens and Willow.

By the next day, Monday, I am furious and am experiencing the negative emotional state that requires Vine and Vervain Bach Remedies. I fire off a rather sharp email to the education department at Nelsons the homeopathic manufacturers in Wimbledon. I then worry myself sick about not being good enough and being overlooked. Eventually I pluck up the courage to respond to the invitation to phone the new Head of

Education. After a discussion in which we clear the air and get to know each other a bit, I am provisionally offered a place on the training course. Almost speechless with relief, I apologise for my graceless communications. "You can by me a pint next week when we meet at the trainers' day", he says.

It is with a lighter heart that I drive home that evening. It is bright sunshine – amazing for this horrible spring and summer. The big white tour buses are out in force, like lumbering wasps with turned in antennae. As I drive past a local village I see our Roman Soldier marching down the road. He is an elderly man who has suffered a stroke and has been determined ever since to walk every day. The twist to the story is that he does it in some form of authentic Roman costume, all historically correct. The first time I saw him I thought he was a ghost.

I call in at mums that teatime. "The washer's broken and I've flooded the kitchen floor." I set to cleaning up. I call in a repair firm that I have a long-standing relationship with. The young man who calls went to school with Steven and takes some time to show mum pictures of his two babies. Once again, I am reminded of what will never be and it chokes me, and my light mood evaporates.

I pull away from her house and look to turn left up the narrow road as there are cars parked all the way along to my left. I ease cautiously out of the junction so that I can see the traffic. Just as well, careering along the middle of the road towards me are two bicycles. To the rear is a red bike that weaves gaily under the burden of carrying two lanky lads. The pillion rider has his legs dangling to the ground and his backside dangerously close to the spinning rear wheel. The other bike is steaming ahead, and carries a bonny boy with dark curls and a big grin, his legs pumping furiously as he stands in his pedals and gives it rock-all. I have stopped and wait patiently for them to negotiate the row of parked cars. As he shoots past he turns to look at me and gives me a big 'thumbs up' in acknowledgement. The boys look so happy, so full of life that I grin with pleasure as I pull away. At the same time my heart aches for the loss of my boy who will never again pedal a bike nor sire me grandchildren with dark curls and a big grin. I am baffled that I can both grin and feel such sorrow in the same sunlit moment.

It is nine months since Steven died and that's the time it takes to conceive, nurture and birth a baby. My belly is huge with grief, held in and hidden. Time to begin to let this energy dissipate out into the air. I lose 7lbs in four weeks, but my belly is hanging on and hanging out.

Thursday 21st – the longest day

It is a silver white morning, damp with a promise of warmth to come. The sun is nowhere to be seen but is bathing the greenness of the garden in an eye-watering grey light. The rain hovers in the air, undecided. Kia cat crouches on my lap as I reflect on the view from the open window. I can see Steven's two anvils and Geoffrey the miner, a garden ornament, all 12 inches of him. He was painted sandstone yellow so that Steven could spot him right at the bottom of the garden. Hidden by the vibrant wild rose is the low yew tree chosen by Steven when he was about 8 – a slow spreading fixture of our garden that quietly grows in bulk each year. Under its low protective branches Gerry cat's grave is hidden, marked by a crouching cat cast in sandy stone. The cat is no longer in the open but hiding underneath the branches. 'Professor Gerry' lies much quieter in death then he ever was in life, a wild, mad and beautiful friend to my son. Across the green space, now snuggled tight by the edge of the greenhouse is Dusty's grave, marked by a flat stone 'Here lies Dusty, a much-loved cat'. The words carefully painted by Steven bereft of his first feline friend. All I can see and feel in the brightening morning is Steven and his cats, from the old cat nestled under my ribs, to the luminous view into the green and grey of the garden. Young Nellie cat is hopping about like a rabbit just for the joy of it. My eyes prickle with tears. Every cool breath confirms that I am alive and alone without my dead and disappeared son.

Saturday 30th

I am tidying the cupboards. I find that we still have onion soup in the pantry and hoisin duck in the freezer. I doubt Steven fancies either of them now.

The Co-operative dividend statement arrives and comes with an ironic twist. We have gained 2,458 points and £56 by using the Co-operative funeral service. Well, every cloud has a silver lining as they say.

July and August 2012

July

I am shattered and precede Ian up to bed. I lie awake, tossing and turning, hot and bothered and totally ill at ease. It is well after 11pm and I hear the phone ring. My heart jumps into my throat – a call at this time of night usually means my mum is in trouble. I take a deep breath and let Ian deal with the initial details. I hear the rumble of his voice and quick steps through the kitchen and the slam of the door. He has taken the phone out into the garage. I try not to tense up, but it is obviously something he does not want me to overhear. He is gone about 5 minutes. I listen to him switching off downstairs and preparing to come up. "Who was on the phone?" My nerves are strained, and I know that I will not like the answer. "It was Eve. She was phoning to express her condolences about Steven. She says she has only just found out." I swear and interrogate him further. "She said her mother died this year as well, so she knows how we must be feeling." I swear some more. Absolutely bloody typical and thoughtless to think that 11.30pm is a good time to call. Ian has managed to be polite and calm and I am fuming with anger and dislike.

My health is wrecked but I am feeling more optimistic. I saw my GP yesterday and I have agreed that I need to have further investigations. Ian has delivered his first training as a MIDAS driver trainer and I am very proud. It has given us something new to share and talk about as trainers! He rewards my interest with the first edible tomato from the greenhouse – a real privilege. The fruits are very late this year because of the lack of light and warmth.

Later that evening I wait until Ian has gone out. I watch the video of Steven at Christmas 2010 and indulge in a good cry. His song and words are true and prophetic. He struggles to sing 'Well, I won't back down' (Tom Petty) then gives up saying he "can't do it anymore." I find his CDs and begin to sort them out properly, cataloguing songs and changing files to mp3's. I try Steven's CD 'Fusion' again and am amazed to find music tracks on the disc that previously wouldn't play. I cry some more. His amazing voice and the black humour and wisdom of his lyrics are vibrant and strong. This is the man that the Mental Health Services wrote off. I am proud, sad and heart-broken I miss him so much. Even Kia cat is twisting her ears and trying to find out where his voice is coming from.

I am nervous about my journey to Chichester for the Bach training. I am awake early and the radio alarm is playing Mozart. I lie there trying to rouse myself. The familiar creak of the floorboard outside Steven's room makes my heart leap with hope. Fat cat Nellie is lying asleep across my feet, so she is not responsible. The thought of Steven, maybe close by, comforts me and I get out of bed to begin another part of the journey. I silently ask that he might help me along today if he can – this is a different way of grieving.

The journey to Chichester and my training is uneventful and I stay with Cara another Bach Practitioner. She is exactly what I need. She has long endured the death of her daughter and can relate to my loss. The advice she gives me is simple yet profound: "When you are struggling, just do one week at a time. If you can't cope with that then do one day at a time, or just one hour, or just survive the next two minutes." At the end of my stay, I send her some Plymouth gin as a thank you having drunk all of hers.

On my return, Ian is beginning to talk more about Steven. One Saturday night we play music, drink, talk and cry. We discuss the 'Trust' again. Will it be for the homeless or for those with mental health problems?

The next day we go out, just because we can. The day is hot and lit with brilliant sun. We spend the day by the sea. I am exhausted, but I enjoy Ian's company, the weather, the freedom and the fish and chips. We trawl the beach and bring some offerings back to sit beside the photo of Steven, small stones, feathers, shells and a delicate crab carapace that has the look of a linen fabric and is as fragile as a life. The tribute is finished off with a sprig of spicy smelling tagetes, picked from a municipal planter.

Drew and Sindy come for dinner and I am moved to see that it is important enough for them to come 'dressed'. They are both turned out in their quirky best, with Drew in an Indian tunic and Sindy in black velvet. We all chat easily but Steven is not really discussed – the elephant in the room. Drew becomes much more relaxed when we discuss Steven's drum kit and cymbals. I reflect that we are the four people who knew Steven the most intimately.

August

The Bank Holiday weekend is cold and bleak. I think back to last year – 50 weeks since Steven was still breathing. I am tediously going through his medical records. How many times did Steven walk through the door of Community Alcohol Service attempting to engage? What was going on in these meetings? What turned him off? Why could they not work with him? As an alcoholic dependant person why was Thiamine not routinely prescribed or discussed? Why weren't we advised of what was on offer?

I am in pain, physical pain - my bowel, my back, left arm and much more. I examine the pain, talk to it, try to listen to what it is telling me. I hear a litany of 'held in' emotions that now can be allowed to leach their way into my awareness. I choose some Bach remedies. I am so dissatisfied at work and the lack of time in my personal life.

I draw the curtains, light the lamps and switch on the fire. I light Steven's candle, it's become a habit and a comfort. I ponder on 'nearly a year'. Ian is struggling with guilt and grief. "I won't listen to his music yet. To hear his voice is too raw for me. I will go to crematorium, but I won't take flowers I just want to be there." The anniversary of Steven's death approaches. I will be at work and I wonder what time the cemetery gates are shut in the evening. Will I have time to get there? We are building up to it and I light a candle every day. On a sad day I have a chat to his photo and ask him for a bit of help. I walk away with tears running. I am at the other side of the room and turn to see a loose photo, tucked into the frame, slowly flip and slide to the floor. He was listening after all.

My mum is unwell and her left arm is bruised from shoulder to wrist. She gives me a very early birthday gift and again I don't like it. Later that day, feeling isolated I dial a few numbers to make contract with friends. My friend Meg is at home but poorly and I apologise and say that I won't keep her. "No don't hang up, Steven is here", she says. This is unexpected. I do not 'ask' for Steven to contact me as I feel he should be getting on with his new state of being. Nevertheless, I am moved and expectant. "I hate that cat." Meg asks for proof that this is Steven the cat lover. He gives her images of very particular biker boots that belong to a friend – well that can only be Drew and is proof enough for me. The cat he hates is the one that chases his beloved cat girls back into the house from the garden. "I'd have come sooner if I'd known how lovely it is. I'm with my grandfather. I'm sorting my life out." I tell Steven about my progress with Bach and ask him what he thinks. "Good on you, mam." I ask for help with getting his music published. Who should I get to do it? "Bugger that, I'll do it" he states exuberantly. A gentle message for his dad "Remember the quiet times we spent together."

September and October 2012

Well here it is – 'the anniversary'. It is after all just a date, a day on the calendar. I'm so weary today. Thoughts of Steven crowd my mind. I'm feeling very sorry for myself. I am at work and know that I can't visit the crematorium before the gates are locked. Ian goes on his own has a private chat with Steven and leaves him a flower.

That evening I light a new candle for Steven by his photo on the sideboard. What else to do? We think about him every day, and this is just a day that reminds us that time is passing. Time is passing without our son. The depth of my sadness and low mood comes as a surprise to me. I am utterly fed up with listening to other peoples' troubles and feeling obliged to sort them out.

I make myself a big glass of Bach remedies - Olive for my absolute exhaustion, Star of Bethlehem for my sadness and loss and Willow for my overwhelming self-pity. There are a lot of people I love and care about but I'm not getting much comfort from anyone today. What about me! So, I drink my Willow.

Later that week I wallow in a surfeit of whiskey whilst I mark some distance learning for a student. Steven's tracks are playing super loud whilst Ian is out – I need space to weep. The words are poignant, heart-breaking and doom laden. Steven saw his future or lack of it, all mapped out before him. I top up my glass, press play again and try to explain to a student using the written word that they haven't quite 'got it'.

Tuesday 25th September

The day delivers the worst flooding I can ever remember for our area. After a wet trip to outpatients at the local hospital, to find a way forward for health problems, I head for the city and work. One of the hotels on the outskirts has copped it again and the road is impassable. I turn off the main road and go through the mining villages where most of my family were raised. I am an hour later than I should be for work. We are released early at 3.00pm and I decide the motorway is the safest route - well just about. It's closed all the way down to the South. Fortunately, the closure is where I turn off and I make it safely home.

Tuesday 23rd October

I wake from my dream suddenly and with a sense of expectation. In my imagination I have seen and spoken with Steven. He is not a child nor a man, but just Steven. I insist that he takes the mobile phone that I am holding out to him. He reaches out for it, half turning away. He is in a tearing hurry. "Can I have some money for the bus fare?" I hand over the cash and he is away, gone, disappeared. Perhaps he is on some new leg of his journey in Spirit? The conscious 'me' hopes that I have been able to help him. A comforting thought.

The journey to work is slow and sky is grey (the weathermen call it dreek). I think of Steven at some time during every long day, but today I am crying as I drive. What tiny sliver of precious memory has caused this? Then I fix on it. Simon is over from Germany and wants to visit. He is my surrogate son and was Steven's first best friend. He will be bringing his partner, a delightful young woman. And I cry harder, my tears streaming and smearing my face just like fog on the windscreen. Grief it seems becomes a part of you. It is needed to fill the huge chasm left by bereavement.

At work our small team go out for lunch for my belated birthday celebration. No one offers to buy me a drink, even though they seem to be buying for each other. I buy my own without a word to them. I choose soup as I don't fancy the rest of the very basic menu, but send it back just tasted, hardly eaten. I refuse a replacement. I think a good dose of Bach Willow is called for to help me overcome my sulks and resentment.

I leave work early so that I can meet Ian at the hospital to be with mum for her brain scan. We are taken straight in. The operator is pleasant but rushes mum, maybe they want an early finish after her 5.30pm slot. She chooses not to take notice of mum's mobility issues or the fact that she is in a lot of pain. Between us we eventually get mum on her back and lying down. At this stage she is shaking with fear and her hand tremor is very noticeable. As requested, Ian and I leave the room and sit in silence watching the x-ray sign flicker on and off. When we are allowed to re-enter and retrieve her, she is clearly distressed and in pain. Fortunately, she believes that I was sat just behind her all the time. She was unable to check this as her head was strapped down and she has no concept of modern day health and safety. Ian takes charge of the wheelchair, and I drive mum home to give her some tea and settle her for the evening. I feel like I am feeding a budgie in a cage and it makes me very sad.

Ian and I bicker when I return home, but I am grateful that he has a meal ready. I mix a brandy and lemonade which lasts me all evening - I don't like brandy but I need a drink. I wake up with a start at 11.00pm, crumpled on the couch, having slept away my few hours of freedom. I trail after Ian to bed, feeling trapped in a way of life that I am not enjoying and too depressed to heave myself out of it.

Wednesday 24th October

Simon and his lady come to share a meal with us. It's a bit basic, just soup and bread, but the additional alcohol livens things up - two bottles of red wine and a litre of whiskey! We have good music and chat and inevitably we talk about Steven. I am touched when Simon tells me that he believes that Steven was the best Foley artist that he has come across and that he could have probably made a living from it. I have to look it up later to make sure I have understood. Foley is the reproduction of everyday sound effects that are added to film, video and other media in post-production to enhance audio quality. These reproduced sounds can be anything from the swishing of clothing and footsteps to squeaky doors and breaking glass. We enjoy the evening and are sad to see them go. We wonder when we might see them again as Germany is now their home.

Friday 26th October

I lie in bed waiting for the alarm. Nearly every part of my body is aching, and I go through a mental check list to see if I can find something positive. Then suddenly I am reliving my last moments with Steven the evening before he died. Soft dry hair, cool skin and the feeling of his thin, tense body in my arms as I tell him "You don't have to be in pain Sweetie."

November and December 2012

Steven comes to me in a dream. He is a child of 8 or 9, barefooted and tearful. The tops of his feet are bruised blue and pink and they are dirty. I hug him to me – he is tense as I hold him, and he has been crying. His tear stained face is grubby and I can't get to look him in the eyes. He wraps himself tightly around me and I hold onto him with equal firmness. I am conscious of his stifled sobs and his bruised feet as I try to comfort him. I get a sense of the older Steven in his long limbs and bruised skin.

My sister stands behind him – was going to speak but acknowledges that she should stay silent. It is something more than my sister – a younger vibrant, larger than life version with a red dress and lustrous dark hair and a wonderful smile. Perhaps this is my sister's Spirit or her 'out of body' version? Has she brought Steven to me for some purpose, for some mutual comfort? I am so very sad that my son is dead and I can no longer hold him in my arms.

Sunday 16th December

Yesterday we bought Steven a Christmas candle. The existing effort is a poor burner and seems demeaning to his memory. We light his candle most evenings, an acknowledgement that he did exist and that he is remembered. This second Christmas tide without him is bitter-sweet. It is Ian's 60th birthday on the 25th and Steven would have been 33 on the 27th. It seems much more painful approaching this second Christmas without him. Maybe I was numb with shock last year?

I rummage in my Christmas basket, looking for labels and wrapping paper for the last of the family gifts. I find my white fluffy deer antlers and I smile as I try them on and nod my head to make them bounce. Then I reach for the two sparkly Santa hats last worn by my husband and my son and I break down in tears. One hat will not have a head to adorn and my heart aches with sadness. I bring a hat downstairs and I drape it over the corner of Steven's photo frame. I have quite a little shrine sitting on the corner of the sideboard now. Feathers, shells, dried flowers – I'm not sure that Steven would be particularly impressed or grateful. He would probably just laugh at my sentimentality.

I make yet another attempt to de-clutter Steven's room. I rummage in the box that holds items too good for the charity shop. The intention is to give things to his friends or to sell them on eBay. I pull out a hair trimming kit bought as a Christmas gift the year before he died. Steven's beard was famously wild, black and luxuriously soft. He felt it gave him an edge, and of course it covered half his face, so he could hide behind it too. However, it was high maintenance because it grew so fast. He usually kept it clean and trimmed and he was proud of its vigorous growth.

I debate the trimmers. Would anyone want second hand goods of such a personal nature? I begin to undo all the bits and pieces and realise this set is in very good condition. Perhaps he preferred the other set that his dad is now using? I decide to wash and clean the heads and empty them into the bathroom basin. Only one head has been used and I carefully dismantle it into the warm soapy water. I am not emotionally prepared for the sight of long black whiskers floating off into the water. A last sight of something tangible draining down the plughole, I am losing a part of Steven yet again. Instinctively I gather some whiskers between my fingers and then wonder what the purpose is. DNA testing? A memorial locket? I rinse my hands and walk away with a towel clutched to my chest and tears wetting my face.

Thursday 27th December

Steven's birthday and ironically, I must go to hospital for health checks to the same building in which he was born 33 years ago today. Once I am done we travel to the crematorium and arrive empty handed. My eyes well up at the sight of his plaque on a pillar in the garden of remembrance, much loved son and musician. It is just two down from that of Ian's stepmother Ida so they will keep each other company.

The whole garden of remembrance looks wet and dreary today. Why do people leave the wrappings on the flowers that they bring? It just becomes so much ugly litter. I puzzle over the fact that some people have left Christmas cards, dissolving and illegible in the persistent rain. My mood mellows as I acknowledge that every person has different needs when it comes to grief.

The border of Christmas wreaths impresses us with the sheer number of remembrances and the beautiful but fast fading colours. It doesn't make it any easier to be in this sad place. Better to be with my son's words and music than here.

In the evening we go to Drew and Sindy's for a meal and good company. I am in awe of their resilience and ability to live in the moment. We sit together, perhaps the four people who knew Steven the best and remember him with laughter and sadness. Just after his time of birth at 3 minutes past 9.00pm, Drew lights a firework especially kept for the occasion. We stand back in the little garden and wait for it to flare and shoot upwards into the night sky. We are not disappointed, and we send our love with it towards the stars. Gradually its light fades, as did Steven and we turn to go back inside.

"There are many worlds, and this one is done with me"

Steven

Give a dog a bad name

As an adult Steven was continually seen as *'just an alcoholic'* and not as a real person with complex needs.

The list of labels that he was given over his short lifetime demonstrates that he did not receive consistent appropriate support or holistic treatment. Person centred care was non-existent, and interventions seemed to focus on keeping him (and us) quiet rather than supporting him to plan for recovery, stability, education or work. If support had been offered and refused by Steven then we were not made aware of it.

The information that follows is a potted history of the labels and conditions attributed to him and these are from fragmented records which I accessed after his death.

* September 1990 Depression
* April 1993 Asperger's Syndrome
* Summer 1995 Obsessive Compulsive Disorder
* Bi Polar Affective Disorders
* August 2001 Bi Polar Disorder
* October 2001 Obsessive Compulsive Disorder, Bipolar Affective Disorder (rapid cycling) and Alcohol Dependency
* November 2001 Not eligible for psychological therapies (*no full explanation of this decision noted*)
* June 2003 Borderline Personality Disorder

'Service Users with dual needs have tended to receive services delivered in a 'serial' or 'parallel' way, which have been found to be ineffective. 'Serial' refers to the person having to resolve their substance use problem before mental health services become involved. 'Parallel' refers to both mental health and substance

use services providing care at the same time, yet not communicating effectively. Guidance and evidence suggests that services need to work together in collaboration to effectively meet the needs of service users'. Dual Diagnosis a Multi-Agency Strategy September 2005.

- July 2006 'Has not got a serious or treatable mental illness'.
- Anxiety Disorder with Alcohol Dependency *'Steven clearly believed that his problems were due to a severe mental illness and that his alcohol consumption was a form of self-medication'. Community Alcohol Service.*
- February 2007 Bi Polar Disorder *'There is an awful lot that points to a firm diagnosis of Bipolar Disorder in this young man. For a start he clearly described recurrent Major Depressive and recurrent Hypo manic and Manic Episodes. Additionally, when young children have the florid onset of affective disorder type symptoms including depression, OCD and hypo manic features that is very commonly the hallmark of a rip-roaring Bipolar Disorder and I am really sure that this is the case here. Really there is not any other explanation. It is possible of course that the alcohol has been a maintaining factor more recently but that is by no means hopeless. His recent mood incongruent psychosis may have been something of a shift caused by alcohol or simply due to a lack of medical treatment as he was taken off his mood stabiliser'. Prof C 2007.*

- July 2007 Independent Affective Disorders
- October 2007 Mental and Behavioural Disorder due to alcohol use and Personality Disorder
- November 2007 No evidence of Bipolar Symptoms due to Cyclothymia, alcohol and personality traits

- December 2007 Not Bi Polar but has traits of Cyclothymia

- January 2008 Emotionally Unstable Personality Disorder

- March 2008 Emotionally Unstable Personality Disorder with predominant Cyclothymic traits. Prof B in full agreement with this

- June 2011 'We may now need to treat Steven as a case of Bi Polar Disorder'. Prof B

Steven died aged just 31 from acute alcohol toxicity and end stage alcoholic liver disease with a verdict of misadventure recorded by the Coroner. This means that he intended to drink alcohol, but he didn't intend at that time to die from it. My gut feeling is that Steven did intend to die and had been drinking heavily for some weeks after a period of abstinence with a view to 'putting out the lights' (his phrase).

He had struggled since the age of 9 with anxiety, lack of confidence and fragile self-esteem and as he matured his mental state degenerated into a long standing mental health illness. Would all those professionals involved please note that Steven **wasn't** drinking alcohol at the age of 9 and he was never *'just an alcoholic'.* There was always an underlying and primary cause for his drinking, but the professionals could never quite agree on what it was or even admit that it existed. As a result, he didn't get consistent support, treatment or medication and he returned to alcohol again and again to numb his racing brain and his distress. He needed someone other than family to acknowledge his mental distress and to try and help him make sense of his condition and alleviate some of the fear. He wanted to live and to make music and to enjoy time with his friends.

Steven was not ready to make changes to his drinking until the powers that be acknowledged his dual diagnosis and treated him accordingly within Mental Health Services.

His stability was continually threatened by short-sighted professionals, poor support and treatment, all aggravated by a lack of resources within the local Mental Health Service. Prejudice within the professional team who were supposed to be caring for him was a real barrier, as were personality clashes. Not professional or caring at all. Steven's self-esteem was being continually eroded by these issues, with the words *"you are just an alcoholic"* echoing through his mind. This caused him to be stubborn and determined not to engage with those who did not fully understand his illness and his personal situation.

Knowing what I do now, I am baffled that Steven was not classed as a vulnerable adult and therefore supported and treated accordingly. This was noted in one set of notes that I have, but in my view, no one was watching out for him but us. I give due attention to the fact that Steven was never an easy client, but how could he be, given his persistent diagnoses of Asperger's, Bi Polar Disorder, Personality Disorder and Alcohol Dependence and more besides.

Steven did seek out his GP's advice on quite a few occasions but sometimes his physical health was ignored. On telling a GP that he was worried about weight loss he was told to eat more potatoes.

The results of the brain scans which took place in 2007 at a specialist hospital were never shared with Steven. They showed significant brain damage due to alcohol. I am convinced that if he had been told about this he would have tried just that bit harder to reform.

I am also baffled as to why Folic Acid and Thiamine were not prescribed by a GP seeing these results. This did not happen until mid-2010 after Steven had nearly died from alcoholic liver disease. I also note that liver function tests were not carried out on a regular basis until after this hospitalisation. This could be because Steven refused to comply. During the times that he lived with us I do not remember them being offered. His bipolar medication could have contributed to his liver disease and he should have been monitored regularly for this.

There were many times when appointments with the Community Alcohol Services and the Community Mental Health Team were cancelled at short notice, not to materialise again until quite a few weeks or months later. Even his CPN in 2010 and 2011 was away for a long period of time due to illness. No other support was given at that time. This demonstrates a persistent lack of resources in the Mental Health Care System.

The mess that was Steven's adult life centres on labels – if he is assessed as having an *'an enduring mental health illness'* then he has support from specialised teams, and regular visits from a CPN. The term *'enduring mental health'* refers to those with long-term mental health problems, typically schizophrenia or a severe affective disorder such as bipolar. If this label is not allocated, then there is no immediate support and each crisis requires the client to start from scratch to access the services that they need. The appropriate label gives access to the Crisis Team in times of need and ongoing support from a CPN.

Flaws in the system?

Lack of support

Much of what I have documented goes against the guidelines in the Department of Health's (2002) Dual Diagnosis Good Practice Guide which highlighted a lack of integrated care for people with both mental health and substance misuse needs. Historically, services have not addressed the unique problems of those struggling with dual diagnosis; instead, they have treated the mental health problem and substance abuse as separate problems.

When Steven was under the care of the local Community Mental Health Team, response times were varied – from a couple of hours (excellent) to over a week. This was purely to do with a lack of resources in the system. In the months after Steven's death I was shocked to learn that there were only two members of staff on duty as the Crisis Response Team at any one time and they covered a huge geographical area.

Mistakes and misinformation seemed to build right from the first realisation that Steven was unwell. Family Psychology was initially useful, but Steven was discharged in 1992. We were not officially informed of a diagnosis of Asperger's until a meeting at school attended by the Educational Psychologist and one of the Family Psychologists. It was mentioned in passing and no real emphasis was given to it. We were given no advice and no follow up, so as Steven became more unwell we didn't know what we should do.

Our GP had provided a medical note for the school that stated that Steven was occasionally too depressed to attend, but no medication was prescribed until January 1996 when he was given Prozac. No talking therapies other psychiatric assessments were offered over this period.

In the summer of 1996 aged 16, Steven was desperate for relief from his depression and OCD. I took him to the GP asking for a referral to a psychiatrist. Due to a lack of resources within the service nothing was available 'for at least 6 months'. I had no concept of being able to challenge this wait and as a result I felt the only way forward was to ask for a private referral. This was given and a couple of weeks later Steven was seen at Yorkvale. He was prescribed Tofranil with a diagnosis of OCD. Steven was excited at the idea that a solution had been found. He had an immediate and severe negative reaction to this drug. A letter from the Yorkvale sent to our GP admits that maybe he should have been given a lower dose than that which was prescribed! This was not seen by me until after Steven died.

Our attempt at getting support via the NHS and our GP at the end of 2006 was a total failure. The referral went to Dr M again. We did not know that we would be referred to the same Psychiatrist who had overturned the initial bipolar diagnosis all those years ago. The GP had no idea who we would see because of shortages of staff within the Community Mental Health Team. Steven and Dr M had no therapeutic relationship whatsoever and Dr M continually insisted that Steven was **'just an alcoholic'.**

Steven was never offered a residential place of safety where he could tackle his addiction to alcohol and have his mental health stabilised. I believe that if it had been offered or if he had been sectioned during his hospital stay in March 2010 he might be still alive and enjoying a useful life today.

The lack of resources within the system forced us to 'go private' when we could, and I appreciate that this may have contributed to a lack of continuity of care. We foolishly believed that our GP had the resources and information to actively follow through but of course we did not understand the system. When there was no assertive outreach from services, we fooled ourselves into thinking we had solved the problem and that Steven was as good as he was going to be. Mental Health Services do not seem to work in tandem with GP practices. In fact, the NHS seems to have a fragmented approach and really needs to look at patients in a more holistic way.

I believe even now that the Mental Health Services struggle to support individuals who are unlucky enough to have a dual diagnosis - a mental health illness alongside a dependency on drugs or alcohol. Their own strategy instructs them to work closely together. This rarely happened for Steven until Ian and I began to cause a fuss. It felt like we had to do it all and become his care co-ordinators. Through our own ignorance and shortcomings, we didn't do a very good job.

According to my local authority's web site – 'If you feel ready to make changes to your drug and/or alcohol use you will be allocated a dedicated worker. Your worker will support you to make positive changes. The package of care and support will be personalised around your needs with recovery being the main objective. Your family/carer can also receive dedicated support.'

Services

The lack of funding and resources within Mental Health Services impacts on every aspect of patient care and staff wellbeing. Without cash, vacancies go unfilled, staff are under pressure, appointments disappear or have lengthy gaps in between. Training and continuing professional development are a challenge. The lack of 'slack' within the system hinders recovery and means that professional help cannot be accessed when needed.

No adequate service was available when Steven was 16 and we took him back to the GP for help. Correspondence sent to our GP talked of a 6 month wait for clients in a neighbouring area and no willingness nor ability to take clients from our area. No support was in place here because vacancies had not been filled. It is at this point that we should have protested. We were ignorant of how to get the service that Steven needed.

People who are mentally unwell, and are 'in the system', can access the Crisis Response Team for their area quite quickly. This information is given in their Care Plan. If they are not 'in the system' or have been 'dumped' then access is only via the GP or Accident and Emergency. Steven was never seen in Accident and Emergency by a psychiatrist when needed. The quickest response that he had in these circumstances was to come back 24 hours later to be assessed. When admitted to a medical ward via Accident and Emergency it was a very rare occurrence for a psychiatrist to be available. It does seem that there is currently a desire for positive change. Our Mental Health Trust quotes on their web site: 'Our Crisis Team staff work closely with emergency departments to make sure that people can be treated for a mental health illness where needed.' When he was within the system, we usually had support quite quickly either at home or by meeting the Crisis Team at a local hospital.

Diagnosis

If you have a label for your condition, then you will receive the care attributed to that label. This can be a double-edged sword. I accept that mental health diagnosis is a challenging issue. What I don't understand is how Steven could be given so many different labels and also be told that he did not have a mental health problem. This resulted in fragmented and sometimes inappropriate care pathways. Does this disagreement relate to a lack of skill amongst practitioners or the constraints of a system under pressure?

Diagnosis needs management – when a letter is received from a consultant what is the correct action for a GP? What is communicated to the patient? What action is taken to promote health and minimise harm? Surely there is a duty to provide continuation of care and assertive outreach for those who really need it.

Steven was discharged from CAMHS with a diagnosis of Asperger's Syndrome written in his records. We were not officially told of this and no support or advice was given for the future. It seems that anxiety, obsessive compulsive disorder (OCD) and depression are common in people within the autism spectrum. 'Even though mental illness can be more common for people on the autism spectrum than in the general population, the mental health of autistic people is often overlooked.'
http://www.autism.org.uk/about/health/mental-health.aspx

When Steven suffers with myocardial inflammation in 1999, no one troubles to make the link between alcohol and this heart condition. At that point we are becoming aware that he drinks heavily.

In July 2001 he is given a diagnosis of bipolar by Prof A and is prescribed some relevant medication that seems to help over the next few months. When he finally gets to hospital, in the September of that year, to be 'dried out' he is reassessed by a different psychiatrist, Dr M, and he leaves hospital in October 2001 on just antidepressants. The original diagnosis of bipolar has been overturned and his medication changed.

In December 2001 after a severe deterioration, our GP referred Steven to the Mental Health Team again. They refuse to accept him, saying his troubles are all to do with alcohol abuse. All this is without seeing him again in the flesh, or troubling to reassess him. Someone, somewhere also decides that there is a risk of violence to others. This is only noted in a letter from a psychiatrist that I do not recognise nor remember seeing Steven. Surely his parents, carers and next of kin, should have been told or warned about this? Information needs to be shared with carers who have a duty to challenge it or corroborate it. I certainly would have challenged this statement as Steven was never a danger to others, just himself. This is just one example of misinformation that I gleaned from his medical records after his death.

Communication and information

There was little constructive communication between services and us as carers during the periods of time that Steven was living with us. So where is the specific information and support for carers? Who takes responsibility for informing carers of what is going on?

Whilst I agree that the patient is entitled to their privacy, in cases where a patient is seriously ill, or dying or would benefit from specific nursing care then carers must be educated, involved and supported. This is for the benefit of all involved and is a lynch pin contributing to successful outcomes. We always had to make the first move to get any information at all and it was apparent that the right hand didn't know what the left hand was doing.

There is a need for better collaboration between Community Drug and Alcohol Teams and Mental Health Teams as noted under the governments Dual Diagnosis Policy.

In conclusion

This story is true as far as memory and my notebooks serve. I am not in the business of laying down blame to any one individual. The NHS and its Mental Health Services are precious but are chronically underfunded and resourced. I applaud the current movement that encourages an increased awareness of mental ill health, but an increased demand and heightened expectations may result in many more people like Steven being let down.

Steven was a vulnerable adult and many safeguarding issues were obvious. No professional except Prof C even touched on this let alone acted on it. His warning was not heeded. So where is the first line of defence? Who was really bothered about saving Steven from himself except for us? We all had a profound loss of hope due to confusing and probably incorrect diagnoses, with no clear pathway of care in the very beginning, with needs not met.

Steven was never 'just an alcoholic'. He was my sweet-natured gentle little lad who grew in to an anxious and distressed teenager and then into a mentally unwell man. This story may well have focussed upon the difficult times, but I choose to remember our son as the talented, funny and caring individual that he was.

Steven's many obsessions as a child were huge fun to join in with. His collection of clocks, his detailed drawings of electrical equipment, his desire to know all about fungi, space, cats, cars, vets, the Goons, geraniums, anvils, pianos and keyboards, street lighting and lamps – all of this kept us busy as a family. His self-taught ability to renovate and mend vintage electrical instruments kept him occupied, and all gave him a purpose in life when he was unable to work.

Friends and family will know that he didn't just mend instruments, he taught himself to play – bass and slide guitar, keyboards of any description, drums. Supported by musically talented friends, he composed and sang songs, created tunes and recorded them.

This story is his legacy to go alongside over 50 songs and many poems. I will never have grandchildren and Ian and I will spend our last years alone. What is left behind is precious to me. I can still listen to his songs and imagine that he is back in the room. I read his words and he stands behind my right shoulder, his voice speaking softly inside my head.

Ian and I have both wondered what was the purpose of it all? What is the point of raising a child with love and dedication only to become bereft and empty? It would be easy to fall into a pit of hopelessness, but I believe that we have avoided this. We are not the only parents to outlive a cherished child, so we must get on with it the best that we can and make something of our later years.

We have free will. We also have the Soul's mission. The two do not necessarily jog along smoothly and peaceably together. Some Souls have chosen to endure pain, suffering and ignorance until they have assimilated enough 'how not to do it' for the benefit of their next earthly escapade. Steven endured. His kindness, wit and musical ability were gifts given to him to allow him to endure humiliation, fear, loneliness and self-loathing. Steven's way of being tested friendships and family relationships. This was part of his mission; to stretch and temper other Souls and give them the opportunity to grow, learn, express kindness, tolerance and understanding. His desire to 'rescue' others, and his empathy and willingness to help, may have been his undoing. After much pain and heartache, his Soul learned not to interfere in the lives of others who were also experiencing painful lessons. We cannot deny the Soul its mission, only delay it.

I do have hope that things are changing for the better. It is of paramount importance that accessible training and supervision for all substance abuse and mental health staff are funded and that the money is ring-fenced. In my reading, I have come across a plethora of toolkits, policies, guidelines and the like, all relating to what should happen when someone is living with a dual diagnosis or a mental illness. They look impressive on paper, but if they cannot be implemented because of the fear of culture change, prejudice towards people with dual diagnosis or lack of funding then many more people like my son will suffer. As I write this I am wondering what is my mission now, what path? Steven was given as a son to Ian and I for a reason and I cannot allow the experience and knowledge I have gained to go to waste.

"The Soul endures, man endures, and we turn the other cheek."

A Dean of Princeton University
(a Buddhist Priest).

Not just an Alcoholic

Steven Midgley and Clare Midgley

Glossary of terms and medication

Acamprosate: Helps maintain abstinence from alcohol in patients with alcohol dependence. Should be part of a comprehensive management program that includes psychosocial support.

ADHD: Attention deficit hyper activity disorder.

Agoraphobic or agoraphobia: An extreme or irrational fear of open or public places. People affected find it very difficult to leave their homes.

Alcoholic polyneuropathy: Alcohol can be toxic to nerve tissue. People who drink too much may start to feel pain and tingling in their limbs. This is known as alcoholic neuropathy. This causes damage in the peripheral nerves.

Alzheimer's/Alzheimer's disease: The most common type of dementia, a progressive neurological disease which affects multiple brain functions, including memory.

Amitriptyline: Belongs to a group of medicines known as tricyclic antidepressants. It has been traditionally prescribed for the treatment of depression, but can also be used in smaller doses to treat nerve pain.

Ascites: An accumulation of fluid in the abdominal cavity. It is common in people with cirrhosis and it usually develops when the liver is starting to fail. In general, the development of ascites indicates advanced liver disease and patients should be referred for consideration of liver transplantation.

Asperger Syndrome: Is a lifelong developmental disability that affects how people perceive the world and interact with others. It is a form of autism.

Bach Rescue Remedy™: Is one of the original flower remedies discovered by Dr Bach in the 1930s. It helps with any emergency situation and calms stressful or frightening situations. Visit: www.bachcentre.com for more information.

Bipolar Disorder: Is characterised by extreme mood swings. These can range from extreme highs (mania) to extreme lows (depression). It is sometimes referred to as manic depression.

CAMHS: Child and Adolescent Mental Health Services for those aged under 18.

Carbamazepine: Used occasionally as part of the treatment for bipolar disorder. This is because it can modify some types of pain, and control some mood disorders.

Chlorpromazine: Also marketed under the trade names Thorazine and Largactil amongst others, is an antipsychotic medication. It is primarily used to treat psychotic disorders such as schizophrenia. It has many other uses including the treatment of bipolar disorder.

Citalopram: Is an antidepressant belonging to a group of drugs called selective serotonin reuptake inhibitors (SSRI's). Citalopram is used to treat depression.

Clonazepam (brand name Rivotril): Is used alone or in combination with other medications to control certain types of seizures. It is also used to relieve panic attacks.

Clozaril: An antipsychotic medication. It's used to treat severe schizophrenia or reduce risk of suicidal behaviour in people with schizophrenia or similar disorders.

Cognitive Behavioural Therapy (CBT): Is a talking therapy that can help you manage your problems by changing the way you think and behave.

CPN (Community Psychiatric Nurse): A psychiatric nurse based in the community rather than a psychiatric hospital. They form an integral part of Community Mental Health Teams. They are often patients' key workers within the NHS Mental Health system and are often the first port of call for further referrals to psychiatrists, psychotherapists and other mental health professionals.

Cyclothymia: Cyclothymic disorder causes mood changes – from feeling low to emotional highs. People with Cyclothymia are at risk of developing bipolar disorder, so it's important to get help before reaching this later stage.

Depakote™: See Valproate semi-sodium.

Diazepam: Is used to treat anxiety disorders, alcohol withdrawal symptoms or muscle spasms. It is sometimes used with other medications to treat seizures.

Electro Convulsive Therapy (ECT): Formerly known as electroshock therapy and often referred to as shock treatment. It is a standard psychiatric treatment in which seizures are electrically induced in patients to provide relief from psychiatric illnesses.

Epilepsy: Is a common condition that affects the brain and causes frequent seizures.

Fender Rhodes: This is an electric piano invented by Harold Rhodes, which became particularly popular throughout the 1970s. Like a piano, it generates sound using keys and hammers, but instead of strings, the hammers strike thin metal tines, which are then amplified via an electromagnetic pickup which is plugged into an external keyboard amplifier and speaker.

Foetal alcohol syndrome: If a woman drinks alcohol during pregnancy, she risks damaging her baby. Sometimes this can result in mental and physical problems in the baby, called foetal alcohol syndrome.

Gliniks and Gambis: Imaginary giant visitors to Steven's room at night. Shaped like scissors, walking they terrified him. I later worked out that they may have been the reflections of car headlights onto the ceiling.

GUM clinic: Sexual health or genitourinary medicine (GUM) clinics offer a range of services, including those to do with emergency contraception and any sexually transmitted disease.

Haloperidol: An antipsychotic medicine. It works by changing the actions of chemicals in your brain. Haloperidol is used to treat schizophrenia. It is also used to control motor and speech tics in people with Tourette's syndrome.

Hammond C3: The Hammond organ is an electric organ, invented by Laurens Hammond and John M.Hanert and first manufactured in 1935. Various models have been produced, most of which use sliding drawbars to create a variety of sounds.

Homoeopathy: Is a natural form of medicine used by over 200 million people worldwide to treat both acute and chronic conditions. It is based on the principle of 'like cures like'. In other words, a substance taken in small amounts will cure the same symptoms it causes if taken in large amounts.

Kelvin: The base unit (in the international system of units of measurement) of thermodynamic temperature, equal in magnitude to the degree Celsius.

Lactulose: Used to treat constipation but also useful in treating high blood ammonia, which can lead to Hepatic encephalopathy. This is the occurrence of confusion, altered level of consciousness and coma because of liver failure. This can also be a side effect of the administration of valproic acid.

Laudanum: A sedative derived from opium.

Leslie Speaker: The Leslie speaker is a combined amplifier and loudspeaker that projects the signal from an electric or electronic instrument and modifies the sound by rotating the loudspeakers. It is most commonly associated with the Hammond organ.

Librium™ (Chlordiazepoxide): Is a sedative and hypnotic medication of the benzodiazepine class; it is used to treat anxiety, insomnia and withdrawal symptoms from alcohol and/or drug abuse.

Lithium: Is most commonly used to treat bipolar disorder. Lithium is not a sedative, euphoriant or depressant and it can be taken at the same time as other medications such as tranquilizers or antidepressants.

Lustral™: The active ingredient sertraline hydrochloride, which is a type of antidepressant known as a selective serotonin reuptake inhibitor (SSRI).

Manic depressive: Someone suffering from manic depression or bipolar disorder

Metacam™: Is a non-steroidal anti-inflammatory drug (NSAID) which is a type of painkiller used for the treatment of pain in dogs and cats.

Milk Thistle (Silybum marianum): Has been used for 2,000 years as a herbal remedy for a variety of ailments particularly liver, kidney and gall bladder problems.

Monoamine Oxidase Inhibitor Antidepressants (MAOIs): Are chemicals which inhibit the activity of the monoamine oxidase enzyme family. They have a long history of use as medications prescribed for the treatment of depression.

Moog synthesizer: Any analogue synthesizer designed by Robert Moog, or manufactured by Moog Music, and is commonly used as a generic term for older-generation analogue music synthesizers.

MRI (Magnetic resonance imaging): Is a type of scan that uses strong magnetic fields and radio waves to produce detailed images of the inside of the body.

OCD: Obsessive Compulsive Disorder is a common mental health condition in which a person has obsessive thoughts and compulsive behaviour.

Olanzapine: An antipsychotic prescribed for the relief of symptoms of schizophrenia, or alternatively the treatment and/or prevention of high mood swings or mania.

Oramorph: Is a liquid form of morphine, often used as a pain killer. In small doses it can be used for the long term relief or chronic breathlessness.

Personality Disorder: There are many categories of personality disorder. Borderline personality disorder (BPD) is a disorder of mood and how a person interacts with others. It's the most commonly recognised personality disorder. A person will be different in how they think, perceive, feel or relate to others.

PETT Scan: Positron emission trans axial tomography. A sophisticated type of brain imaging which, amongst other uses, can be used to observe brain activity in people with schizophrenia, substance abuse, mood disorders and other psychiatric conditions.

Post-natal depression: A type of depression that some women develop after having a baby. More than one in 10 women gets post-natal depression, which often starts within one or two months of giving birth. However, it can start several months after having a baby. For some women, their depression starts while they are pregnant.

Post-traumatic stress: Is a mental health condition that's triggered by a terrifying event — either experiencing it or witnessing it. Symptoms may include flashbacks, nightmares and severe anxiety, as well as uncontrollable thoughts about the event.

Prozac (Fluoxetine): Is a selective serotonin reuptake inhibitor (SSRI) antidepressant. It can be used to treat major depressive disorder, bulimia nervosa (an eating disorder), obsessive-compulsive disorder and panic disorder.

Psychoses: Plural - any of several major mental illnesses that can cause delusions, hallucinations, serious defects in judgment and other cognitive processes, and the inability to evaluate reality objectively.

Rivotril: See Clonazepam

Seasonal affective disorder (SAD): Is a form of depression that people experience at a particular time of year or during a particular season. It is usually associated with the lower levels of daylight in the winter.

Schizophrenia: A chronic and severe mental disorder that affects how a person thinks, feels and behaves. People with schizophrenia may seem like they have lost touch with reality.

Seroxat (Paroxetine): Is prescribed for depression, anxiety disorders and obsessive-compulsive disorder (OCD). A selective serotonin reuptake inhibitor (SSRI) antidepressant.

Sertraline: Generic term for the brand name Lustral™

SSRI: A selective serotonin reuptake inhibitor antidepressant. Brain cells, called neurons, release chemicals which go on to stimulate other neurons. This leads to electrical impulses which result in many functions controlled by the brain. Serotonin is one such chemical in the brain. Once released, it stimulates other neurons and is then taken back up into the neuron cells and recycled. SSRIs increase the amount of circulating serotonin available in your brain. Altering the balance of the chemicals in the brain can help with the symptoms of depression, anxiety disorders and OCD.

Tofranil ™: Generic name Imipramine is a tricyclic antidepressant used to treat depression but has other uses as well.

Tramadol: A narcotic based pain reliever that is dangerous in overdose and addictive.

Tryptophan: Is an essential amino acid needed for general growth and development, producing niacin and creating serotonin in the body. Serotonin is thought to produce healthy sleep and a stable mood.

Unipolar mood disorder: A major depression, also known as unipolar or major depressive disorder, which is characterised by a persistent feeling of sadness or a lack of interest in outside stimuli.

Valium™: See Diazepam

Valproate Semi-Sodium: A mood stabiliser. It is used to treat the psychiatric illness bipolar affective disorder or manic depression, brand name Depakote™

Wiccan: Also known as Pagan Witchcraft. A contemporary Pagan and religious movement. It was developed in England during the first half of the 20th century and was introduced to the public in 1954 by Gerald Gardner, a retired British civil servant.

Wurlitzer EP: A stringless electric piano, using felt covered hammers which strike metallic reeds.

Resources - accessing services and how to get help and information

NHS 111: This is your first point of contact if you cannot phone or contact your own GP. Telephone 111 from any phone or Textphone: 18001 111. It is available 24 hours a day, 365 days a year. Calls are free from landlines and mobile phones.

Bipolar UK: Supporting individuals with the much misunderstood and devastating condition of bipolar and their families and carers. Telephone support and access to support groups and information visit https://www.bipolaruk.org or telephone 0333 323 3880

Carers Trust: A major charity for, with and about Carers visit https://carers.org or telephone 0300 772 9600 in England

Carers UK: Making life better for Carers in England. Visit www.carersuk.org or telephone 020 7378 49999 in England

Drinkaware: Lists national organisations that can help you drink less as well as sharing information about alcoholism. Visit https://www.drinkaware.co.uk/alcohol-support-services/

Mental Health Foundation: Good mental health for all. Information, research, education see: https://www.mentalhealth.org.uk/

Mind: For better mental health visit: https://www.mind.org.uk/ or telephone 0300 123 3393 or text 86463

NHS Choices: Comprehensive health and services information including many mental health conditions, addictions as well as physical illnesses and conditions. Visit http://www.nhs.uk/

NHS England: To find out the standards of care you should expect visit https://www.england.nhs.uk/mental health/adults/

Personality Disorder: This is an information site with excellent resources. It highlights how 'patchy' and inconsistent support is throughout the UK. Visit http://personalitydisorder.org.uk/

Rethink mental illness: A better life for everyone affected by mental illness. Support and information: https://www.rethink.org/ or telephone 0300 5000 927

SANE: A UK mental health charity. For good information, education and support visit http://www.sane.org.uk/ or telephone Saneline 0300 304 7000

The National Autistic Society: Provides information, support and pioneering services and campaign for a better world for autistic people including those with Asperger Syndrome http://www.autism.org.uk/ or telephone 0808 800 4104

The Samaritans: Offer a safe place for you to talk any time you like, in your own way about whatever's getting to you visit https://www.samaritans.org or telephone 116 123 from any phone free of charge.